Keys to the adults of seed and leaf beetles of Britain and Ireland
(Coleoptera: Orsodacnidae, Megalopodidae and Chrysomelidae)

By David Hubble

FSC
BRINGING
ENVIRONMENTAL
UNDERSTANDING TO ALL

© FSC 2012
ISBN 978 1 908819 08 6
Occasional Publication 156

Contents

Acknowledgements   iv

Introduction   1

Collection of adults and juvenile stages   1

Identification   3

Typical morphology   4

Glossary   5

Categories for scarce or rare species   7

Checklist   9

Keys for the identification of
British seed and leaf beetles   23

Key to Subfamilies and small families   23

Keys to genera and species   27

Key A: Subfamilies Bruchinae and
Amblycerinae   27

    Key A1: Genus *Bruchus*   29

    Key A2: Genus *Callosobruchus*   31

    Key A3: Genus *Bruchidius*   33

Key B: Family Megalopodidae
(Subfamily Zeugophoridae)   34

    Key B1: Genus *Zeugophora*   34

Key C: Subfamily Donaciinae   35

    Key C1: Genus *Macroplea*   36

    Key C2: Genus *Plateumaris*   36

    Key C3: Genus *Donacia*   37

Key D: Subfamily Criocerinae   41

    Key D1: Genus *Oulema*   42

Key E: Subfamily Cryptocephalinae   44

    Key E1: Genus *Cryptocephalus*   45

Key F: Family Orsodacnidae
(Subfamily Orsodacninae)   51

    Key F1: Genus *Orsodacne*   51

Key G: Subfamily Chrysomelinae   51

    Key G1: Genus *Timarcha*   53

Key G2: Genus *Chrysolina*   54

Key G3: Genus *Gastrophysa*   57

Key G4: Genus *Phaedon*   58

Key G5: Genus *Hydrothassa*   59

Key G6: Genus *Prasocuris*   59

Key G7: Genus *Chrysomela*   60

Key G8: Genus *Gonioctena*   60

Key G9: Genus *Phratora*   62

Key H: Subfamily Galerucinae   63

    Key Ha: Tribe Galerucini   64

    Key Ha1: Genus *Galeruca*   66

    Key Ha2: Genus *Luperus*   67

    Key Ha3: Genus *Lochmaea*   67

    Key Ha4: Genus *Galerucella*   68

    Key Hb: Tribe Alticini   69

    Key Hb1: Genus *Psylliodes*   74

    Key Hb2: Genus *Chaetocnema*   78

    Key Hb3: Genus *Altica*   80

    Key Hb4: Genus *Epitrix*   82

    Key Hb5: Genus *Crepidodera*   82

    Key Hb6: Genus *Neocrepidodera*   84

    Key Hb7: Genus *Podagrica*   84

    Key Hb8: Genus *Mantura*   85

    Key Hb9: Genus *Batophila*   86

    Key Hb10: Genus *Longitarsus*   86

    Key Hb11: Genus *Phyllotreta*   101

    Key Hb12: Genus *Aphthona*   106

    Key Hb13: Genus *Apteropeda*   109

    Key Hb14: Genus *Sphaeroderma*   110

Key I: Subfamily Cassidinae   110

    Key I1: Genus *Cassida*   111

References and further reading   115

Online resources   120

Appendix A   121

Image credits   123

Index   125

Acknowledgements

A test version of this key was circulated by AIDGAP/FSC in 2010 and my thanks go to Rebecca Farley-Brown who produced and distributed it, and collated the resulting feedback. I am also grateful to the many people who tried the test key and provided valid criticisms and feedback – in some cases suggesting new (and much improved) key structures and identification features, and in orders entering into ongoing correspondence regarding areas of taxonomic uncertainty. I have not aimed to name testers individually as the list would inevitably be incomplete, but it is true to say that this book would not have been completed without them.

Next, I would like to thank two staff from the Biological Records Centre. Dr Helen Roy was central in encouraging this endeavour and initially involving me as the national organiser of the Leaf and Seed Beetle Recording Scheme which was the initial spur that drove me to fill a gap in the UK's beetle identification literature. Similarly, invaluable help was given by Björn Beckmann who tracked down and provided a wide range of 'venerable' journal articles that I wouldn't otherwise have had access to.

I am also grateful to Darren Mann of the Oxford University Museum of Natural History for access to the Hope Entomological Collections (invaluable during the latter stages of rewriting the *Longitarsus* key) and to the Hampshire Museums Service for access to their collection.

I would like to thank Steve Lane, for his many helpful comments and suggestions.

Lastly, I would like to thank my wife (and occasional 'beetle widow') Kate for putting up with my endless hours of typing, retyping, drawing, redrawing, peering into microscopes, and poring over heaps of books and articles.

INTRODUCTION

The chrysomelids include a number of species of popular interest, either because of their attractive metallic coloration or status as pests in farms and gardens. However, although there are a number of identification works covering the Chrysomelidae of all or various parts of Europe and the Palaearctic, there has been no simple, affordable, single identification guide in English to the species found in Britain and Ireland. Instead, those seeking to identify and study these beetles have had to accumulate a wide range of books and journal articles, some rather obscure and/or expensive, and some not available in English. Since the publication of the excellent Atlas of British and Irish species (Cox, 2007) brought together distribution and other information on this group, the need to fill the remaining gap in identification literature has been highlighted. As accurate identification is essential in order to study and conserve any species, I hope that this volume will prove to be a significant step forward for entomologists, ecologists and others interested in the fauna of the British Isles.

The species covered in this work comprise the Chrysomelidae (277 species including the Bruchinae, previously considered a family rather than subfamily), Orsodacnidae (2 species, previously placed in the Chrysomelidae) and Megalopodidae (3 species, also previously in the Chrysomelidae). Aside from the recent addition of *Longitarsus symphyti* (Harrison, 2010), the systematic list (p. 9) follows Duff's 2008 checklist, with species included in the Irish checklist (Anderson *et al.*, 2005) marked with an asterisk. The brief ecological notes are largely adapted from Cox (2007) which I see as an essential companion volume.

COLLECTION OF ADULTS AND JUVENILE STAGES

For details of the timing of adult activity, see Cox (2007) which gives a month-by-month bar chart for each species. Most species show a peak of activity somewhere between late spring and early autumn, a pattern generally well demonstrated by e.g. *Cryptocephalus* and *Luperus*. However, this pattern is not always clear as some species can be collected throughout the year, albeit in much-reduced numbers during winter months e.g. several species of *Chrysolina* and *Phaedon*, as well as many of the 'flea beetles' (subfamily Galerucinae, Tribe Alticini). Some others (such as several *Chaetocnema* species) have a single generation per year but show a double peak of activity, the first being overwintering adults and the second being newly developed adults.

While capture of the adults of many species is fairly straightforward (notwithstanding their ability to fly or drop to the ground when disturbed), this is not always the case e.g. the 'flea beetles' are able to escape very effectively by jumping while some of the 'reed beetles' occur on vegetation overhanging water-bodies and can be difficult to reach from dry land. Juvenile stages (larvae and pupae) are relatively immobile, but often hidden. The collection method used varies not only by species but also by season within a single species (i.e. active adults may be found in different locations to those hibernating, aestivating or in diapause). In combination, the following simple methods should cover much of the chrysomelid community and do not require particularly expensive or specialised equipment:

Pooter – essential for capturing beetles when hand-searching or using a sweep net or beating tray. Its use may need to be swift in order to capture flea beetles before they jump.

Hand-searching – particularly useful in grass tussocks, flood debris and dead bulrushes, beneath bark, stones and leaf rosettes, and at or around the uppermost roots revealed when lower leaves are moved aside. Such methods may be used to find juvenile stages as well as sheltering adults. A range of donaciines may be collected by pulling up the rhizomes and roots of aquatic plants (using a hook or grapple in deeper water) and searching the washed samples for brown, oval cocoons or small, white, slightly curved larvae. A rake can be used to collect more easily dislodged plant material. Larvae can be collected this way from late summer to late winter and cocoons from late summer to spring (Stainforth, 1944), although this method is destructive of the habitat and so should be used sparingly, noting possible requirements for permission to collect.

Evidence from leaves – larvae of some species produce leaf mines which may be tentatively identifiable to species, though identification can only be confirmed directly from larvae or pupae in mines, or adults raised from juvenile stages. To obtain a possible identification of a leaf mine, look carefully at features such as the shape of the mine, where it starts and finishes, the frass pattern within it (hold it up to the light or use a light box or other lighting from beneath) and whether pupation occurs within the mine or externally (in which case there should be a tiny exit hole or slit). It is essential to note the date and the host plant species. You can then compare your specimen with those presented in online resources such as the excellent British Leafminers (www.leafmines.co.uk). Other observations of leaves may provide evidence of feeding, such as the series of holes left in reeds by some donaciines, and the shot-holes characteristic of many flea beetles.

Sweep net – best used for erect plants (including reeds and sedges where a number of donaciines may be captured) rather than those with a sprawling or rosette-like habit; try to avoid wet or very windy conditions. Key habitats for sweeping are fields and their margins, damp meadows with adjacent woodlands, and undergrowth in open woodland. A water net may be required for collection of aquatic donaciines and needs a mesh coarser than that of a sweep net, though not so coarse that small beetles can escape through it. A long-handled clap net (essentially a closeable sweep net) may be more practical for inaccessible locations.

Beating tray – used to collect specimens from bushes and trees as well as from dense stands of vegetation such as reeds and bulrushes. Tapping overhanging marginal and aquatic vegetation may cause beetles to fall onto the water surface where they can be collected, or into a sweep net held beneath the plants. Similarly, quickly submerging a piece of vegetation causes beetles to detach and float to the surface where they can be collected as they are unable to fly.

Sieving of soil and plant litter – particularly useful for collecting juvenile stages as well as inactive adults. Note that a large amount of material may be required in order to obtain a small number of specimens.

There are a number of other methods which require more sophisticated equipment and/or return visits. These include pitfall traps, water traps, Malaise traps, flight interception traps, suction traps, light traps and suction samplers. See Oldroyd (1970), Cooter & Barclay (2006) and Cox (2007) for more detail about these as well as the methods listed above. For information about raising adults from larvae or pupae, see Oldroyd (1970) which covers insects in general, Burakowski (1993) or Cooter & Barclay (2006), both of which cover a range of beetle groups, or Steinhausen (1996) which specifically considers chrysomelids.

Where identification in the field is not possible, specimens will need to be taken, possibly for dissection. Information on specimen preparation is given in Cooter & Barclay (2006) and whenever collecting specimens it is essential to work one of the several sets of ethical guidelines that aim to reduce the impact of entomological study. A widely cited collecting code in the UK (JCCBI, 2002) is available online from Invertebrate Link (www.royensoc.co.uk/InvLink/Index.html), with an associated statement on the appropriate role of legislation in this area of study also available (JCCBI, 2008). It is important not to over-collect a particular species or location. This applies to juvenile stages at least as much as it does to adults.

IDENTIFICATION

Where possible, simple keys to external features leading to species-level identification by use of a hand lens are given. In many cases, finer examination is required using a binocular microscope, and in some cases (especially within the Galerucinae), identification to species requires dissection of (usually male) genitalia. Where this may remain insufficient and/or there is ongoing taxonomic confusion, further references are given. Unless stated otherwise, dorsoventral figures of aedeagi all show the dorsal view. In many cases, the outline of the aedeagus, especially the shape of the apex, may be sufficient; in others, finer detail may be required. It is worth noting that even with genitalia there may be some variation between individuals, though this is usually minor and the figures offered here should prove adequate for identification to species. Practical aspects of the dissection and examination of beetle genitalia are beyond the scope of this book, but there is excellent coverage of this and other curatorial aspects of the study of Coleoptera in Cooter & Barclay (2006).

Where length measurements are given, these are from British references where available, otherwise from further afield and in all cases exclude appendages. Note that size ranges do vary between authors (possibly due to genuine variation in sizes from different areas) and so should be treated as guidelines rather than being absolutely definitive. A species described as '2.5-3.5 mm' could reasonably be found as a 2.4 mm or 3.6 mm specimen, but not 5.0 mm.

When considering colours, it is worth noting that in many texts, coleopterists have traditionally used specialist terms e.g. piceous (a dark colour which may have a greenish or yellowish sheen), testaceous (yellowish, usually dusky rather than bright, but applied to any yellowish to yellow-red shade), rufous (reddish), pitchy (blackish-brown but, like 'piceous' a rather variable term) and fuscous (brown to tawny-brown). In the keys presented here, I have generally avoided these terms and have instead given colours their everyday names.

The keys presented here cover only adults. For information on the identification of immature stages, see the list of sources given in Cox (2007). There are no comprehensive guides to bruchid and chrysomelid larvae in English, though there is a relatively recent work in Russian covering the Russian fauna (Zaytsev & Medvedev, 2009).

Typical morphology

The figures below show generalised versions of the main features used in this key. Other features are figured as required throughout the text.

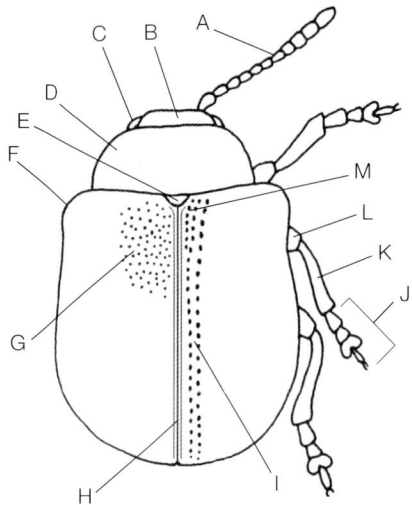

A   antenna
B   vertex (top) of head
C   eye
D   pronotum
E   scutellum
F   elytral 'shoulder'
G   elytra with random punctures

H   elytral suture
I   elytra with punctate striae
J   mid tarsus
K   mid tibia
L   mid femur
M   scutellary stria

Figure 1. Generalised dorsal view

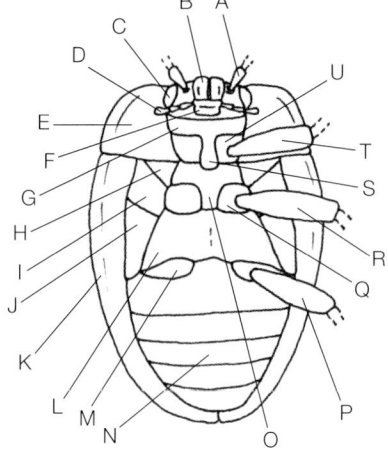

A   antenna
B   mandible
C   eye
D   maxillary palp
E   underside of pronotum (hypomera)
F   labrum and clypeus
G   prosternum
H   mesepisternum
I   mesepimeron
J   metepisternum
K   epipleura of elytron

L   metasternum
M   hind coxa
N   abdominal sternite (no. 3 of 5)
O   mesosternum
P   hind (meta) femur
Q   mid coxa
R   mid (meso) femur
S   intercoxal prosternal process
T   front (pro) femur
U   front coxa

Figure 2. Generalised ventral view

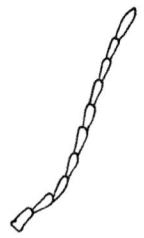

Figure 3. Filiform antenna (*Psylliodes*)

Figure 4. Serrate antenna (*Bruchidius*)

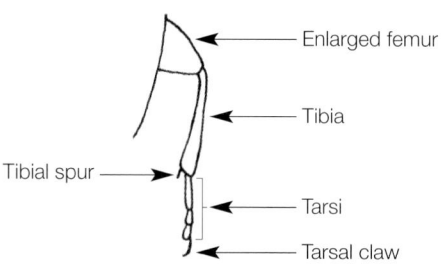

Enlarged femur

Tibia

Tibial spur

Tarsi

Tarsal claw

Figure 5. Flea beetle hind leg (*Phyllotreta*)

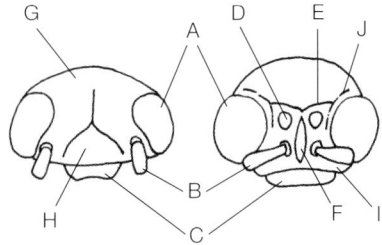

A eye
B 1st antennal segment
C labrum
D callus or bulge above
   antennal base
E groove or sulcus
   above bridge

F carina/keel
G vertex/top of head
H frons/front of head
I gena/jowl
J orbital line

Figure 6. Generalised front of head and mouthparts

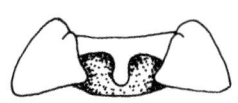

Figure 7. Open coxal cavities

Figure 8. Closed coxal cavities

GLOSSARY

Aedeagus. Male genital structure, sometimes considered the equivalent of the penis, although they are analagous structures.

Apical. Relating to the tip i.e. away from the point of attachment (cf. basal).

Basal. Relating to the area near the point of attachment (cf. apical).

Bicolorous. With two distinct colours.

Bilobed. With two lobes.

Clypeus. The hardened plate (sclerite) forming the lower margin of the 'face'.

Concave. Curved inwards.

Concolorous. The same colour.

Convex. Curved outwards (if very convex, could be called 'domed').

Coxa (pl. coxae). Basal segment of the front leg where it attaches to the body. May be specified as front (procoxa), middle (mesocoxa) or hind (metacoxa).

Disc. The main surface area of a body part (pronotum or elytra) away from edges, corners etc.

Dorsal. Relating to the upper surface.

Elytron (pl. elytra). Wing case.

Epimeron (sometimes 'epimere'). The rear half of the side wall of a thoracic segment.

Epipleuron (pl. epipleura). That part of the edge of the elytron which is reflexed (folded) onto the underside of the beetle.

Femur (pl. femora). The 3rd segment of the leg, and often the largest (the first two are small and so the femur is the first long one to project from the body).

Filiform. Thread-like.

Frons. Front sclerite of the head, between the antennal bases and below the vertex. May be broad or narrow and may bear frontal lines or ridges.

Gena (pl. genae). The 'jowl' or side of the head/face.

Interstices. Of the elytra, the spaces between straie.

Labrum. The 'upper lip', a movable plate on the front of the head forming part of the mouthparts.

Lateral. Relating to the side/s.

Longitudinal. Running from front to back.

Margin. A delineated edge or rim, may be expanded to form a flange.

Maxilla (pl. maxillae). One of the two components of the mouthparts just behind the jaws.

Maxillary palp. A jointed structure arising from the maxilla.

Metasternum. Rear thoracic segment seen ventrally; directly in front of first abdominal segment.

Montane. Relating to mountains or similar uplands.

Pectinate. With narrow parallel projections giving a comb-like shape.

Pitchy. Blackish-brown, sometimes with a yellowish, greenish or reddish sheen or tinge.

Pronotum. The dorsal plate between the head and elytra. It is the dorsal plate of the 1st thoracic segment.

Pubescent. With shiny hairs or down.

Pygidium. Last dorsal segment of the abdomen.

Quadrate. Forming a rectangle approximately as wide as long.

Rostrum. Beak-shaped structure at the front of the head.

Scutellum. The very small, usually triangular or rounded plate just behind the pronotum where the bases of the elytra meet. Not visible in some species.

Serrate. Saw-like.

Seta (pl. setae). Bristle or hair-like structure.

Sclerite. Any of the chitinous plates forming the exoskeleton.

Shagreening/shagreened. With the surface bearing extremely fine sculpturing like sharkskin or a microscopic mosaic (as opposed to puncturation, although the surface between punctures may be shagreened).

Sinuate. Curved/wavy.

Stenophagous. Eating only a single or restricted range of food plants. Compare with **monophagous** (feeding strictly on a single food plant), **oligophagous** (feeding on a restricted range of food plants, but more than one) and **polyphagous** (feeding on a wider range of food plants).

Stria (pl. striae). Grooves or lines on the elytra, may be punctured. Note that the suture may also be striate.

Suture. The line where the elytra meet; may include the margins.

Tarsus (pl. tarsi). The 'foot', attached to the tibia and consisting of several segments.

Tibia (pl. tibiae). The 4th segment of the leg, the second long one projecting from the body.

Transverse. Wider than long.

Trapezoidal. Forming a trapezium e.g. with the front edge shorter than the rear edge and so having angled sides.

Truncate. Cut off, blunt.

Unicolorous. Single-coloured.

Ventral. Relating to the lower surface.

Ventrite. Lower plate.

Vertex. Top of the head.

CATEGORIES FOR SCARCE OR RARE SPECIES

Any species listed in the relevant Red Data Book (RDB) are considered rare and/or threatened and are given an RDB code in the text. Any species considered nationally scarce are similarly given an N code, either Na or Nb. These codes are explained as follows:

RDB1: Endangered. These species are in danger of extinction (or are believed, but not yet known, to be extinct) and are unlikely to survive if factors affecting them continue to do so. They include species known only from a single 10 km grid square, species only found in especially vulnerable habitats, species which have declined rapidly and continuously and are found in no more than five 10 km grid squares, and species believed to be extinct but which would need protection if rediscovered.

RDB2: Vulnerable. These species are likely to become Endangered if factors affecting them continue to do so. They include species declining throughout their range, in vulnerable habitats and/or whose populations are low.

RDB3: Rare. These species have small populations and are at risk. They are found in no more than fifteen 10 km grid squares.

RDBI: Indeterminate. These species are *considered* to be in one of the categories RDB1-3, but there is not enough information to determine which.

RDBK: Insufficiently Known. These species are *suspected* of being in one of the categories RDB1-3 but there is not enough information to know for certain. They may be:

Recently discovered/recognised in Britain;

Known from only a few locations, or a single location, but belonging to poorly recorded or taxonomically difficult groups;

Known from only a few locations, or a single location, inhabiting inaccessible or infrequently sampled (though widespread) habitats. Examples include some moorland and agricultural habitats;

Known from only a few locations, or a single location, and of questionable native status, but not clearly a recent colonist, vagrant or introduction.

Na. These species do not fall into an RDB category but are uncommon and believed to occur in no more than thirty 10 km grid squares.

Nb. These species do not fall into an RDB category but are uncommon and believed to occur in between 31 and 100 10 km grid squares.

BAP: UK Biodiversity Action Plan. These species are known to require priority conservation action and have been listed within the UK BAP.

Note that these categories have been superceded by the 2001 IUCN Red List categories (version 3.1) but these have not yet been applied to most groups of beetles (including the Chrysomelidae) and so RDB codes are retained here. For more on the IUCN categories, see IUCN (2010). N codes and RDB codes are described in Hyman & Parsons (1992).

The RDB status above applies specifically to Britain (i.e. omits Ireland), while the UK BAP refers to the UK (i.e. includes Northern Ireland but omits the Republic of Ireland). The Irish Red List No. 1 (Foster *et al.*, 2009) covers water beetles (at the time of writing it is available for download from http://www.npws.ie/publications/redlists/RL1.pdf), the following species from the subfamily Donaciinae being included:

Regionally Extinct (RE)
Plateumaris affinis [given as *rustica* (Kunze)]
Donacia semicuprea

Critically Endangered (CR)
Plateumaris braccata (Scopoli) [given as *bracata*]

Vulnerable (VU)
Donacia aquatica
Donacia cinerea

Nelson *et al.* (2007) provides a critical review of Irish donaciine records while Foster & Nelson (2010) list donaciine records from 2008 and 2009. Both of these sources have been used to incorporate information on Irish distribution into the keys to species within the Donaciinae.

CHECKLIST
(from Duff 2008, plus species due for inclusion in the 2012 update)

Family MEGALOPODIDAE Latreille, 1802
Family author: M.L. Cox

Subfamily ZEUGOPHORINAE Böving & Craighead, 1931

   ZEUGOPHORA Kunze, 1818
     flavicollis (Marsham, 1802)
     subspinosa (Fabricius, 1781)
     turneri Power, 1863

Family ORSODACNIDAE Thomson, C.G., 1859
Family author: M.L. Cox

   ORSODACNE Latreille, 1802
    ORSODACNA Latreille, 1804
     cerasi (Linnaeus, 1758)
     humeralis Latreille, 1804
      lineola (Panzer, 1795) non (Fabricius, 1781)

Family CHRYSOMELIDAE Latreille, 1802
Family author: M.L. Cox

Subfamily BRUCHINAE Latreille, 1802

   BRUCHUS Linnaeus, 1767
    MYLABRIS Geoffroy, 1762
    LARIA sensu auctt. non Scopoli, 1763
     atomarius (Linnaeus, 1761) *
      fahraei Gyllenhal, 1839
      viciae sensu Fowler, 1890 non Olivier, 1795
     brachialis Fåhraeus, 1839
     ervi Frölich, 1799
     loti Paykull, 1800
     pisorum (Linnaeus, 1758)
      pisi Linnaeus, 1767
     rufimanus Boheman, 1833 *
      affinis sensu auctt. Brit. non Frölich, 1799
      velutinus Mulsant & Rey, 1858
     rufipes Herbst, 1783
      luteicornis sensu auctt. Brit. non Illiger, 1794

BRUCHIDIUS Schilsky, 1905
BRUCHUS sensu Fowler, 1890 partim non Linnaeus, 1767
cisti (Fabricius, 1775)
unicolor (Olivier, 1795)
canus (Germar, 1824)
debilis (Gyllenhal, 1833)
cisti '(Paykull, 1800)' sensu Joy, 1932
incarnatus (Boheman, 1833)
olivaceus (Germar, 1824)
canus sensu auctt. Brit. non (Germar, 1824)
unicolor sensu Schilsky, 1905 non (Olivier, 1795)
varius (Olivier, 1795) 631
villosus (Fabricius, 1793) *
cisti sensu (Paykull, 1800) non (Fabricius, 1775)
ater (Marsham, 1802) non (Scriba, 1790)
fasciatus sensu auctt. non (Olivier, 1795)

ACANTHOSCELIDES Schilsky in Küster & Kraatz, 1905
obtectus (Say, 1831)
obsoletus sensu auctt. non Say, 1831

CALLOSOBRUCHUS Pic, 1902
chinensis (Linnaeus, 1758)
pectinicornis (Linnaeus, 1767)
maculatus (Fabricius, 1775)
quadrimaculatus (Fabricius, 1793)

Subfamily DONACIINAE Kirby, 1837

MACROPLEA Samouelle, 1819
HAEMONIA Dejean, 1821
appendiculata (Panzer, 1794) *
equiseta (Fabricius, 1798)
mutica (Fabricius, 1793)
curtisi (Lacordaire, 1845)

DONACIA Fabricius, 1775
aquatica (Linnaeus, 1758) *
dentipes Fabricius, 1793
bicolora Zschach, 1788 *
bicolor auctt. (misspelling)
sagittariae Fabricius, 1793
cinerea Herbst, 1784 *
clavipes Fabricius, 1793 *
menyanthis Fabricius, 1801
menyanthidis Gyllenhal, 1813
crassipes Fabricius, 1775 *
dentata Hoppe, 1795 *

    impressa Paykull, 1799 *
    marginata Hoppe, 1795 *
       limbata Panzer, 1796
       lemnae Fabricius, 1801
    obscura Gyllenhal, 1813 *
    semicuprea Panzer, 1796 *
    simplex Fabricius, 1775 *
       linearis Hoppe, 1795
    sparganii Ahrens, 1810
    thalassina Germar, 1811 *
    versicolorea (Brahm, 1791) *
    vulgaris Zschach, 1788 *
       typhae Ahrens, 1810

PLATEUMARIS Thomson, C.G., 1859
    DONACIA sensu Fowler, 1890 partim non Fabricius, 1775
       affinis (Kunze, 1818) *
       braccata (Scopoli, 1772) *
       discolor (Panzer, 1795) *
       sericea (Linnaeus, 1758) *

Subfamily CRIOCERINAE Latreille, 1804

LEMA Fabricius, 1798
    cyanella (Linnaeus, 1758) *
       puncticollis Curtis, 1830

OULEMA des Gozis, 1886
    erichsoni (Suffrian, 1841)
    melanopus (Linnaeus, 1758) *
       melanopa auctt.
    obscura (Stephens, 1831) *
       gallaeciana (Heyden, 1870)
       lichenis sensu (Weise, 1882) non (Voet, 1806)
    rufocyanea (Suffrian, 1847) *
       melanopus sensu auctt. partim non (Linnaeus, 1758)
       duftschmidi (Redtenbacher, 1874)
    septentrionis (Weise, 1880) *

CRIOCERIS Geoffroy, 1762
    asparagi (Linnaeus, 1758)

LILIOCERIS Reitter, 1912
    CRIOCERIS sensu Fowler, 1890 partim non Müller, O.F., 1764
       lilii (Scopoli, 1763) *

Subfamily CRYPTOCEPHALINAE Gyllenhal, 1813
    Tribe CLYTRINI Kirby, 1837

LABIDOSTOMIS Dejean, 1836
    tridentata (Linnaeus, 1758)

CLYTRA Laicharting, 1781
    CLYTHRA Fabricius, 1798 (misspelling)
    laeviuscula Ratzeburg, 1837
    quadripunctata (Linnaeus, 1758) *

SMARAGDINA Dejean, 1836
    CYANIRIS Dejean, 1836 non Dalman, 1816
    GYNANDROPHTALMA Lacordaire, 1848
    GYNANDROPHTHALMA Jacquelin du Val, 1865
    affinis (Illiger, 1794) *

    Tribe CRYPTOCEPHALINI Gyllenhal, 1813

CRYPTOCEPHALUS Geoffroy, 1762
    aureolus Suffrian, 1847 *
    biguttatus (Scopoli, 1763)
    bilineatus (Linnaeus, 1767)
    bipunctatus (Linnaeus, 1758)
    coryli (Linnaeus, 1758)
    decemmaculatus (Linnaeus, 1758)
    exiguus Schneider, 1792
    frontalis Marsham, 1802
    fulvus (Goeze, 1777)
    hypochaeridis (Linnaeus, 1758)
        cristula Dufour, 1843
    labiatus (Linnaeus, 1761) *
    moraei (Linnaeus, 1758)
    nitidulus Fabricius, 1787
        ochrostoma Harold, 1872
    parvulus Müller, O.F., 1776
        nigrocoeruleus (Goeze, 1777)
    primarius Harold, 1872
    punctiger Paykull, 1799
    pusillus Fabricius, 1777 *
    querceti Suffrian, 1848
    sexpunctatus (Linnaeus, 1758)
    violaceus Laicharting, 1781

Subfamily LAMPROSOMATINAE Lacordaire, 1848

OOMORPHUS Curtis, 1831
LAMPROSOMA sensu auctt. non Kirby, 1818
concolor (Sturm, 1807) *

Subfamily EUMOLPINAE Hope, 1840

BROMIUS Dejean, 1836
ADOXUS Kirby, 1837
obscurus (Linnaeus, 1758)

Subfamily CHRYSOMELINAE Latreille, 1802

TIMARCHA Samouelle, 1819
goettingensis (Linnaeus, 1758) *
coriaria (Laicharting, 1781)
tenebricosa (Fabricius, 1775) *

CHRYSOLINA Motschulsky, 1860
CHRYSOMELA sensu auctt. non Linnaeus, 1758
americana (Linnaeus, 1758)
banksi (Fabricius, 1775) *
brunsvicensis (Gravenhorst, 1807)
didymata sensu auctt. Brit. non (Scriba, 1791)
caerulans (Scriba, 1791)
cerealis (Linnaeus, 1767)
fastuosa (Scopoli, 1763) *
graminis (Linnaeus, 1758)
haemoptera (Linnaeus, 1758)
herbacea (Duftschmid, 1825)
menthastri (Suffrian, 1851)
menthrasti (Fowler, 1890) (misspelling)
hyperici (Forster, 1771) *
intermedia (Franz, 1938)
crassicornis (Helliesin, 1911) non (Fabricius, 1775)
latecincta sensu auctt. partim non (Demaison, 1896)
hellieseni Silfverberg, 1977
marginata (Linnaeus, 1758)
oricalcia (Müller, O.F., 1776) *
orichalcia auctt. (misspelling)
hobsoni (Stephens, 1831)
polita (Linnaeus, 1758) *
sanguinolenta (Linnaeus, 1758) *
marginalis sensu auctt. non (Duftschmid, 1825)
staphylaea (Linnaeus, 1758) *
staphylea (Fowler, 1890) (misspelling)

varians (Schaller, 1783) *
violacea (Müller, O.F., 1776)
    goettingensis sensu (Linnaeus, 1761) non (Linnaeus, 1758)

GASTROPHYSA Dejean, 1836
GASTROIDEA Hope, 1840
polygoni (Linnaeus, 1758) *
viridula (De Geer, 1775) *

PHAEDON Latreille, 1829
armoraciae (Linnaeus, 1758) *
cochleariae (Fabricius, 1792) *
    regnianum Tottenham, 1941
concinnus Stephens, 1831 *
tumidulus (Germar, 1824) *

HYDROTHASSA Thomson, C.G., 1859
glabra (Herbst, 1783)
    aucta (Fabricius, 1787)
hannoveriana (Fabricius, 1775)
    hannoverana Fowler, 1890 (misspelling)
marginella (Linnaeus, 1758) *

PRASOCURIS Latreille, 1802
HELODES Paykull, 1799 non Latreille, 1796
junci (Brahm, 1790) *
phellandrii (Linnaeus, 1758) *

PLAGIODERA Dejean, 1836
versicolora (Laicharting, 1781) *
    armoraciae sensu (Fabricius, 1775) non (Linnaeus, 1758)

CHRYSOMELA Linnaeus, 1758
MELASOMA Stephens, 1831
aenea Linnaeus, 1758 *
populi Linnaeus, 1758
tremula Fabricius, 1787
    tremulae auctt. (misspelling)
    longicollis (Suffrian, 1851)

GONIOCTENA Dejean, 1836
PHYTODECTA Kirby, 1837
decemnotata (Marsham, 1802)
    rufipes (De Geer, 1775) non (Linnaeus, 1758)
olivacea (Forster, 1771) *
pallida (Linnaeus, 1758) *
viminalis (Linnaeus, 1758)

PHRATORA Dejean, 1836
> PHYLLODECTA Kirby, 1837
>> *laticollis* Suffrian, 1851 *
>>> *cavifrons* Thomson, C.G., 1866
>> *polaris* Schneider, 1886
>> *vitellinae* (Linnaeus, 1758) *
>> *vulgatissima* (Linnaeus, 1758) *

Subfamily GALERUCINAE Latreille, 1802
> Tribe GALERUCINI Latreille, 1802

GALERUCELLA Crotch, 1873
> *calmariensis* (Linnaeus, 1767) *
> *lineola* (Fabricius, 1781) *
> *nymphaeae* (Linnaeus, 1758) *
> *pusilla* (Duftschmid, 1825) *
> *sagittariae* (Gyllenhal, 1813) *
>> *fergussoni* Fowler, 1910
>> *grisescens* sensu auctt. Brit. non (Joannis, 1866)
> *tenella* (Linnaeus, 1761) *

PYRRHALTA Joannis, 1865
> GALERUCELLA sensu Fowler, 1890 partim non Crotch, 1873
>> *viburni* (Paykull, 1799) *

XANTHOGALERUCA Laboissière, 1934
> *luteola* (Müller, O.F., 1766)

GALERUCA Geoffroy, 1762
> ADIMONIA Laicharting, 1781
> GALLERUCA Fabricius, 1793 (misspelling)
>> *laticollis* (Sahlberg, C.R., 1838)
>>> *interrupta* sensu auctt. non Illiger, 1802
>> *tanaceti* (Linnaeus, 1758) *

LOCHMAEA Weise, 1883
> LOCHMAEATA Strand, E., 1935
>> *caprea* (Linnaeus, 1758) *
>>> *capreae* auctt. (misspelling)
>> *crataegi* (Forster, 1771) *
>> *suturalis* (Thomson, C.G., 1866) *

DIABROTICA Dejean, 1836
> *virgifera* LeConte, 1858

PHYLLOBROTICA Dejean, 1836
> *quadrimaculata* (Linnaeus, 1758) *

LUPERUS Geoffroy, 1762
> *flavipes* (Linnaeus, 1767)
> *longicornis* (Fabricius, 1781)
>> *rufipes* sensu auctt. Brit. ? (Scopoli, 1763)

CALOMICRUS Dillwyn, 1829
> LUPERUS sensu Fowler, 1890 partim non Müller, O.F., 1764
>> *circumfusus* (Marsham, 1802)
>>> *circumfuscus* auctt. (misspelling)
>>> *nigrofasciatus* sensu Weise, 1886 non (Goeze, 1777)

AGELASTICA Dejean, 1836
> *alni* (Linnaeus, 1758)

SERMYLASSA Reitter, 1912
> SERMYLA Chapuis, 1875 non Adams, 1854
>> *halensis* (Linnaeus, 1767) *

Tribe ALTICINI Spinola, 1844

LUPEROMORPHA Weise, 1887
> *xanthodera* (Fairmaire, 1888)

PHYLLOTRETA Dejean, 1836
> *atra* (Fabricius, 1775) *
> *consobrina* (Curtis, 1837) *
>> *hintoni* Donisthorpe, 1944
> *cruciferae* (Goeze, 1777)
> *diademata* Foudras, 1860
> *exclamationis* (Thunberg, 1784) *
> *flexuosa* (Illiger, 1794) *
>> *sinuata* (Stephens, 1831)
> *nemorum* (Linnaeus, 1758) *
> *nigripes* (Fabricius, 1775) *
> *nodicornis* (Marsham, 1802) *
> *ochripes* (Curtis, 1837)
> *punctulata* (Marsham, 1802) *
>> *aerea* Allard, 1859
> *striolata* (Fabricius, 1803)
>> *vittata* sensu auctt. non (Fabricius, 1801)
> *tetrastigma* (Comolli, 1837)
> *undulata* Kutschera, 1860 *
> *vittula* (Redtenbacher, 1849) *

APHTHONA Dejean, 1836

 ?atratula Allard, 1859 *
  atrovirens sensu auctt. Brit. non Förster, 1849
 atrocaerulea (Stephens, 1829)
  cyanella (Redtenbacher, 1849)
  puncticollis Allard, 1866
 euphorbiae (Schrank, 1781) *
  virescens Foudras, 1860
  aeneomicans sensu auctt. non Allard, 1875
 herbigrada (Curtis, 1837)
 lutescens (Gyllenhal, 1808) *
 melancholica Weise, 1888 *
  venustula sensu auctt. Brit. non Kutschera, 1861
 nigriceps (Redtenbacher, 1842)
  pallida sensu auctt. Brit. partim non Bach, 1856
 nonstriata (Goeze, 1777) *
  coerulea (Fourcroy, 1785)
 pallida (Bach, 1856)

LONGITARSUS Berthold, 1827

 absynthii Kutschera, 1862
  absinthii auctt. (misspelling)
 aeneicollis (Faldermann, 1837) *
  suturalis (Marsham, 1802) non (Fabricius, 1775)
  nigricollis (Foudras, 1860)
 aeruginosus (Foudras, 1860)
 agilis (Rye, 1868)
 anchusae (Paykull, 1799) *
 atricillus (Linnaeus, 1761) *
 ballotae (Marsham, 1802) *
  cerinus sensu auctt. Brit. partim non (Foudras, 1860)
 brunneus (Duftschmid, 1825) *
  castaneus sensu auctt. Brit. non (Duftschmid, 1825)
 curtus (Allard, 1860) *
 dorsalis (Fabricius, 1781)
 exoletus (Linnaeus, 1758) *
  femoralis (Marsham, 1802)
 ferrugineus (Foudras, 1860) *
  waterhousei Kutschera, 1864
 flavicornis (Stephens, 1831)
  tabidus sensu auctt. partim non (Fabricius, 1775)
  jacobaeae sensu auctt. partim non (Waterhouse, G.R., 1858)
  rufescens Fowler, 1890
 fowleri Allen, 1967
  abdominalis sensu Fowler, 1890 non (Duftschmid, 1825)
 ganglbaueri Heikertinger, 1912 *
  piciceps sensu auctt. non (Stephens, 1831)
  senecionis Brisout, 1873 non (Motschulsky, 1851)

gracilis Kutschera, 1864 *
    poweri (Allard, 1866)
holsaticus (Linnaeus, 1758) *
jacobaeae (Waterhouse, G.R., 1858) *
    tabidus sensu auctt. partim non (Fabricius, 1775)
kutscherae (Rye, 1872) *
    atriceps Kutschera, 1863 non (Stephens, 1831)
longiseta Weise, 1889
    clarus Allen, 1967
luridus (Scopoli, 1763) *
    brunneus sensu auctt. non (Duftschmid, 1825)
    castaneus (Duftschmid, 1825)
    fusculus sensu auctt. Brit. non Kutschera, 1864
lycopi (Foudras, 1860)
    abdominalis sensu (Allard, 1860) non (Duftschmid, 1825)
melanocephalus (De Geer, 1775) *
    piciceps (Stephens, 1831)
membranaceus (Foudras, 1860) *
    cerinus sensu auctt. Brit. partim non (Foudras, 1860)
    teucrii (Allard, 1860)
nasturtii (Fabricius, 1793)
nigerrimus (Gyllenhal, 1827) *
nigrofasciatus (Goeze, 1777) *
    patruelis (Allard, 1866)
    distinguendus (Rye, 1872)
obliteratoides Gruev, 1973
obliteratus (Rosenhauer, 1847)
    pulex sensu Fowler, 1890 non (Schrank, 1781)
ochroleucus (Marsham, 1802) *
parvulus (Paykull, 1799) *
    pumilus (Illiger, 1807)
    ater sensu Fowler, 1890 non (Fabricius, 1775)
pellucidus (Foudras, 1860) *
    medicaginis (Allard, 1860)
plantagomaritimus Dollman, 1912
pratensis (Panzer, 1794) *
    pusillus (Gyllenhal, 1813)
    collaris (Stephens, 1831)
    bearei Kevan, 1967
quadriguttatus (Pontoppidan, 1763)
reichei (Allard, 1860)
    fusculus Kutschera, 1864
rubiginosus (Foudras, 1860) *
    flavicornis sensu (Allard, 1860) non (Stephens, 1831)
rutilus (Illiger, 1807)
succineus (Foudras, 1860) *
    laevis sensu (Allard, 1860) non (Duftschmid, 1825)

        suturellus (Duftschmid, 1825) *
            thoracicus (Stephens, 1831)
        symphyti (Heikertinger, 1912)
        tabidus (Fabricius, 1775)

ALTICA Geoffroy, 1762
    HALTICA Illiger, 1801
        brevicollis Foudras, 1860
            coryli (Allard, 1860)
        carinthiaca Weise, 1888
        ericeti (Allard, 1859) *
            longicollis (Allard, 1860)
            britteni Sharp, 1914
            sandini Kemner, 1919
        helianthemi (Allard, 1859) *
            pusilla (Duftschmid, 1825) non (Müller, O.F., 1776)
        lythri Aubé, 1843 *
            tamaricis sensu auctt. Brit. partim non Schrank, 1785
        oleracea (Linnaeus, 1758) *
            ampelophaga sensu auctt. Brit. non Guérin-Méneville, 1858
            ytenensis Sharp, 1914
        palustris Weise, 1888 *

HERMAEOPHAGA Foudras, 1860
        mercurialis (Fabricius, 1793) *

BATOPHILA Foudras, 1860
        aerata (Marsham, 1802)
        rubi (Paykull, 1799) *

LYTHRARIA Bedel, 1897
    OCHROSIS sensu Fowler, 1890 non Foudras, 1860
        salicariae (Paykull, 1800) *

OCHROSIS Foudras, 1860
    CREPIDODERA sensu Fowler, 1890 partim non Dejean, 1836
        ventralis (Illiger, 1807) *

NEOCREPIDODERA Heikertinger, 1911
    CREPIDODERA sensu auctt. non Dejean, 1836
    ASIORESTIA Jacobson, 1925
        ferruginea (Scopoli, 1763) *
        impressa (Fabricius, 1801)
        transversa (Marsham, 1802) *

DEROCREPIS Weise, 1886
    CREPIDODERA sensu Fowler, 1890 partim non Dejean, 1836
        rufipes (Linnaeus, 1758) *

HIPPURIPHILA Foudras, 1860
  modeeri (Linnaeus, 1761) *

CREPIDODERA Dejean, 1836
  CHALCOIDES Foudras, 1860
    aurata (Marsham, 1802) *
    aurea (Fourcroy, 1785) *
      helxines sensu auctt. non (Linnaeus, 1758)
    fulvicornis (Fabricius, 1793) *
      smaragdina Foudras, 1860
    nitidula (Linnaeus, 1758)
    plutus (Latreille, 1804)
      chloris Foudras, 1860

EPITRIX Foudras, 1860
  EPITHRIX Foudras, 1860
    atropae Foudras, 1860
    pubescens (Koch, J.D.W., 1803)

PODAGRICA Dejean, 1836
    fuscicornis (Linnaeus, 1767)
    fuscipes (Fabricius, 1775) *

MANTURA Stephens, 1831
    chrysanthemi (Koch, J.D.W., 1803) *
    matthewsii (Curtis, 1833)
    obtusata (Gyllenhal, 1813)
    rustica (Linnaeus, 1767)

CHAETOCNEMA Stephens, 1831
  PLECTROSCELIS Dejean, 1836
    aerosa (Letzner, 1847)
    arida Foudras, 1860
      aridula sensu auctt. Brit. partim non (Gyllenhal, 1827)
    concinna (Marsham, 1802) *
    confusa (Boheman, 1851)
    hortensis (Fourcroy, 1785) *
    picipes Stephens, 1831
      concinna sensu auctt. partim non (Marsham, 1802)
      laevicollis (Thomson, C.G., 1866)
      heikertingeri Lubischev, 1963
    sahlbergii (Gyllenhal, 1827) *
    subcoerulea (Kutschera, 1864)

SPHAERODERMA Stephens, 1831
> *rubidum* (Graëlls, 1858) *
>> *testaceum* sensu auctt. partim non Fabricius, 1775
> *testaceum* (Fabricius, 1775) *
>> *cardui* (Gyllenhal, 1813)

APTEROPEDA Dejean, 1836
> *globosa* (Illiger, 1794) *
> *orbiculata* (Marsham, 1802) *
> *splendida* Allard, 1860

MNIOPHILA Stephens, 1831
> *muscorum* (Koch, J.D.W., 1803) *

DIBOLIA Latreille, 1829
> *cynoglossi* (Koch, J.D.W., 1803)

PSYLLIODES Berthold, 1827
> *affinis* (Paykull, 1799) *
> *attenuata* (Koch, J.D.W., 1803) *
> *chalcomera* (Illiger, 1807)
> *chrysocephala* (Linnaeus, 1758) *
>> *anglica* (Fabricius, 1775)
>> *luridipennis* sensu auctt. partim non Kutschera, 1864
> *cucullata* (Illiger, 1807)
> *cuprea* (Koch, J.D.W., 1803) *
>> *instabilis* sensu auctt. Brit. non Foudras, 1860
> *dulcamarae* (Koch, J.D.W., 1803) *
> *hyoscyami* (Linnaeus, 1758)
> *laticollis* Kutschera, 1860
>> *weberi* Lohse, 1955 657
> *luridipennis* Kutschera, 1864
>> *hospes* sensu auctt. non Wollaston, 1854
> *luteola* (Müller, O.F., 1776)
> *marcida* (Illiger, 1807) *
> *napi* (Fabricius, 1793) *
> *picina* (Marsham, 1802) *
> *sophiae* Heikertinger, 1914
>> *cyanoptera* sensu auctt. non (Illiger, 1807)

Subfamily CASSIDINAE Gyllenhal, 1813

PILEMOSTOMA Desbrochers, 1891
> CASSIDA sensu Fowler, 1890 partim non Linnaeus, 1758
>> *fastuosa* (Schaller, 1783)

HYPOCASSIDA Weise, 1893
> *subferruginea* (Schrank, 1776)

CASSIDA Linnaeus, 1758

denticollis Suffrian, 1844
  chloris sensu auctt. Brit. non Suffrian, 1844
flaveola Thunberg, 1794 *
hemisphaerica Herbst, 1799 *
murraea Linnaeus, 1767
  maculata Linnaeus, 1767
nebulosa Linnaeus, 1758
nobilis Linnaeus, 1758 *
prasina Illiger, 1798 *
  sanguinolenta sensu auctt. Brit. non Müller, O.F., 1776
  chloris Suffrian, 1844
rubiginosa Müller, O.F., 1776 *
  viridis sensu Scopoli, 1763 non Linnaeus, 1758
sanguinosa Suffrian, 1844 *
vibex Linnaeus, 1767 *
viridis Linnaeus, 1758 *
  equestris Fabricius, 1787
vittata de Villers, 1789

KEYS FOR THE IDENTIFICATION OF BRITISH SEED AND LEAF BEETLES

A dichotomous key to subfamilies is provided below, and provides a starting point for unknown specimens of leaf beetles. It is followed by keys to genera and species, and users can move straight to these if the subfamily is known.

KEY TO SUBFAMILIES AND SMALL FAMILIES

1 Head covered by pronotum, not visible from above; mouthparts directed backwards. Elytral margins flattened, giving a wide rim; often the whole beetle has a flattened appearance, though some may be fairly convex overall. Often rounded in dorsal view, sometimes broadly oval, never truly elongate. Known as 'tortoise beetles' (Fig. 9) .... **Key I: Subfamily Cassidinae** (p. 110)

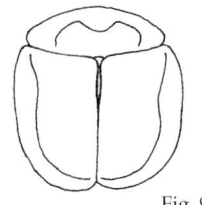

Fig. 9

Confirmatory characters: Small to medium-large beetles (4.0-10.0 mm long). Highly flattened, more or less rounded and usually splayed out to some extent around the edges.

- Not with highly flattened elytral margins or the general form indicated above 2

2 Eyes deeply notched at the front. Antennae usually serrate, sometimes filiform. Elytra generally blackish or brownish with a mottled pattern, 10 distinct striae, and recumbent pubescence. Head usually deflexed, neck long with front of head extended into a short, wide, flattish rostrum or 'muzzle'. Top of head usually with a central longitudinal ridge. Hind femora often swollen or with teeth on the underside (but femoral development **not** as in the 'flea beetles' of Subfamily Galerucinae, Tribe Alticini) (see Fig. 10 for features of the head mentioned here) ....
.... **Key A: Subfamilies Bruchinae and Amblycerinae** (p. 27)

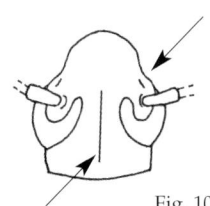

Fig. 10

Confirmatory characters: 1.7-5.3 mm long (with head deflexed). Four tarsal segments on front, middle and hind legs, with some two-lobed segments. Often associated with Rosaceae, Fabaceae and Apiaceae. Commonly known as seed beetles (sometimes other names such as 'bean weevils').

- Eyes not deeply notched at the front; may be notched at the inner edge, or entirely un-notched. Head not extended into a 'muzzle' at the front. Other features variable, but not combined as above 3

3 Head clearly (though variably) angled and constricted behind eyes (Fig. 11). Pronotum without side margins **4**

- Head without this constriction, or if with such a constriction, 5-7 mm long and yellow with four black spots on the elytra (*Phyllobrotica quadrimaculata* qv). Pronotum usually with side margins (though not in *Bromius*, *Orsodacne* and some *Cryptocephalus*) **6**

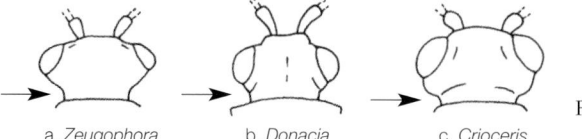

a. *Zeugophora*   b. *Donacia*   c. *Crioceris*   Fig. 11

4 Elytra with punctures in rows **5**

- Elytra with random punctures ....
.... **Key B: Family Megalopodidae (Subfamily Zeugophorinae)** (p. 34)

Confirmatory characters: 2.5-4.0 mm long and weakly elongated. Yellow pronotum coarsely punctured with a broad central lateral spine on each side (Fig. 12). Elytra irregularly and coarsely punctured but not striate. Elytral suture has a rim along the entire length (Fig. 13). Claws with a blunt appendage beneath (Fig. 14) though this may be hard to see. Other features broadly similar to Orsodacnidae.

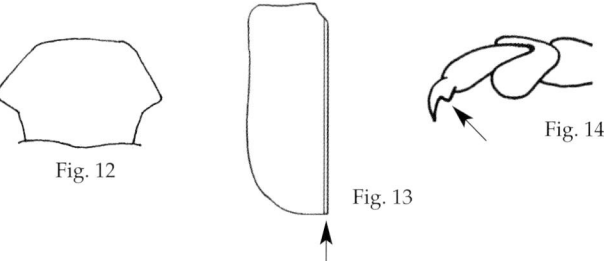

Fig. 12   Fig. 13   Fig. 14

5 First antennal segment clearly elongate and considerably longer than segment 2 (Fig. 15). Scutellum slightly pubescent. Eyes not notched ..... **Key C: Subfamily Donaciinae** (p. 35)

Confirmatory characters: 4.5-13.0 mm long. Of characteristic appearance (Fig. 16a), usually with metallic coloration and long antennae, they are unlikely to be confused with any other chrysomelid group. They are usually active in sunshine and may be readily visible in large numbers. Commonly known as reed beetles.

- First antennal segment rounded to oval; may be longer than segment 2, but not clearly elongate. Scutellum hairless. Eyes notched on inner edge, though this may be slight (e.g. in *Oulema*) .... **Key D: Subfamily Criocerinae** (p. 41)

Confirmatory characters: Distinctive; narrow, elongate with rectangular elytra (Fig. 16b) and often vividly coloured (some are metallic). Pronotum narrower than elytra at shoulders and never bordered. Includes lily and asparagus beetles.

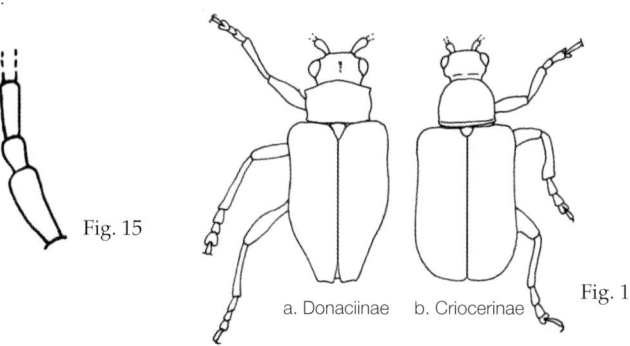

Fig. 15   a. Donaciinae   b. Criocerinae   Fig. 16

6   Fourth abdominal sternite strongly constricted in the middle (Fig. 17); if only slightly constricted, then antennae serrate. Females with a round dent in the 5th abdominal sternite (Fig. 17) ....
.... **Key E: Subfamily Cryptocephalinae** (p. 44)

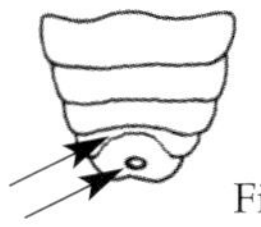

Confirmatory characters: Parallel-sided with the head largely or entirely hidden from above by the bulging pronotum, especially in *Cryptocephalus*. Antennae long and filiform in *Cryptocephalus* (most species, and the majority of specimens), serrate in *Labidostomis*, *Clytra* and *Smaragdina* (Tribe Clytrini). All are distinctly coloured and mostly stenophagous (feeding on a single food-plant or a limited range).

Fig. 17

-   Fourth abdominal sternite not, or only slightly, constricted in the middle. Antennae not necessarily serrate. Females without a round dent in the centre of the 5th abdominal sternite (Fig. 18) 7

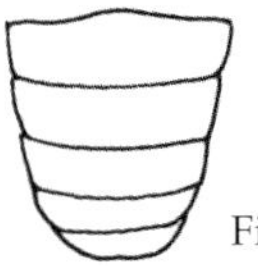

Fig. 18

7   Antennal bases beneath side margin of head, separated by about twice the length of the 1st antennal segment (Fig. 19) 8

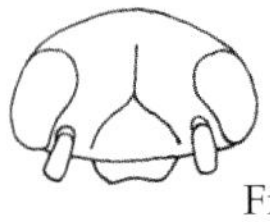

Fig. 19

-   Antennal bases on forehead (i.e. between or in front of the eyes), no further apart than the length of the 1st antennal segment (Fig. 20). Includes the flea beetles with enlarged hind femora (see Fig. 5) and the ability to jump .... **Key H: Subfamily Galerucinae** (p. 63)

Confirmatory characters: Small to medium in length.

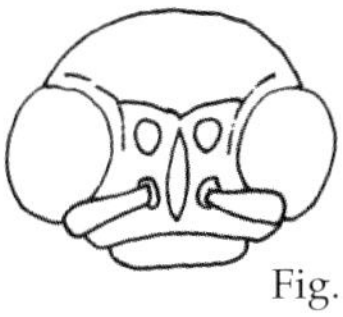

Fig. 20

8   Front coxae rounded (Fig. 21) 9

Fig. 21

-   Front coxae transverse (Fig. 22) 10

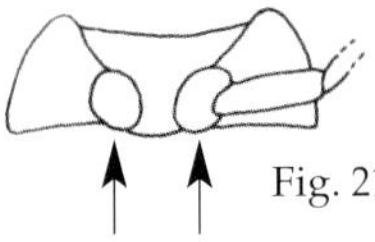

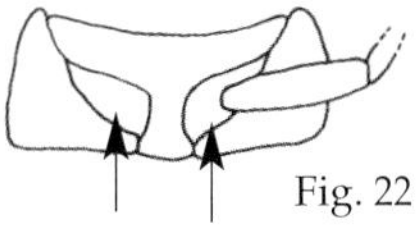

Fig. 22

9 Antennal segments 7 and 9-11 widened (Fig. 23). Elytral epipleura with three depressions, hind one deepest (Fig. 24) .... **Subfamily Lamprosomatinae (*Oomorphus concolor*)**

Confirmatory characters: 2.5-3.5 mm, oval, convex and hairless. Brassy, shiny black or brilliant bronze. Antennae short, black and bluntly-toothed; second segment red-brown, segments 7 and 9-11 swollen. Pronotum and elytra finely punctured. In ventral view, elytral epipleura with three depressions, the hind one deepest.

A single species *Oomorphus concolor*. Egg-shaped oval (Fig. 25), convex and hairless. Usually brassy. Antennae short, black and bluntly-toothed; first segment red-brown. Pronotum and elytra finely punctured. Tibiae dilated and smooth on outer side (Fig. 26). Males and females difficult to separate. Widespread across southern England and Wales, some scattered northerly records. Adults may be beaten from ivy growing on tree trunks.

- Antennal segments enlarge more or less gradually towards the tip. No epipleural depressions .... **Subfamily Eumolpinae (*Bromius obscurus*)**

Confirmatory characters: 5.0-6.0 mm, elongate (for chrysomelids), dark-coloured, non-metallic with pale pubescence. Elytral epipleura without depressions, antennae with segments gradually increasing in size towards the tip.

A single species, *Bromius obscurus*. Uniformly black with dull yellow-grey pubescence. Four basal antennal segments orange-red. Males and females difficult to separate. Adults feed on various willowherbs, making 'scribbling' marks. Endangered (RDB1), found in a single 10 km square on the Cheshire-Staffordshire border.

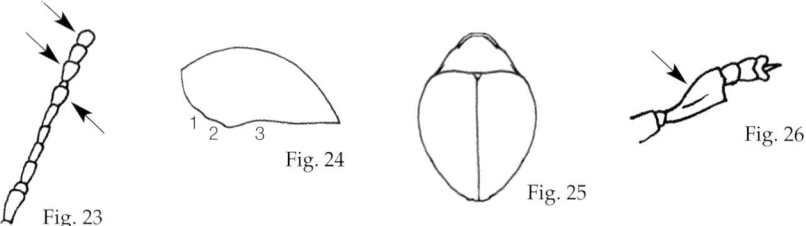

Fig. 23   Fig. 24   Fig. 25   Fig. 26

10 Head elongate in front of antennal bases. Pronotum without side margins, narrowed towards the rear, considerably narrower than front of elytra (Fig. 27) .... **Key F: Family Orsodacnidae (Subfamily Orsodacninae)** (p. 51)

Confirmatory characters: 4.0-8.0 mm long. Pale brown to black. Head with a narrow neck so that the eyes are some distance from the front edge of the pronotum. Pronotum without lateral teeth. Elytra elongate and randomly punctured, rounded at apex (in some specimens elytral punctures tend to run in longitudinal lines near the middle but overall the randomness should be clear).

Further features if required: Antennae filiform with segment 1 bulbous, 2 quadrate and 3-11 elongate; segments 7-10 about 1.5 times longer than wide (Fig. 28). Antennae inserted behind the mandibles but forward of the front edge of the eyes; insertions widely separated, a little wider than the length of the basal segment. Eyes entire (not notched). Procoxae transverse (visible from the side). Third tarsal segment bilobed, on middle and hind legs, deeply so (Fig. 29). Colour varies from dark blue to yellow or a combination of these and a casual glance in the field suggests a robust cantharid (soldier beetle), but broader and more convex.

- Head not elongate in front of antennal bases. Pronotum with side margins, not constricted at rear, where it is, at most, slightly narrower than front of elytra (Fig. 30) .... **Key G: Subfamily Chrysomelinae** (p. 51)

Confirmatory characters: 2.5-18.0 mm. Brightly coloured and usually shining metallic species. Hairless, generally round or oval (some may be elongate for chrysomelids, but still oval) and very convex – often the 'typical' leaf-beetle shape and colour. Antennae often gradually thicken towards the tip; inserted beneath side margin of head and widely placed, further apart than the length of the basal joint. Head not elongate in front of antennal bases. Pronotum with a side margin, not narrowed at the rear, and no more than slightly narrower than the front of the elytra. Mostly stenophagus (feeding on a single food-plant or a limited range), found by beating shrubs or trees or general sweeping.

Several species are crop pests including the notorious and unmistakeable yellow and black Colorado potato beetle (*Leptinotarsa decemlineata*) (Fig. 31) with its equally distinctive red and black larva (Fig. 32). It is not included here as it has not yet become established in Britain although this may change if climate change produces winters warm enough for adult survival. It is a notifiable quarantine pest; adults or larvae suspected of being this species should be placed in a container and sent to Fera (The Food Environment Research Agency), Sand Hutton, York YO41 1LZ, along with a detailed description of where and when found. Note that Fera was previously known as the Central Science Laboratory.

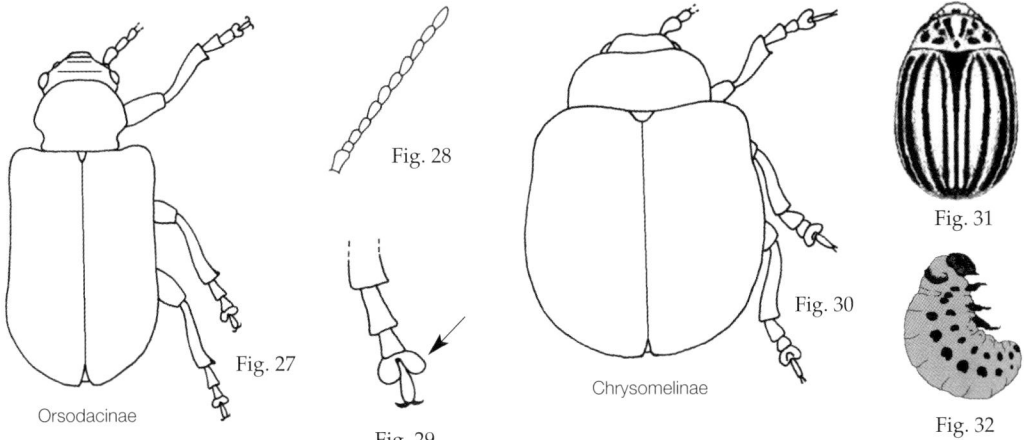

Fig. 28

Fig. 31

Fig. 30

Fig. 27

Orsodacinae

Chrysomelinae

Fig. 29

Fig. 32

KEYS TO GENERA AND SPECIES

KEY A: SUBFAMILIES BRUCHINAE AND AMBLYCERINAE

1 Hind tibiae with two long movable apical spurs (Fig. 33). Hind coxae about twice as wide as hind femora, which are narrow without ventral teeth .... **Subfamily Amblycerinae**

Confirmatory characters: In Britain, a single species of this subfamily has been recorded, *Zabrotes subfasciatus* (Mexican bean beetle). Males with uniform pale brown pubescence on the dark cuticle; females with pronotum and elytra clearly marked with a white pubescent pattern on the dark cuticle. Elytra squat and broad. Hind femora with a longitudinal ventral groove bordered by sharp, untoothed keels. 1.8-2.5 mm. Originally from the Americas, it is now found in many tropical and subtropical areas and is a pest of beans (*Phaseolus*). Although recorded on imported produce, it is an introduced species which is not considered established and so is not listed in Duff (2008), although it is described and figured in Cox (2001) and included, without a map, in Cox (2007).

- Hind tibiae with a single long apical spur (Fig. 34), or two short apical spurs (Fig. 35); in either case they are immobile. Hind coxae less than twice as wide as hind femora, which are thickened (with or without one or more teeth) .... 2 (**Subfamily Bruchinae**)

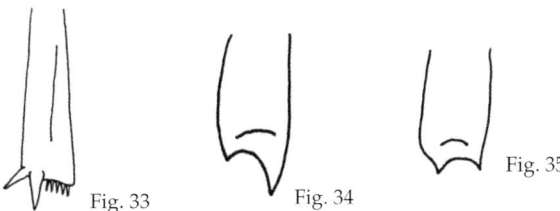

Fig. 35

Fig. 33   Fig. 34

2 Pronotum wide, sides at least slightly notched, sometimes with a small tooth at the front edge of the notch (Fig. 36). Hind femora ventrally with a large tooth on the inner keel. Males usually with middle tibiae usually bearing a spur, or 1 or 2 teeth, at and/or near the apex .... Key A1: Genus *Bruchus* (p. 29)

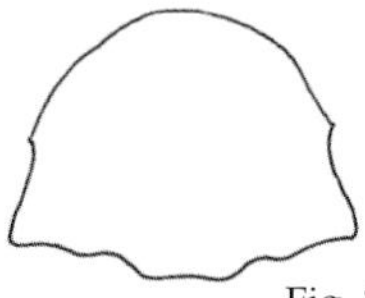

Fig. 36

– Pronotum not notched; narrows conically towards the front (Fig. 37), less so in *Bruchidius villosus*, with all dark legs and uniform pubescence dorsally. Hind femora not as above. Males without teeth or a spur on the mid-tibiae 3

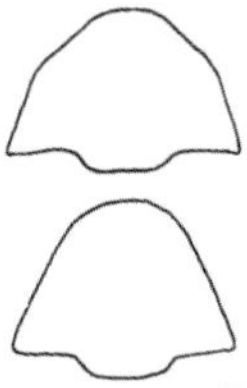

Fig. 37

3 Rear of pronotum with a double callus in the centre bearing dense white pubescence. First hind tarsal segment clearly longer than others combined. Hind femora ventrally usually with a tooth on both inner and outer keels .... Key A2: Genus *Callosobruchus* (p. 31)

– Rear of pronotum not as above. First hind tarsal segment may be equal to, shorter than or no more than slightly longer than others combined 4

4 Hind femora ventrally with large backwards-pointing tooth in the apical half, followed by two or three (rarely one) smaller teeth (Fig. 38). Pronotum with scale-like pubescence obscuring otherwise clear microsculpturation .... *Acanthoscelides obtectus* (dried bean beetle)

Fig. 38

Confirmatory characters: Antennae dark grey, segments 1-5 and 11 often reddish. Elytral pubescence forming numerous faint spots. Most of abdomen, tips of elytra, and legs yellowish-red, except underside of mid and hind femora (black). 2.5-3.0 mm.

Distribution: Since the 1920s, an introduced pest of dried foods. Scattered, mostly in south and south-east England.

– Hind femora without teeth ventrally (rarely with a very small spine). Pronotum without scale-like pubescence; microsculpturation not obscured .... Key A3: Genus *Bruchidius* (p. 33)

Key A1: Genus *Bruchus*

The middle tibiae of male *Bruchus* have one or two spurs at or near the apex; these spurs are not present in females.

1 Hind tibiae with two apical spurs more or less equal in length. Lobes of 3rd hind tarsal segment as long as 2nd segment in males, a little shorter in females (Fig. 39). Pygidium with white T-shaped pubescent patch which has dark spots on either side (Fig. 40). Males with mid tibia bearing a single sharp apical spur (similar to Fig. 44 but sharper). 3.4-4.5 mm .... *pisorum* (pea beetle)

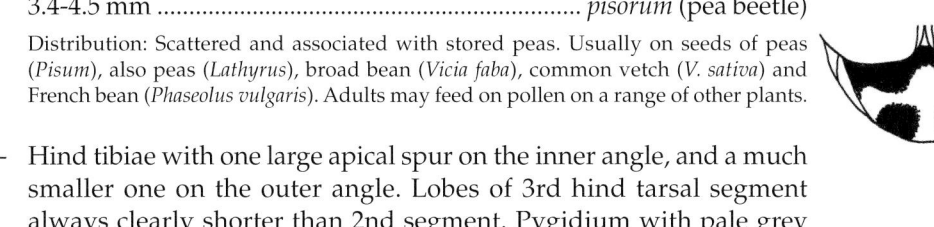

Fig. 39

Fig. 40

Distribution: Scattered and associated with stored peas. Usually on seeds of peas (*Pisum*), also peas (*Lathyrus*), broad bean (*Vicia faba*), common vetch (*V. sativa*) and French bean (*Phaseolus vulgaris*). Adults may feed on pollen on a range of other plants.

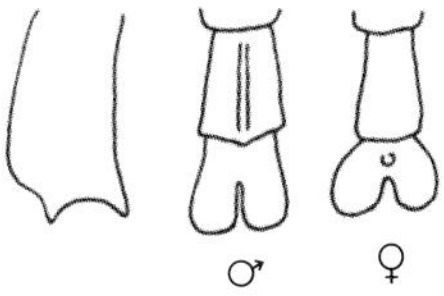

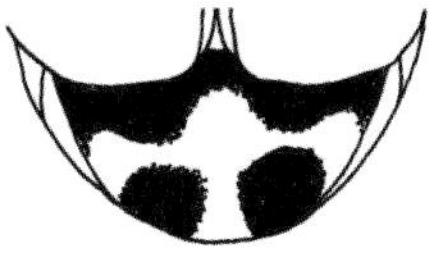

- Hind tibiae with one large apical spur on the inner angle, and a much smaller one on the outer angle. Lobes of 3rd hind tarsal segment always clearly shorter than 2nd segment. Pygidium with pale grey (to whitish) pubescence, sometimes with faint darker spots on either side. 1.7-5.3 mm 2

2 Pronotum and elytra black with recumbent (not scale-like) pubescence. Pronotum bell-shaped, rounded at the front; lateral teeth very small, may be almost absent (Fig. 41). Males with two spurs close together on middle tibiae. 1.7-2.9 mm .... *loti*

Distribution: Widespread, often on legumes, in a range of habitats.

- Scutellum and centre of rear edge of pronotum at least with scale-like pubescence. Elytra usually with pale patches of scale-like pubescence. Pronotum with sides rounded towards front angles; front edge usually straight, though this straight section may be very short; lateral teeth more clearly developed (Fig. 42). 1.8-5.3 mm 3

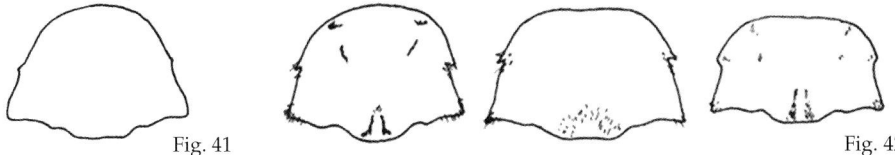

Fig. 41

Fig. 42

3 Pronotum at least 1.5 times as wide as long. 1.8-4.0 mm 4

- Pronotal width no more than 1.4 times length. 2.5-5.3 mm 5

4 TRIPLET – read all three parts

Note that, in general form, *rufipes* and *brachialis* appear similar and may be found together; see the notes at the end of this triplet, adapted from Hammond & Harvey, 2011.

- Pronotum and elytra with dense, uniform golden pubescence and several white markings. Antennae with first 4 or 5 antennal segments orange (sometimes all orange). Males with a single apical spur on the middle tibiae. 3.0-4.0 mm .... *ervi*

Distribution: A very rare introduction found breeding in imported lentils in a shop in East Sussex in 1985.

- Patches of denser pale pubescence appearing as more or less white spots, especially across the elytral shoulders and on the elytral disc. Front and middle legs, and first 4 or 5 antennal segments orange, rarely black (sometimes middle legs may be partly and variably darkened). Antennae sometimes yellow or orange in males. Males with two spines near apex on inner edge of middle tibiae; distance between tips no more than length of longest spine (Fig. 43b). Males with the front tibia not swollen. Males with the distal end of the middle tibia bearing a stout projection with a pair of thorn-like points. 1.8-3.1 mm ...... *rufipes*

Distribution: Widespread south from the Midlands, often on legumes, in a range of habitats.

- Pronotum and elytra dark (brownish to blackish) with variable white to cream or pale brown markings formed from irregular dorsal pubescence, the surface appearing flecked with pale grey against a brown-grey background. Front legs and antennae orange (middle legs may be orange or dark). Males with a single apical spur on the middle tibiae, the tip of the spur very slightly bifurcated. Males with the front tibia variably swollen. Males with the distal end of the middle tibia bearing a rather narrow (more or less flat-ended) blade-like projection. 1.8-3.1 mm .... *brachialis*

Distribution: From 2010, established in south Essex (Hammond & Harvey, 2011) on fodder vetch (*Vicia villosa*); known from numerous vetches (*Vicia*) in many countries outside the UK and is likely to expand its range.

Separation of *rufipes* and *brachialis*

Antennal segments of *brachialis* are more clearly broadened than in *rufipes*, especially in males. Male *brachialis* have antennae a unicolorous orange-yellow, while those of male *rufipes* are very variable, from a unicolorous orange-yellow, to those with slightly darker distal segments, those with only segments 1-4 reddish colour, and others with the antennae more or less completely dark. Female *brachialis* usually have bicoloured antennae with (at least) segments 1-5 orange-red and the distal one or two also reddish, with three or more intermediate segments more or less black. Female *rufipes*, like males, have variably coloured antennae, but most segments (at least 6-11) are more or less black. Segments 1-4 (or 5) may be orange-red colour, or relatively dark, sometimes such that the antennae are effectively unicolorous black.

The middle and hind legs in *brachialis* are more or less unicolorous black in both sexes. The front legs are uniformly orange-yellow in males; in females at least the tarsus and tibia of the front legs are of a similar orange-yellow colour but the front femur is variably darker, especially towards the base. In *rufipes* only the hind legs are always dark; front and middle legs may be paler orange-yellow to reddish-brown in both sexes, though more commonly in males, especially in individuals with unicolorous orange-yellow antennae. In both sexes, the front and middle legs are often darker, occasionally more or less uniformly black.

The front tibia of male *brachialis* is variably swollen, unlike that of male *rufipes*. The distal end of the middle tibia is modified in male *brachialis*, bearing a rather narrow (more or less flat-ended) blade-like projection; in male *rufipes* a stouter projection is seen which bears a pair of thorn-like points.

In *brachialis* the dorsal pubescence is irregular, but far less patchy than in *rufipes*, and the surface appears to be flecked with pale grey against a brown-grey background. Distinctively paler patches or spots are only seen around the scutellum and centrally at the base of the pronotum. In *rufipes*, patches of denser pale pubescence appear as more or less white spots, especially across the elytral shoulders and on the elytral disc.

5 Scale-like pubescence on the pronotum sparse; a dense patch around centre of the rear edge, a few small spots on top, around lateral teeth and rear angles. Males with tibial spur located away from inner apical angle (Fig. 43a). 2.5-3.6 mm .... *atomarius*

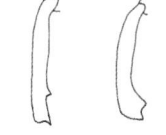

a. *atomarius* b. *rufipes*

Fig. 43

Distribution: Scarce (Nb), widespread but local and not found in Scotland. Mainly on Fabaceae, sometimes other plants including trees and umbellifers.

- Scale-like pubescence on the pronotum moderately dense, especially around centre of the rear edge and rear angles. Males with long middle tibial spur at inner apical angle (Fig. 44). 3.1-5.3 mm .... *rufimanus* (bean seed beetle)

Fig. 44

Distribution: Widespread but local in various habitats; a pest of stored beans, otherwise on a range on mainly leguminous plants.

Key A2: Genus *Callosobruchus*

In males the apical abdominal segment is much reduced, while in females it is well developed and distinct. See individual species descriptions for differences between male and female antennae.

1 Hind femora with the inner tooth small or absent, much smaller than the tooth on the outer keel which extends much further from the femora than the inner tooth (Figs 45, 47). Fig. 45 is a side view of the hind femora, showing the variation in inner tooth size on the keel which runs longitudinally – in Fig. 54a, the keel is untoothed; in Fig. 45b, a small inner tooth is present. The keel usually bears several tiny teeth behind the inner tooth. Tip of aedeagus narrowly pointed with a few small bristles where the tip begins to widen (Fig. 46). Male antennae weakly serrate, female antennae clearly serrate. 2.6-4.0 mm .... *analis*

Distribution: An Asian pest of legumes with one imported specimen collected in 1911.

- Hind femora with inner tooth almost as large as outer tooth (Figs 48, 50, 52). Aedeagus with tip differently shaped and a different arrangement of bristles 2

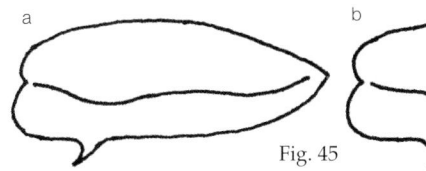

Fig. 45

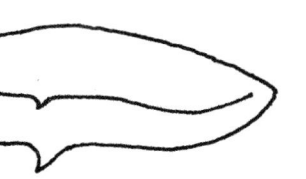

Fig. 46

Fig. 47

2   Abdominal sternites 2-4 without a broad band of dense white pubescence laterally. Hind femora with two teeth extending about the same distance (Fig. 48). Tip of aedeagus broadly triangular with numerous basal bristles (Fig. 49). Male antennae no more than weakly serrate; female antennae clearly serrate with segment 11 more than twice as long as wide 2.7-3.8 mm .... *maculatus* (cowpea seed beetle)

     Distribution: An African pest of stored legumes, especially chick pea (*Cicer arietinum*), occasional records from such produce.

\-   Abdominal sternites 2-4 with a broad band of dense white pubescence laterally, different in colour and density to the rest of the abdominal setae. Hind femora with one spine extending a different distance than the other (Figs 50, 52). Tip of aedeagus with shorter and/or sparser basal bristles and more narrowly triangular, sometimes spear-shaped (Figs 51, 53). 2.2-3.0 mm 3

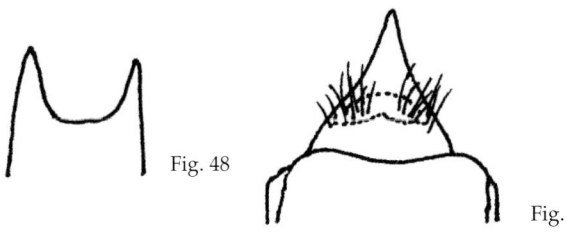

Fig. 48   Fig. 49

3   Two teeth on hind femora; the outer one slightly longer than the inner one (Fig. 50). Tip of aedeagus spear-shaped (Fig. 51). Male antennae pectinate; female antennae serrate with segment 11 oval and clearly less than twice as long as wide .... *chinensis* (adzuki beanseed beetle)

     Distribution: An Asian pest of stored legumes, recorded occasionally in Britain in or near such produce, occasional wild records from umbellifers.

\-   Two teeth on hind femora; the inner one slightly longer than the outer one (Fig. 52). Tip of aedeagus narrowly triangular but not spear-shaped (Fig. 53). Male antennae serrate; female antennae weakly serrate with segment 11 an elongate oval .... *rhodesianus*

     Distribution: An African pest of legumes.

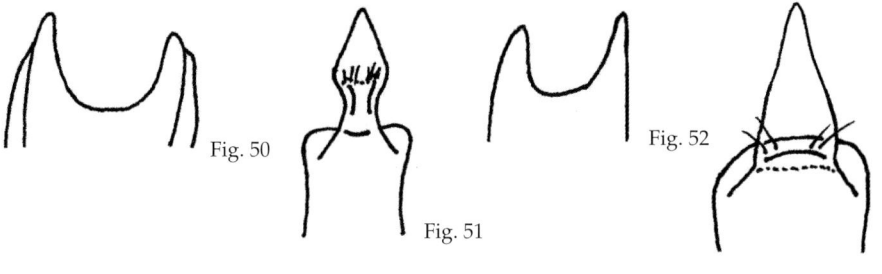

Fig. 50   Fig. 52

Fig. 51   Fig. 53

C. analis and *C. rhodesianus* are introduced species which are not considered established and so are not listed in Duff (2008), although they are described and figured in Cox (2001) and included, without maps, in Cox (2007). Note that the aedeagus of *C. rhodesianus* is only weakly chitinised and so care is required to avoid damage during dissection (Southgate 1958).

Key A3: Genus *Bruchidius*

In males, the last tergite folds around the end of the abdomen and is therefore visible in ventral view along with a indent at the tip of the final sternite (Fig. 54). In females, the last tergite is barely visible and there is no corresponding indent (Fig. 55).

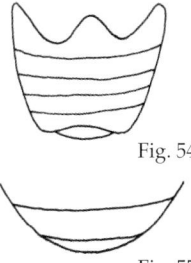

Fig. 54

Fig. 55

1 Pronotum and elytra with a clear pattern formed of whitish, golden, pale and dark brown scale-like pubescence. 2.5-3.0 mm .... *varius*

Confirmatory characters: Legs reddish with basal parts of femora, apices and the inner edges (often) of the hind tibiae and tarsi brownish to black. Males with antennae two thirds of body length, segments 9-11 reddish-orange. Females with antennae less than half body length, segment 11 (and sometimes 10) reddish.

Distribution: First recorded in Britain in 1994, now scattered in south and south-east England in mixed vegetation in a variety of habitats. Mainly on red clover (*Trifolium pratense*) and zigzag clover (*T. medium*), also gorse (*Ulex europaeus*), sea club-rush (*Bolboschoenus maritimus*) and possibly a range of other species.

- Pronotum and elytra without this pattern 2

2 Elytra blackish, or reddish except for darker base and suture. Legs reddish with black femoral bases. Antennae entirely reddish (sometimes yellowish to brownish); two thirds of body length. 2.5-3.5 mm .... *incarnatus*

Distribution: A very rare introduction likely to be associated with imported beans or similar produce.

- Pronotum and elytra with uniform unpatterned pubescence. Legs almost entirely blackish. Males with antennae reaching no further than mid-point of elytra, segments 5-10 blackish. Females with antennal segments 10 and 11 blackish. 1.9-3.4 mm 3

3 Pronotum almost twice as wide as long (Fig. 56). Pygidium broad. Antennae short, reaching just past pronotum; first 4 segments reddish at least on the underside (sometimes dark brown or black above). 2.4-3.2 mm .... *villosus*

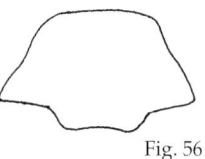

Fig. 56

Distribution: Widespread in a range of habitats, usually on broom (*Cytisus scoparius*) sometimes on a variety of other species.

- Pronotum narrowing towards front, appearing conical and no more than 1.5x as wide as long (Fig. 57). Pygidium elongate. Antennae entirely black, reaching to around mid-point of elytra. 1.9-3.4 mm 4

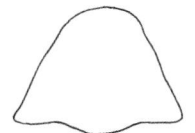

Fig. 57

4 Pronotum with fine uniform punctures. Dorsal pubescence short, fine, silvery white and sparse. Ventral pubescence usually the same colour as dorsally, sometimes darker with some golden setae. Pygidium with a pointed tip. 2.3-3.4 mm .... *cisti*

Distribution: Widely scattered on various plants in a range of habitats in England and Wales.

- Pronotum with coarse non-uniform punctures; spacing irregular, large deep punctures with smaller, shallower ones in between. Dorsal pubescence long, thick and golden (obscures the integument). Ventral pubescence silvery white. Pygidium with a rounded tip. 1.9-2.8 mm .... *olivaceus*

Distribution: Endangered (RDB1) and possibly extinct. Associated with sainfoin (*Onobrychis viciifolia*) on calcareous grassland and agricultural land; possibly also found on rock-roses (*Cistus*), brideworts (*Spiraea*) and the introduced scorpion senna (*Hippocrepis emersus*).

KEY B: FAMILY MEGALOPODIDAE (SUBFAMILY ZEUGOPHORINAE)

A single genus in the UK; larvae are legless, flattened leaf-miners. Males and females are difficult to separate, but dissection is unnecessary as the species can be identified using colours and surface features.

Key B1: Genus *Zeugophora*

1 Yellowish dorsally with black hind thoracic segment and abdomen. 3.2-3.6 mm ...... *turneri*

Distribution: In broad-leaved woodland, Scotland only.

- Elytra black. Pronotum orange-yellow. 2.5-3.5 mm 2

2 Head black between the eyes (sometimes all black from above), pronotum sparsely punctured. 2.5-3.5 mm .... *flavicollis*

Distribution: Sparsely scattered (south-east and central England only) and Vulnerable (RDB2) in broad-leaved woodland and on commons. On poplars (*Populus*) and sometimes willows (*Salix alba* and *S. caprea*).

- Head entirely yellow, pronotal disc densely and coarsely punctured. 2.7-3.5 mm (usually less than 3.0 mm) .... *subspinosa*

Distribution: Widespread, somewhat scattered and locally common in various habitats; previously listed as Scarce (Nb). Adults on poplars (*Populus*), especially aspen (*P. tremula*) saplings and sometimes willows (*Salix*) or, probably accidentally, hazels (*Corylus*).

KEY C: SUBFAMILY DONACIINAE

Males have front tarsi dilated; this is not the case in females. See individual species accounts for other features such as femoral teeth which may be used to separate males and females.

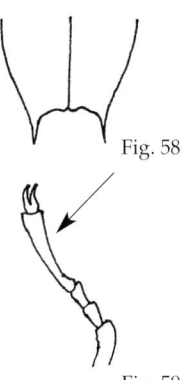

1 Dull yellowish with grey or black head and elytral striae. Elytral apex sinuate and toothed at the rear corners (Fig. 58). Tarsi long and slender with 3rd segment simple. Final tarsal segment (with claws) longer than others combined (Fig. 59). 5.0-7.5 mm ....
.... Key C1: Genus *Macroplea* (p. 36)

Distribution: Usually underwater on plants.

Fig. 58

Fig. 59

- Metallic, elytra without tooth at the end. Tarsi not elongated; 3rd segment lobed. 5.0-12.0 mm 2

Distribution: Usually on water plants.

2 Legs relatively stout, hind femora typically 2.5-3 times as long as their widest point (excluding femoral teeth), and not strongly constricted towards the base. Elytra dorsally 'vaulted' and rounded at the end; widest after the middle when viewed from side (Fig. 60), though may be less distinctly widened than in the figure. Suture sinuate near tip (Fig. 61). Mandibles protruding .... Key C2: Genus *Plateumaris* (p. 36)

- Legs relatively spindly, hind femora typically more than 3 times as long as their widest point (excluding femoral teeth), and may be strongly constricted towards the base forming a club-like shape. Note that in some species, particularly *versicolorea* (but also *obscura* and *dentata*, and especially males), the femoral length:width ratio may overlap with that of *Plateumaris*. Elytra dorsally somewhat flattened and truncate at the end; tapers more or less evenly when viewed from the side (Fig. 62). Suture straight to the tip. Mandibles short, not protruding .... Key C3: Genus *Donacia* (p. 37)

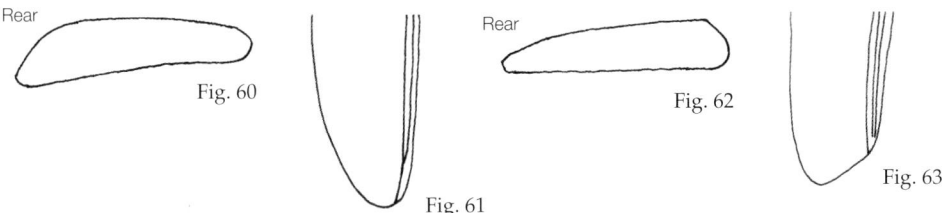

Rear

Fig. 60

Fig. 61

Rear

Fig. 62

Fig. 63

Key C1: Genus *Macroplea*

1 Spine at end of elytra narrow and sharply pointed, with a wider indent alongside its base (Fig. 64). Median lobe of aedeagus wider and sharply narrowed at the end with a small central lip (Fig. 65). Last antennal segment with a length:width ratio of approximately 6.6; antennae usually longer overall. 6.0-7.5 mm ....… *appendiculata*

Distribution: Rare (RDB3) on various plants in canals, lakes, rivers and drainage channels. In Ireland, scattered mainly in central areas; recent records from the Grand, Royal and Barrow Canals, the 'lower River Shannon', Fermanagh, Galway and Sligo.

- Spine at end of elytra thicker and blunter with a narrower indent alongside its base (Fig. 66). Median lobe of aedeagus narrower and more gradually narrowed at the end where it is blunt without a small central lip (Fig. 67). Last antennal segment with a length:width ratio of approximately 5.7; antennae usually shorter overall. 5.0-7.0 mm .... *mutica*

Distribution: Rare (RDB3) on various plants in brackish water, usually coastal, sometimes inland; mainly in eastern England.

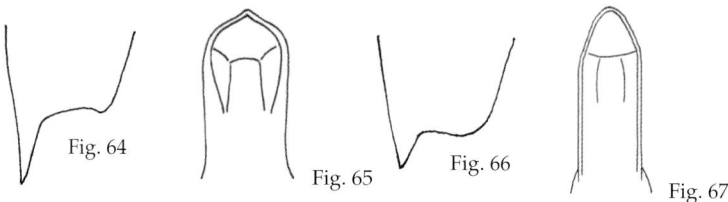

Fig. 64

Fig. 65   Fig. 66

Fig. 67

Key C2: Genus *Plateumaris*

1 Pronotum hairless apart from (at most) a few bristles towards the rear; abdomen the same colour as the rest of the body. Elytra each with two impressions near the suture, one about a third of the way from the front edge, the other about a third of the way from the rear edge. Males and females both have a strong tooth on the hind femora (Fig. 68). 5.5-8.5 mm 2

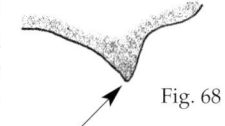

Fig. 68

- Pronotum very finely pubescent; abdomen brown or reddish and different from the rest of the body. Elytra without impressions. Males have a strong tooth on the hind femora, females have no tooth or a blunt angular protrusion (Fig. 69). 5.0-11.5 mm 3

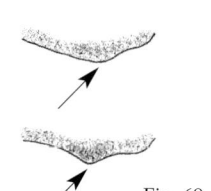

Fig. 69

2 Pronotal disc obliquely wrinkled with puncturation stronger in the mid-line. Colour metallic but variable, sometimes black. In males, antennal segment 4 approximately 2.0 times as long as wide. Median lobe of aedeagus narrows evenly towards the pointed tip (Fig. 70). 6.6-8.0 mm .... *discolor*

Distribution: Widespread and common in boggy areas, wet heaths and mires, and around various water-bodies. Usually on sedges (*Carex*), sometimes on cottongrasses (*Eriophorum*; larvae and cocoons are found on the roots and rhizomes), sweet-grasses (*Glyceria*) and cotton deergrass (*Trichophorum alpinum*). In Ireland, widespread, though sparse in the SW.

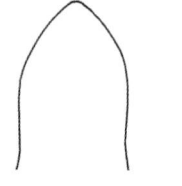

Fig. 70

- Pronotal disc with fine, even punctures; smoother, without oblique wrinkles. Colour as *P. discolor* above. In males, antennal segment 4 approximately 2.6 times as long as wide. Median lobe of aedeagus narrows unevenly towards the tip which bears a small central lip (Fig. 71). 5.5-8.5 mm .... *sericea*

Distribution: Widespread and common on vegetation in various non-acidic aquatic habitats. Mainly on bur-reeds (*Sparganium*) especially branched bur-reed (*S. erectum*). Widespread in Ireland.

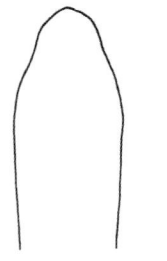

Fig. 71

> Take care with the separation of *P. discolor* and *P. sericea* as intermediate forms are quite common and dissection of males may be required.

3 Pronotum narrowing to the rear and with a small lump on each side protruding out from the side margin of the thorax (just behind the weak front angle), and edged with small dents (Fig. 72). Black with a green or violet reflection, pronotum often greenish or bluish. Antennae, legs and abdominal sternites reddish-brown. 8.5-11.5 mm .... *braccata*

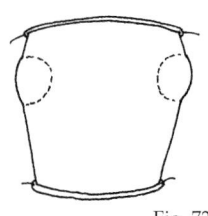

Fig. 72

Distribution: Scarce (Na) at the margins of various water-bodies on common reed (*Phragmites australis*); larvae and cocoons also known from various sedges (*Carex*). In Ireland, rediscovered as a single female specimen from a reedbed near Oilgate, Wexford in 2008, the first Irish record since 1936 (Foster *et al.* 2007, Reynolds & Foster 2009).

- Pronotum more or less rectangular, without the small lump (or if present, much reduced) seen in *P. braccata* and other *Plateumaris* (Fig. 73). The front angle of the pronotum is prominent. Males black with purplish reflection, sometimes reddish-brown basally, females coppery. Antennae and legs orange-brown. 5.0-9.0 mm .... *affinis*

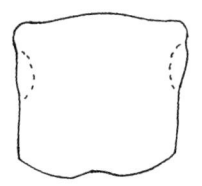

Fig. 73

Confirmatory characters: Pronotum with more-or-less even, dense punctures along the middle.

Distribution: Scarce (Na) but widespread and may be locally common, mainly on sedges (*Carex*) at lake and canal margins, sometimes on other plants. In Ireland, a few old records from Donegal, the most recent from 1913; no more recent specimens.

Key C3: Genus *Donacia*

1 Pronotum and elytra with short pale pubescence; with the underlying colour usually bronze, rarely metallic dark green, the dorsal colour overall appears shiny silver-grey or pale brownish .... *cinerea*

Confirmatory characters: Front tibiae widen towards the apex where there is a small projection on the outer edge (Fig. 74); this character may be very weak in males. 7.3-10.5 mm.

Distribution: Scarce (Nb) on emergent vegetation growing in still water at the edges of various non-flowing water-bodies. In Ireland, scattered in central areas; recent records from Westmeath, Leitrim and Limerick.

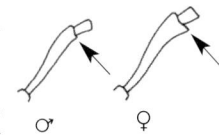

♂   ♀

Fig. 74

- Not pubescent, colour variable. 5.4-10.8 mm 2

2   Antennae and legs, including tarsi, entirely reddish-brown. 8.3-10.5 mm .... *clavipes*

Confirmatory characters: Pronotum with transverse wrinkles and fine, random punctures.

Distribution: Scarce (Nb) in various water-bodies and wet areas. Adults on common reed (*Phragmites australis*). Larvae and cocoons on roots of *P. australis*; also known from rhizomes of sedges (*Carex*). In Ireland, widepread but scattered, mainly to the north and west.

-   Antennae and legs, including tarsi, at the most only partly reddish-brown. 5.4-10.8 mm ... 3

3   Antennae and legs, except claws, entirely black with weak metallic reflection, or legs may be brightly metallic. 6.0-10.7 mm 4

-   Legs partly reddish-brown (the black colour may well cover most of the legs, so this needs to be checked carefully); antennae may be reddish-brown (whole or in part) or entirely dark. 5.4-10.8 mm 10

4   Pronotal disc clearly and coarsely punctured (punctures not necessarily densely packed or numerous). 6.6-10.7 mm 5

-   Pronotal disc with no (or a few indistinct) punctures, but with transverse wrinkles (Fig. 75). 6.0-8.5 mm .... *sparganii*

Confirmatory characters: Elytra shiny. Long hind femora with one large (and often 1 or 2 small) teeth before the apex on the underside.

Distribution: Scarce (Na), usually on floating leaves of bur-reeds (*Sparganium*), sometimes on various river-bank plants.

Fig. 75

5   Elytra green, blue-green along suture, wide reddish band outside this (may be partly golden, coppery, blue or purple). 6.7-8.8 mm .... *aquatica*

Confirmatory characters: Hind femora with one spine.

Distribution: Rare (RDB3) in sedge-dominanted aquatic vegetation by open water, also with rushes (*Juncus*) beside upland tarns. In Ireland, scattered in central-western areas with recent records from Fermanagh, Clare, Galway and Offaly.

-   Elytra without colour along suture, sometimes with anterior quarter-length red, blue or purple patch. 6.6-10.7 mm 6

6   Pronotum strongly wrinkled with few punctures (Fig. 76), though these are coarse. Elytra bronze-brown, edges greenish, usually with anterior fifth red, blue or purple (markings may be missing). 8.0-10.0 mm .... *marginata*

Confirmatory characters: Hind femora with one spine.

Distribution: Widespread and locally common on emergent vegetation in various wet habitats, including *Phragmites australis* reedbeds. Adults on branched bur-reed (*Sparganium erectum*), larval cocoons also known from sweet-grasses (*Glyceria*) and common club-rush (*Schoenoplectus lacustris*). In Ireland, very scattered, mainly in the south and east.

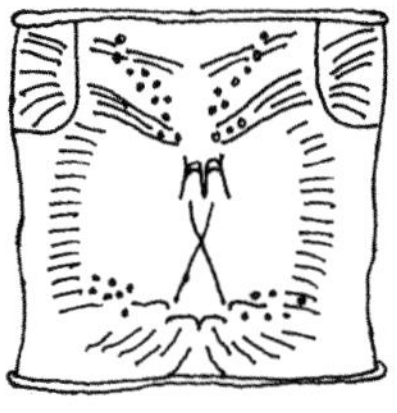

Fig. 76

-   Pronotum not (or weakly) wrinkled with many punctures. No red, blue or purple markings on elytra. 6.6-10.7 mm 7

7   Usually a distinct short scutellary stria on the elytra (Fig. 77). Front
     edge of pronotum straight or weakly convex. 6.6-8.4 mm 8

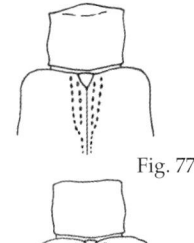

Fig. 77

-    Short scutellary stria usually indistinct/confused (Fig. 78). Front edge
     of pronotum may be weakly concave or convex. 8.0-10.7 mm 9

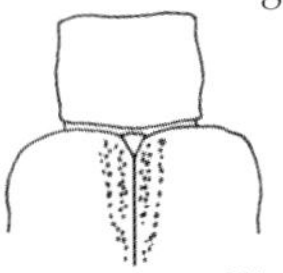

Fig. 78

8   Hind femora with tooth small or absent. Elytra with suture raised to
     a small point at the apex (Fig. 79). Median lobe of aedeagus narrower,
     gradually broadening towards the tip which narrows more gradually
     and has a less distinct central lip (Fig. 80). 6.7-8.4 mm .... *impressa*

     Confirmatory characters: Hind femora with one spine. Usually deep brass or bronze.

     Distribution: Scarce (Na) but widespread and may be locally common, usually on
     common club-rush (*Schoenoplectus lacustris*) or sedges (*Carex*), but sometimes on other
     plants, at the edges of various water-bodies and wet areas. In Ireland, widespread in
     central and western areas.

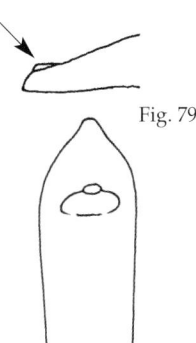

Fig. 79

Fig. 80

-    Hind femora with a long sharp tooth (may be reduced). Elytra usually
     without suture raised. Median lobe of aedeagus broader and more-
     or-less parallel-sided, gradually narrowing at the tip which has a
     distinct central lip (Fig. 81). 6.6-8.3 mm .... *thalassina*

     Confirmatory characters: Silvery pubescence beneath. Brass, bronze or greenish.

     Distribution: Scarce (Nb) though widespread, usually on common spike-rush
     (*Eleocharis palustris*) or other vegetation by various water-bodies and wet areas. Similar
     ecological requirements to *D. impressa* though the two species are not found together.
     In Ireland, widespread, mainly in the north and west.

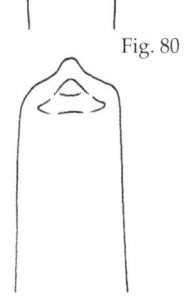

Fig. 81

9   Dorsal surface and legs dull deep bronze, no green reflection. Large
     femoral tooth (Fig. 82). 8.1-10.7 mm .... *obscura*

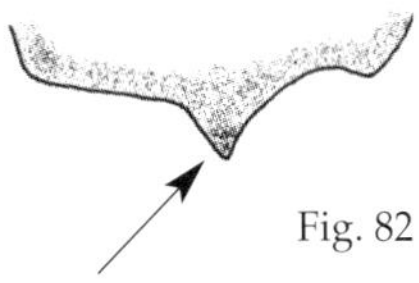

     Distribution: Scarce (Na), mainly in the north and west. On vegetation dominated by
     club-rushes (Cyperaceae) and sedges (Cyperaceae) in boggy areas by acidic water-
     bodies. In Scotland, particularly associated with beak-sedges *Rhynchospora*. In Ireland,
     widely scattered but uncommon.

Fig. 82

-    Dorsal surface and legs bright golden green or darker greenish
     bronze; occasionally blue. Small femoral tooth (Fig. 83). 8.0-10.2 mm
     .... *bicolora*

     Confirmatory characters: Golden pubescence beneath.

     Distribution: Vulnerable (RDB2) on branched bur-reed (*Sparganium erectum*) beside
     various water-bodies, occurring with adults of *D. simplex*. Larval cocoons also known
     from roots of common club-rush (*Schoenoplectus lacustris*). In Ireland, widespread in
     central and western areas and possibly under-recorded.

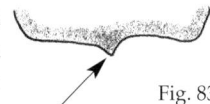

Fig. 83

10 Hind tibiae and femora not toothed. 5.4-10.8 mm 11

- Hind tibiae (ventral ridge) and femora toothed. 6.2-10.8 mm 13

11 Pronotum with two elongate dimples joined by a groove along the mid-line (Fig. 84). Disc shiny between punctures. No groove along inner margin of eyes. 5.8-7.8 mm .... *semicuprea*

Confirmatory characters: Shiny copper colour. Short pubescence on underside, legs, antennae and head makes these areas appear pale grey.

Distribution: Locally common on reed sweet-grass (*Glyceria maxima*), sometimes plicate sweet-grass (*G. notata*), around various water-bodies. Larval cocoons also known from branched bur-reed (*Sparganium erectum*). In Ireland, a small number of old records, the most recent being from the late 1910s; no more recent records.

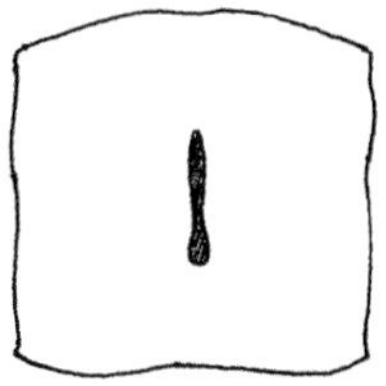

Fig. 84

- Pronotum without dimples, though faint groove may be present. Disc dull between punctures. Groove on head along inner margin of eyes. 5.4-9.4 mm 12

12 Elytra with a longitudinal band (red, blue, purple, golden, brassy or a combination of colours); rarely all dark green. Dorsal part of front tibiae darkened, only partly reddish. Front edge of pronotum with a tiny protuberance (Fig. 85). Tips of elytra slightly concave when viewed from above. Median lobe of aedeagus gradually and somewhat unevenly narrowed towards the tip, with a sharper point (Fig. 86). 6.2-9.0 mm .... *vulgaris*

Distribution: Widespread and may be locally abundant. On a range of plants in and around various water-bodies and wet areas. Widespread in Ireland.

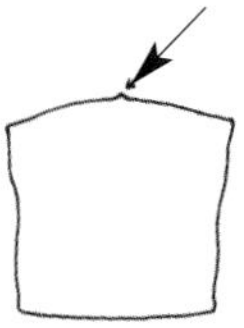

Fig. 85

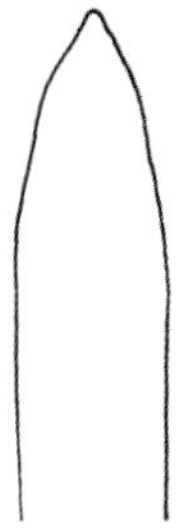

- Elytra all the same colour, tips not concave when viewed from above. Dorsal part of front tibiae entirely reddish. Front edge of pronotum without a tiny protuberance. Median lobe of aedeagus more abruptly and evenly narrowed towards the tip, with a blunter, more rounded point (Fig. 87). 5.4-9.4 mm .... *simplex*

Distribution: Probably the most widespread and common species of British *Donacia*. In a wide variety of water-bodies and wet areas, on various plants, particularly bur-reeds (*Sparganium*). The much rarer *D. bicolora* may also be present. Widespread in Ireland.

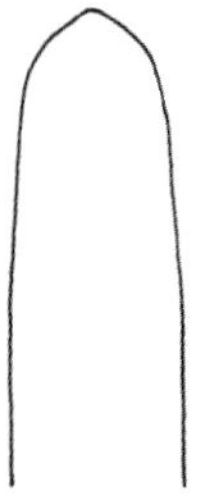

Fig. 86

Fig. 87

13 Pronotum strongly wrinkled with coarse punctures. 6.2-8.9 mm ... 14

- Pronotum weakly wrinkled with sparse, shallow punctures (or none) .... *crassipes*

Confirmatory characters: Hind femora with one blunt tooth, or with two well separated teeth further apart than the length of the anterior tooth (Fig. 88a,b). 8.1-10.8 mm.

Distribution: Scarce (Nb) with a scattered distribution. On the upper surface of leaves of water-lilies (*Nymphaea* and *Nuphar*) in various water-bodies. In Ireland, likely to be widespread but under-recorded.

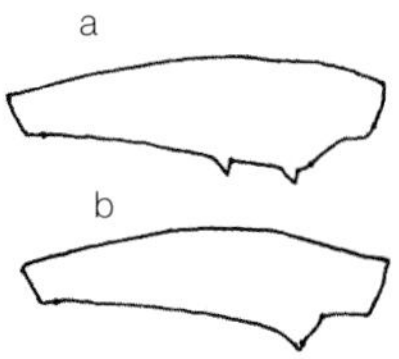

a

b

Fig. 88

14 Elytra dull. Ventral half of femora pale reddish; dorsal half dark metallic. Hind femora with two teeth, the larger one on the ventral surface, slightly posterior to the smaller one (Fig. 89). 7.0-8.8 mm .... *dentata*

Fig. 89

> Distribution: Scarce (Na), only in the south. Usually on arrowhead (*Sagittaria sagittifolia*) in dykes; may also be associated with water-plantains (*Alisma*) and yellow water-lily (*Nuphar lutea*). In Ireland, a small number of old records from Kerry; no recent records, and old records are somewhat uncertain.

- Elytra shiny. Ventral half of femora almost entirely dark; apical two thirds of femora almost entirely black. In males, hind femora with two small teeth of approximately equal size side by side. In females, hind femora with a very small, very blunt tooth, may be absent. 6.2-8.9 mm .... *versicolorea*

> Distribution: Widespread, but not common. In various water-bodies, especially on broad-leaved pondweed (*Potamogeton natans*), sometimes on other plants. In Ireland, widespread mainly at or near the coast; likely to be under-recorded as a late summer species associated with less rich waters than most other *Donacia*.

KEY D: SUBFAMILY CRIOCERINAE

For most species, separation of males and females is not straightforward prior to dissection where required. However, in *Crioceris asparagi*, males have longer, more strongly curved front tibiae than females.

1 Head, legs and underside of body black, pronotum and elytra bright red. Pronotum strongly narrowed at, or just behind, middle. 6.0-8.0 mm, the largest British species in this sub-family .... *Lilioceris lilii* (lily beetle)

> Distribution: On various plants of the family Liliaceae, almost always in gardens and plant nurseries.

Elytra not red. 3.0-6.5 mm.. 2

2 Head blue-black, often with a metallic green reflection. Pronotum red, often with a dark spot. Elytra predominantly blue-black, each with yellow margins and apices and three yellow marks of variable size (Fig. 90). 5.0-6.5 mm .... *Crioceris asparagi* (asparagus beetle)

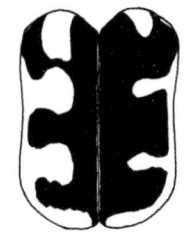

Fig. 90

> Distribution: Widespread and locally common on asparagus (*Asparagus officinalis*; wild and cultivated), especially in the south-east.

> Note that the continental *C. duodecimpunctata* has been found in Britain but has not become established. It is orange-yellow with dark tarsi and antennae, and 12 black spots on the elytra.

- Not as above; often dark metallic blue or similar. 3.0-5.0 mm 3

3 Pronotum constricted at the mid-point (Fig. 91) or occasionally further back but in any case the constriction of the sides does not match up with the transverse furrow. 3.5-5.0 mm .... *Lema cyanella*

Distribution: Widespread on various thistles (*Cirsium, Carduus*, and the introduced *Silybum*), in a wide range of habitats.

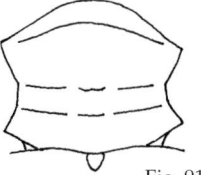

Fig. 91

- Pronotum not constricted at the mid-point; narrowed further back and this constriction lines up with the transverse furrow (Fig. 92). 3.0-4.8 mm .... Key D1: Genus *Oulema* (below)

Fig. 92

Key D1: Genus *Oulema*

1 Pronotum, femora and tibiae red or orange-red. 4.0-5.3 mm 2

- Pronotum, femora and tibiae dark blue (may be greenish or almost black). 3.0-4.5 mm 3

2 Relatively small and flat. Punctures coarse. In males, the flagellum of aedeagus is thin and relatively pointed (Fig. 93). In females, the spermathecal duct (sd) is long, clearly longer than the width of the terminal portion of the bursa copulatrix (bc) where it is attached (Fig. 94). 4.0-4.8mm .... *rufocyanea*

Distribution: Widespread and common on cereals and wild grasses in a range of habitats.

- Relatively large and domed. Punctures moderate in size. In males, the flagellum of aedeagus is thick and blunt (Fig. 95). In females, the spermathecal duct (sd) is short, its length approximately the same as the width of the terminal portion of the bursa copulatrix (bc) where it is attached (Fig. 96). 4.3-5.3mm .... *melanopus* (cereal leaf beetle)

Distribution: Widespread and can be common, especially in England and Wales, on cereals and grasses in a range of habitats. Oats and barley are preferred over wheat, which is in turn preferred over rye, maize and wild grasses.

For more on the separation of *O. rufocyanea* and *O. melanopus* using features of their genitalia, see Cox (1995). Note that work is ongoing regarding the identity of a possible melanic form of *O. melanopus*.

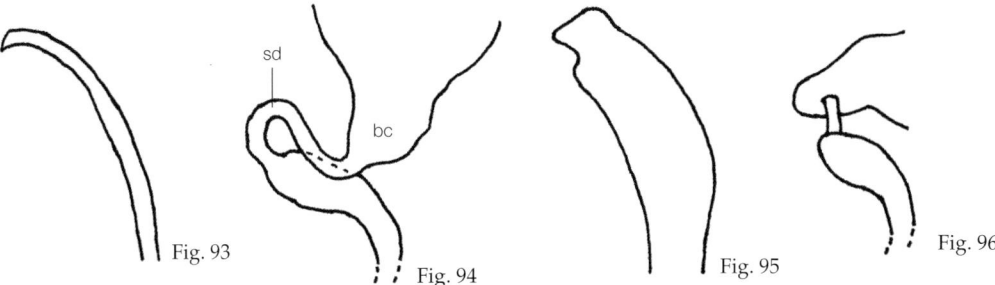

Fig. 93   Fig. 94   Fig. 95   Fig. 96

3 Metallic blue (sometimes greenish or almost black). Angle at widest point of pronotum well defined, not highly rounded (Fig. 97). Relatively short with elytra 1.25 times as long as wide. Pronotum relatively small (length about 0.30 that of elytra). 3.0-4.2 mm ... *obscura*

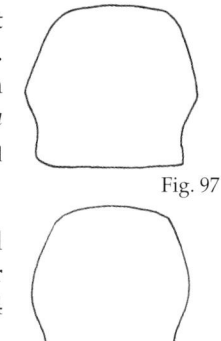

Fig. 97

Distribution: Widespread and common on a range of plants, especially grasses and cereals, in various habitats.

- Metallic blue. Angle at widest point of pronotum clearly rounded (Fig. 98). Elytra 1.30-1.45 times as long as wide. Pronotum longer (length 0.35-0.40 that of elytra). 4.0-4.5 mm **4**

Fig. 98

4 Front thoracic segment black without metallic reflection (or if present, very weak). Elytral punctures less coarse overall, especially where they become finer towards the rear. Lamella of the aedeagus broad and blunt (Fig. 99)... *septentrionis*

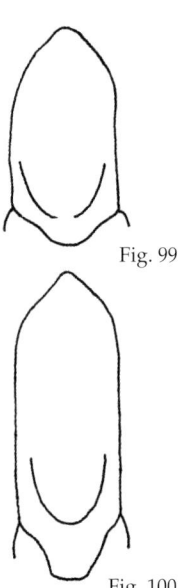

Distribution: Ireland only. On oats (*Avena*) and bulrushes (*Typha*) in various habitats, often close to water.

Fig. 99

> The status of *O. septentrionis* in Ireland is currently under review as there is evidence from dissections of the aedeagal flagellum that specimens from Ireland and Normandy are a melanic form of *O. melanopus*. The final outcome of this work is awaiting publication.

- Front thoracic segment with a definite metallic reflection. Elytral punctures coarser overall, particularly towards the rear. Lamella of the aedeagus relatively elongate and somewhat pointed (though generally not sharply so) (Fig. 100) .... *erichsoni*

Distribution: Rare (RDB3), usually on floating sweet-grass (*Glyceria fluitans*), mainly in wet peat cuttings or trenches with little other vegetation, or on heaths. Recently recorded only from Somerset.

Fig. 100

Separation of *erichsoni*, *obscura* and *septentrionis*

For more about differences of *O. erichsoni*, *O. obscura* and *O. septentrionis*, see Allen (1976) and Cox (2000b). *O. septentrionis* and *O. erichsoni* are very similar and considered by some authors, e.g. Medvedev & Samaderzhenkov (1989), to be the same species, while Cox (2000b) notes similarity of surface features for these two species (and hence their unreliability as diagnostic features if used alone), but gives details of differences in genitalia. However, recent work on records and specimens from Fenno-Scandinavia notes similar differences in genitalia but also mentions that these are not clearly linked to other morphological differences, and indicates a need for more study of these species to determine their status (Wanntorp, 2009). Such work was undertaken by Bukejs (2010). A number of differences were noted, but these do not all agree with those noted by other authors such as Warchałowski (2003) e.g. differences between the shape of the flagellum and aedeagal tip in lateral view. However, as shown in Figs 99 and 100, the lamella of the aedeagus in *O. erichsoni* is more elongate and somewhat more pointed compared with that of *O. septentrionis* which is broader and blunter. Note that Cox (2000b) states that in *O. erichsoni*, about one third of the flagellum projects forwards from the ostium, which is located dorsally before the tip of the median lobe but that in *O. septentrionis*, no part of the endophallus can be seen externally as the flagellum does not protrude from the ostium – this difference is also indicated by the relevant figures in Warchałowski (2003). Note however, that Cox (2000b) also describes the flagellum of *O. septentrionis* as blunt at the tip which does not agree with Bukejs (2010). Current work in the UK includes determining the identity of the 'Somerset *O. erichsoni*' which may prove to be *O. septentrionis*.

KEY E: SUBFAMILY CRYPTOCEPHALINAE

1   Antennae long, filiform. 2.0-8.0 mm ....
.... Key E1: Genus *Cryptocephalus* (p. 45)

\-   Antennae serrate from the 3rd or 4th segment to the tip (Fig. 101).
2.5-9.5 mm .... 2 (Tribe Clytrini)

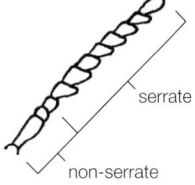

Fig. 101

2   Elytra blue with fine, dense puncturation. Females have a deep circular pit located centrally in the apical abdominal sternite; this is absent in males. 2.5-4.0 mm ....
.... *Smaragdina affinis*

Confirmatory characters: Blue-black head. Pronotum black or blue-black with broad orange to red-brown side margins.

Distribution: Endangered (RDB1). On hazels (*Corylus*), sometimes birches (*Betula*) and Asteraceae in broad-leaved woodland and marshy thickets near rivers; known only from a few sites in Oxfordshire and Gloucestershire; no records since 1965.

> Note that *S. salicina* is known from a single specimen collected in Buckinghamshire in 2010 by sweeping in mixed deciduous hedgerow and scrub habitat on a SW-facing chalk grassland slope (Hubble & Murray, 2011). It is easily separated from *S. affinis* by having an entirely orange to red-brown pronotum. It is also larger at 5.5 mm (for the single British specimen) and differs in the structure of the aedeagus, which is required in order to separate it from some other non-British European species (e.g. using Bienkowski, 2004; Warchałowski, 2003). *S. salicina* is associated with a wide range of scrub tree species, as well as abandoned orchards (Vig & Markó, 2006).

\-   Elytra yellowish-brown or yellowish-red, with or without dark spots. 6.0-9.5 mm 3

3   Head, pronotum, legs and body dark metallic greenish or greenish-blue, elytra yellowish-brown .... *Labidostomis tridentata*

Confirmatory characters: Males have larger heads and longer mandibles with a dorsal projection, the front tibiae are longer and more strongly curved than the other tibiae, and tarsal segments 1 and 2 are longer than the same segments on other legs. Females have a deep circular pit located centrally in the apical abdominal sternite; this is absent in males. 6.0-9.0 mm.

Distribution: Endangered (RDB1) and may be extinct. Rough open ground in woodland; adults usually on birch (*Betula*), feeding especially on the leaves of 5-year old saplings. Known only from a few scattered sites in Hampshire, Kent, Sussex, Worcestershire and Yorkshire.

\-   Pronotum, scutellum, body and legs black, head black with a red spot behind the eyes. Elytra yellowish-red with black spots (Fig. 102) 4

Confirmatory characters: As for *Labidostomis tridentata*, females have a deep circular pit located centrally in the apical abdominal sternite; this is absent in males, though (unlike *L. tridentata*) there may be a broad, shallow, smooth depression.

Fig. 102

4 Pronotum with side margins flattened, broad (especially to the rear) and clearly punctured. Aedeagus elongate with the tip clearly widened in dorsal or ventral view (Fig. 103). 7.4-9.5 mm .... *Clytra quadripunctata*

Distribution: Associated with various ant species; found on trees, shrubs, cock's-foot (*Dactylis glomerata*) and bracken (*Pteridium aquilinum*) in various woodland types, widespread but not common.

Fig. 103

- Pronotum with side margins narrow and smooth. Aedeagus short and slightly widened at the tip in dorsal or ventral view (Fig. 104). 7.5-11.5 mm .... *Clytra laeviuscula*

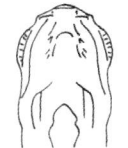

Distribution: Probably extinct in Britain (Cox, 2007), the last record being from Berkshire in 1895. Associated with various ant species and previously known from a range of trees and shrubs in Caledonian pine and birch woodland, and on chalk grassland.

Fig. 104

Key E1: Genus *Cryptocephalus*

Females have a deep circular pit located centrally in the apical abdominal sternite; this is absent in males. In males, the antennal segments are usually more elongate than in females, a difference that is particularly marked in *C. pusillus*.

1 Body usually 2.0-3.5 mm. Elytral punctures in regular rows. Tip of aedeagus formed into three (occasionally two) processes (Fig. 105) and its opening situated apically rather than dorsally. Head and eyes relatively small 2

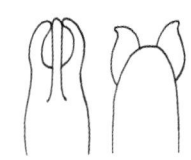

punctiger   exiguus

Fig. 105

- Body usually longer than 3.5 mm. Elytral punctures usually irregular or only partly regular. Opening of aedeagus (except in *C. coryli*) situated dorsally rather than apically. Head and eyes relatively large 9

2 Pronotum clearly punctured or wrinkled 3

Confirmatory character: Upper surface bicolorous, dark bluish (sometimes with metallic reflection) or black.

- Pronotum shiny, sometimes almost glassy; at most with sparse, extremely tiny punctures ... 5

3 Pronotum longitudinally wrinkled. Upper surface black or bicolorous 4

- Pronotum punctured. Upper surface mainly black and dark metallic blue. Head usually with yellow markings on the top above antennae (take care as these can be hard to see). Pronotum black with front and rear angles yellow. Legs yellow to pale brown, sometimes partly dark brown and with hind legs darker. Elytra black with indistinct metallic blue reflection. Scutellum concolorous with dorsal surface, without paler central area. 2.4-3.5 mm .... *punctiger* (blue pepper-pot beetle)

Distribution: Scarce (Na) and listed as a UK BAP species. Very scattered in broad-leaved woodlands and commons, on various trees, usually young birches (*Betula*).

4 Upper surface all black. Pronotal wrinkles shallow. 2.0-3.2 mm ....
.... *exiguus* (Pashford pot beetle)

Confirmatory characters: Legs yellowish except hind femora at least black at the apices.

Distribution: Endangered (RDB1) and listed as a UK BAP species. On various possible host plants (including sorrels (*Rumex*), catchflies (*Lychnis*), thistles (*Carduus* and *Cirsium*), birches (*Betula*) and grey willow (*Salix cinerea*)) in wetlands, particularly mixed fen or fen meadow. Recent records only from Pashford Poors Fen, Suffolk where habitat degradation through drying out has raised concerns that it may be extinct.

- Upper surface bicolorous; pronotum black with fine yellow front and side margins, often two yellow spots near the middle of the base (Fig. 106). Elytra yellow with black suture and longitudinal band (Fig. 107); the yellow part between these black areas sometimes interrupted. Elytra sometimes black with front and side margins yellow. Pronotal wrinkles deep and distinct even if fine. 2.0-3.0 mm .... *bilineatus*

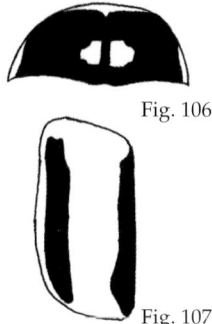

Fig. 106

Fig. 107

Confirmatory characters: Base of antennae and legs entirely yellow.

Distribution: Scarce (Nb) in grassland on chalk downs, lake edges and commons, especially on kidney vetch (*Anthyllis vulneraria*).

5 Upper surface pale, yellow or rusty yellow. Hind margin of pronotum and front margin of elytra usually with a black marginal ridge. Includes pale specimens with a pale brownish spot on the elytral shoulder, often (but not always) also with a pale brownish pattern on the upper surface and/or a narrowly darkened suture 6

- Upper surface bicolorous or black 7

6 Antennal segments 4-10 more elongate, final segment longer than 0.2 mm, as long as or longer than the first segment. Punctures of elytral striae becoming distinctly finer towards the rear. Extent of dark dorsal colour highly variable (from almost all yellow to almost all black), but males often with elytra largely dark brown or black, in females elytra yellow and usually with darkened elytral shoulders, sometimes also with brown spots to the rear, sometimes also the front (Fig. 108). Aedeagus pale with dorsal process very narrow and slightly thickened at the tip (Fig. 109). 2.2-3.0 mm .... *pusillus*

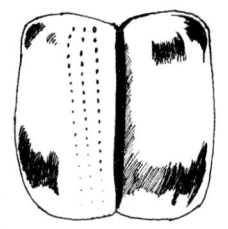

Fig. 108

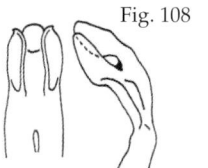

Distribution: Widespread and common on various plants (primarily broad-leaved trees) in a range of habitats.

- Antennal segments 4-10 less elongate, final segment shorter than 0.17 mm, and shorter than the first segment. Punctures of elytral striae do not become distinctly finer towards the rear; however, punctures slightly finer around sides than on top. Males without extensive dark brown or black marks on the elytra, though there may be darkening on the shoulders. Aedeagus black with dorsal process thick and blunt/rounded (Fig. 110). 2.0-3.0 mm .... *fulvus*

Fig. 109

Fig. 110

Confirmatory characters: Femora apically with a small flange on the front upper edge though this can be hard to see (Fig. 111).

Distribution: Widespread on a range of mainly herbaceous plants, especially sheep's sorrel (*Rumex acetosella*), in various mainly open habitats.

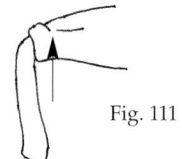

Fig. 111

7 Pronotum black with front margin usually finely yellow, front to half of side margin usually finely yellow-orange; no spot at the hind angles (sometimes a very small yellow area to the side on hind angles and sometimes pale spots on the disc); very finely punctured ..... *frontalis*

Confirmatory characters: Head black with yellow markings on the top above antennae, front at least partly yellow; head may be largely yellow with some black on top. Legs yellow, femora darkened to the rear. Elytra black with front half of side margin and epipleura finely yellow or pale brown. Scutellum usually black with the central area yellow or brown (may be indistinct). 2.3-3.0 mm.

Distribution: Scarce (Na) and scattered in England south of the River Humber. Mainly in mature hedgerows, especially on hawthorn (*Crataegus*).

- Pronotum entirely black 8

8 Small tooth on front margin of prosternum (Fig. 112). Dorsally black. Legs not entirely yellowish; femora, tibiae and tarsi at least partly dark brown or black. Elytral punctures relatively coarse. 2.0-2.8 mm .... *labiatus*
Distribution: Widespread and common on a range of plants in various habitats.

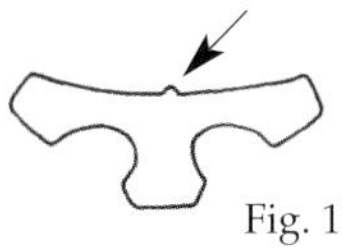

Fig. 112

- Front margin of prosternum without a small tooth. Black pronotum, black to dark brown elytra. Legs yellow, only hind femora slightly darkened. Front of head black, sometimes with small red mark near inner edge of eye. Elytral punctures very fine. 2.5-3.4 mm......... *querceti*

Distribution: Vulnerable (RDB2) on oaks (*Quercus*), sometimes hawthorn (*Crataegus*) and possibly birches (*Betula*). In ancient broad-leaved pasture-woodland, parkland and forests; favours open parkland over woodland with a closed canopy.

9 Head with top yellow-orange, sometimes mostly black (especially in males) with a thin yellowish stripe along the inner edge of the eye. Pronotum orange-red in females, black in males. Elytra orange-red with fine black suture; males sometimes with an indistinct black spot on shoulder, sometimes also on disc. Tip of aedeagus extended to form two short, blunt processes (Fig. 113). 5.8-7.5 mm .... *coryli* (hazel pot beetle)

Distribution: Endangered (RDB1) and listed as a UK BAP species. Recent records from Surrey, Lincolnshire, Nottinghamshire, Berkshire and Hampshire. However, although the Kirkby Moor site in Lincolnshire was thought to have around 90% of the adult population, it appears to have declined and recent surveys have only found this species in Sherwood Forest. It is possible that it remains in at least some of its previous areas such as the Surrey North Downs and nearby in Hampshire, and further work is ongoing to determine its distribution and status. Usually on young birch (*Betula*), sometimes on a range of other trees. In clearing and ride margins in broad-leaved woodland on south-facing slopes, chalk downland, and heathland.

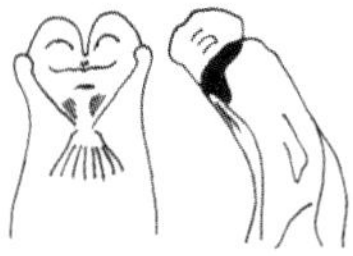

Fig. 113

- Not this combination of characters 10

10 Upper surface black or with clear metallic (bluish, greenish or purplish) sheen 11

- Upper surface with at most a very weak metallic sheen 15

11 Dorsally metallic green. Head with a narrow yellow mark between antennal bases. Pronotum finely punctured, sometimes with yellow spots at the front and rear angles. Front legs and tibiae of middle and hind legs yellow. 3.5-5.2 mm .... *nitidulus*

Distribution: Endangered (RDB1) and listed as a UK BAP species. On a variety of smaller tree species (e.g. birch, hazel and hawthorn) in downland scrub or along woodland rides. Host plants must be south-facing, at the transition between woodland and either grassland or heath, and there must be windbreaks of taller vegetation all round. Recent records only from Surrey.

\-   Upper surface entirely black with metallic (bluish, greenish or purplish) sheen, sometimes just the bases of antennae, clypeus and genae yellowish-reddish 12

12 Clypeus and genae at least partly yellowish .... *parvulus*

Confirmatory characters: Elytra with regularly punctured striae. Pronotum and elytra metallic blue or purple. Pronotum with coarse punctures and in males two distinct oblique impressions (Fig. 114). Legs with a dark metallic blue reflection, yellowish to reddish-brown trochanters and dark brown tarsi. 2.8-4.5 mm.

Distribution: Scarce (Nb) and scattered on various trees in chalk scrub, chalk pits, commons and broad-leaved woodland.

Fig. 114

\-   Clypeus and genae all black 13

13 Short section of side margin towards the rear of the pronotum widened and flattened, the rest of the margin smooth and narrow. Pronotum moderately shiny with scattered punctures. Elytra randomly and coarsely punctured. Elytra and pronotum metallic dark blue usually with green or violet tint, occasionally entirely black forms found. In males, legs and antennae concolorous with elytra and pronotum. In females, legs and antennae similar but may be slightly paler .... *violaceus*

Confirmatory characters: Dense, even pubescence on front of head. 4.0-6.0 mm.

Distribution: On various plants in deciduous woodland but probably extinct in Britain.

\-   Side margin of pronotum widened and flattened throughout, more so towards the rear. Upper surface usually greenish with a faint golden sheen, but this is variable (bluish, purplish, blackish, golden reflection may be stronger or absent) 14

14 Side margin of pronotum more or less straight in side view. Aedeagus only slightly curves downwards at the tip (Fig. 115). 4.6-5.7 mm .... *hypochaeridis*

Distribution: Scattered distribution with clusters on the North Downs along with other limestone areas and some western dune systems. On various yellow flowers in open habitats such as chalk grassland, especially those of the hawkweed/hawkbit group of composites.

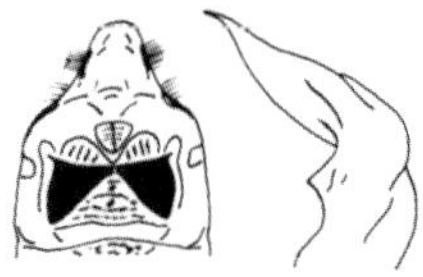

Fig. 115

\-   Side margin of pronotum more or less S-shaped in side view. Aedeagus clearly curves downwards at the tip (Fig. 116). 5.5-7.8 mm .... *aureolus*

Distribution: Scarce (Nb) though widespread and may be locally more common. On yellow flowers in various habitats, especially lightly-grazed grassland, especially those of the hawkweed/hawkbit group of composites.

Fig. 116

15   Pronotum entirely black 16

-       Pronotum bicolorous, not entirely black, though colour may be no more than a fine front margin 18

16   Elytra black with variable oval yellow spot (usually more rounded than in *C. bipunctatus* var. *thomsoni*) at the rear covering one tenth to one third of the elytral length, sometimes with a very small extra spot (Fig. 117); rear with a fine black margin. Head black, sometimes dark brown below antennal bases. Elytra more strongly punctured with intervals slightly convex. 4.5-6.0 mm .... *biguttatus*

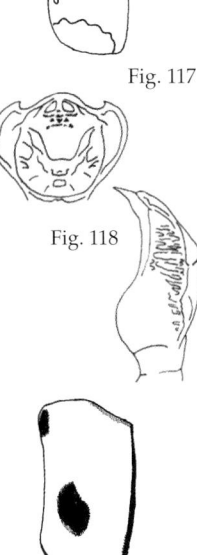

Fig. 117

Fig. 118

Confirmatory character: Aedeagus as in Fig. 118.

Distribution: Vulnerable (RDB2), generally associated with cross-leaved heath (*Erica tetralix*) in southern England, with a few records as far north as Yorkshire.

-       Elytra orange-red, each with a variable black spot near the centre and a smaller one on the shoulder (Fig. 119); these may expand into larger patches or a longitudinal band **OR** elytra black with variable orange spot (often more intensely coloured than in *C. biguttatus*) at the rear – usually crescent or kidney-shaped, sometimes reduced to small oval sections or dashes (Fig. 120) **OR** elytra red to red-brown, each with 5 oblique black spots, variable but usually small (Fig. 122). Head black 17

Fig. 119

17   Elytral punctures in more or less regular rows. Elytra orange-red, each with a variable black spot near the centre and a smaller one on the shoulder (Fig. 119); these may expand into larger patches or a longitudinal band. In var. *thomsoni* elytra black with variable orange spot (often more intensely coloured than in *C. biguttatus*) at the rear – usually crescent-shaped, sometimes reduced to small oval sections or dashes (Fig. 120). Often some microscopic orange coloration near the scutellum. 4.0-6.0 mm .... *bipunctatus*

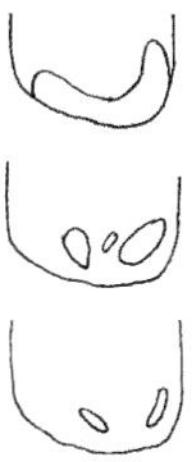

Fig. 120

Confirmatory character: Aedeagus as in Fig. 121.

Distribution: Scarce (Nb) on various plants (especially a range of tree species) in a variety of habitats: broad-leaved woodland, downland, open heaths and gardens. Var. *thomsoni* is very scarce and only recorded in five vice-counties in southern England; the majority of specimens are from Surrey.

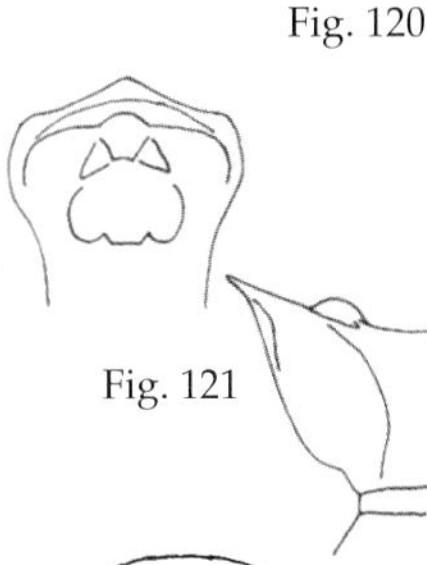

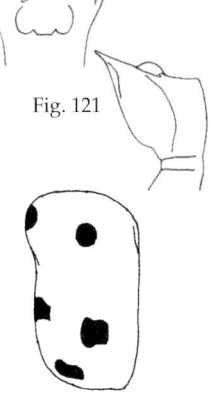

Fig. 121

> More information on the identification and distribution of *C. biguttatus* and *C. bipunctatus* var. *thomsoni* is given in Mann & Barclay (2009), though note that the male genitalia figures were transposed in error in the original publication.

-       Elytral punctures confused. Elytra red or red-brown, each with 5 oblique black spots, variable but usually small (Fig. 122). 4.5-8.0 mm .... *primarius* (rock-rose pot beetle)

Distribution: Endangered (RDB1) and listed as a UK BAP species. On chalk grassland, especially in warm, dry, sheltered conditions on south-facing slopes. Recent records from Gloucestershire and Dorset. Usually on common rock-rose (*Helianthemum nummularium*), possibly on other plants including trees.

Fig. 122

18 Elytral punctures arranged in regular or nearly regular rows at least in the inner half of the elytra 19

- Elytral punctures confused, sometimes forming sections of semi-regular rows here and there. Elytra pale red or orange-red, each usually with three black spots sometimes fused, or partly so, into transverse bands (Fig. 123), sometimes black with a red spot. 4.5-6.5 mm .... *sexpunctatus* (six-spotted pot beetle)

Fig. 123

Confirmatory characters: Head black, pronotum black with orange-yellow markings (Figs 124, 125).

Distribution: Vulnerable (RDB2) and listed as a UK BAP species. On a variety of plants, including scrubby trees, broom (*Cytisus scoparius*), wood spurge (*Euphorbia amygdaloides*) and yellow Asteraceae. Found on chalk grassland with dense scrub, especially on west-facing slopes, and in broad-leaved woodland; in a few widely scattered locations.

Fig. 124

Fig. 125

19 Elytra yellow with 5 black spots (Fig. 126); in var. *bothnicus* entirely black or dark brown). 3.5-5.0 mm ....
.... *decemmaculatus* (ten-spotted pot beetle)

Fig. 126

Confirmatory characters: Head black with yellow markings on top and front. Pronotum black, usually with a narrow yellow or brown stripe (may be much widened).

Distribution: Vulnerable (RDB2) and listed as a UK BAP species. On various willows (*Salix*), also alders (*Alnus*) in broad-leaved woodland, especially on wet hillsides or quaking bogs. Known primarily from two areas in Perthshire and Staffordshire.

- Elytra black with variable yellow or red spot at the rear (rarely dark brown and indistinct); also a yellow side area in the front half (Fig. 127). 3.0-5.0 mm .... *moraei*

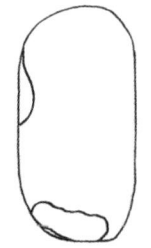

Fig. 127

Confirmatory characters: Pronotum black, usually with a fine yellow front edge and a yellow spot at the rear angles, usually edged by a thin furrow; finely to moderately coarsely punctured.

Distribution: Widespread (especially in the south) on various low vegetation, particularly St John's worts (*Hypericum*), on calcareous soils.

KEY F: FAMILY ORSODACNIDAE (SUBFAMILY ORSODACNINAE)

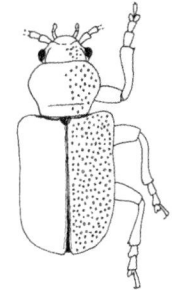

A single genus in the UK. Relatively little is known about the larvae, including where they hibernate, which may be above ground although they are likely to be root feeders (Cox, 1981). The species can be identified using external features, hence there is no need to separate males and females for dissection. Fig. 128 gives the overall shape.

Key F1: Genus *Orsodacne*

Fig. 128

1 Elytra almost hairless, diffusely punctured and with dull interstices. Elytra duller than pronotum. 4.5-6.4 mm .... *cerasi*

  Distribution: Widespread and common in mixed or deciduous woodland. Adults on flowers of woody and herbaceous plants, appearing to favour white flowers.

- Elytra shiny with dense cover of fine hairs and densely punctured. 4.4-7.9 mm ... *humeralis*

  Distribution: A scarce (Nb) species of south-east England west to Hampshire and north to Cambridgeshire and there is a separate group of records north of the Severn estuary in Hereford and Gloucester. In broad-leaved woodland, parks, scrub, heathland, commons and meadows bordering woodland.

  Note that these species are very variable in size and colour. Colour forms include yellow-orange pronotum with yellow elytra, brownish pronotum with elytra yellowish (suture a darker brown), pronotum orange-red with elytra darkened (almost black, sometimes with deep reddish marks at the shoulders, and pronotum and elytra deep brown to almost black.

KEY G: SUBFAMILY CHRYSOMELINAE

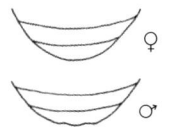

Males usually have front tarsi with either one or the first three segments dilated, and this feature is not seen in females. Also, females have the tip of the rear abdominal sternite smoothly rounded; in males it is slightly indented or sinuous (Fig. 129).

Fig. 129

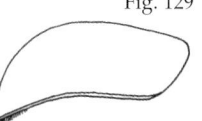

1 Looking from the side, inner edge of elytra with small bristles at or near the tip (Fig. 130; take care as this feature can be difficult to see; if missed, *Chrysolina* may key out as *Chrysomela*, *Gastrophysa*, *Plagiodera* or *Timarcha* hence confirmatory characters may be particularly useful here). 4.5-11.0 mm .... Key G2: Genus *Chrysolina* (p. 54)

Fig. 130

  Confirmatory characters: Tarsal claws without small tooth. Third hind tarsal segment only with a shallow dent at the tip. Last segment of maxillary palp at least as long as the preceding one. Measured along the midline, first abdominal sternite shorter than metasternum. Tibiae not especially dilated, and without a tooth at or near the apex. Pronotum only slightly narrower than elytra where they meet.

- Looking from the side, inner edge of elytra without small bristles at or near the tip. 2.5-18.0 mm 2

2 Elytra with random punctures. 2.5-18.0 mm 3

- Elytral punctures striate. 2.5-12.0 mm 6

3 Large (8.0-18.0 mm) beetles, darkly coloured (not metallic), wingless (elytra fused), nearly spherical, tarsal segments broadly spread, especially in males (Fig. 131). Metasternum very short, constricted either side of the midline (Fig. 132) .... Key G1: Genus *Timarcha* (p. 53)

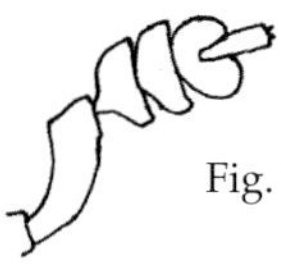

Fig. 131

> Take care with *Chrysolina violacea* which is superficially similar to *Timarcha goettingensis* but has head, pronotum, elytra and underside metallic purple, and tarsi and palps orange brown and paler than the rest of the legs.

Fig. 132

- Winged (elytra not fused); may have some of the characters of *Timarcha* above, but not all. Metasternum longer without such strong constrictions (Fig. 133). 2.5-12.0 mm 3

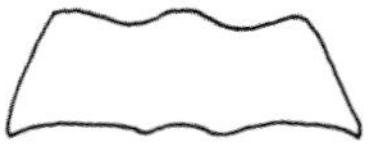

Fig. 133

4 Elytra with a row of punctures along the rear third of the suture which is raised to form a narrow rim (Fig. 134). 3.9-6.0 mm ....
.... Key G3: Genus *Gastrophysa* (p. 57)

Confirmatory characters: Slightly elongate, with elytra more-or-less parallel-sided. Pronotum somewhat bulging/domed. Female abdomen may become swollen, pushing aside elytra. Brightly coloured and metallic. Front coxal cavities open and joined at the rear. Tooth at apex of middle and hind tibiae.

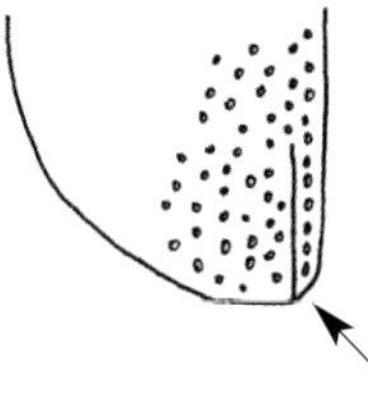

Fig. 134

- Elytra without a row of punctures along the rear third of the suture (at most a short row near the tip) which is not so distinctly raised as a rim. 2.5-12.0 mm 5

5 Elongate to elongate-oval, moderately convex. Bumps to sides of pronotum separated from its upper surface by clear longitudinal dents (Fig. 135) except in *Chrysomela aenea*. Pronotum considerably narrower than front of elytra. 6.3-12.0 mm ....
.... Key G7: Genus *Chrysomela* (p. 60)

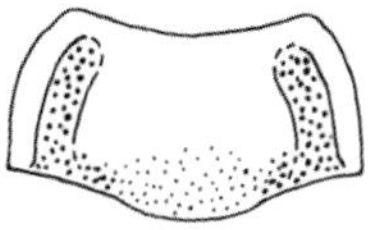

Fig. 135

- Round to rounded-oval, weakly convex. No bumps to sides of pronotum. Pronotum a little narrower than front of elytra. 2.5-4.8 mm
.... *Plagiodera versicolora*

Confirmatory characters: Dorsally metallic blue or green, rarely purplish or black; head, pronotum and elytra usually concolourous, occasionally elytra differs from head and pronotum. Underside, femora and tibiae black. Tip of elytra rounded with dimple (may be very shallow) in the apical angle (Fig. 136). Elytra with narrow, more-or-less even rim, sides slightly indented above this rim. Elytra with distinct shoulders.

Distribution: Mostly in central and southern England usually near water on willows (*Salix*), especially crack-willow (*S. fragilis*), sometimes far from water and/or on poplars (*Populus*) and birches (*Betula*).

Fig. 136

6 Claws without appendages at base. 3.0-6.0 mm 7

- Claws with small appendages at base (Fig. 137). 3.7-7.5 mm 9

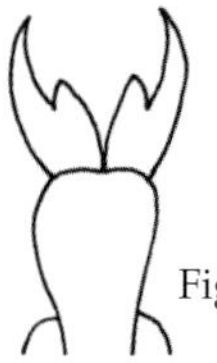

Fig. 137

7 Metasternum with random punctures except for the front outer corner which is not punctured and is separated by a clear border (Fig. 138). This corner area may be more or less densely microsculptured and occasionally a very few punctures can be found within (generally near the border), but clearly not the even puncturation covering the rest of the metasternum. 3.0-4.7 mm .... Key G4: Genus *Phaedon* (p. 58)

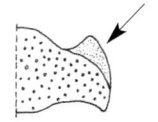

Fig. 138

Confirmatory characters: Rounded, domed oval, metallic. Side borders of elytra reach the tip. Elytra without yellow or reddish lateral stripe.

- Metasternum with uniform coarse punctures, including front outer corner. 4.0-6.0 mm 8

Confirmatory characters: Elytra sometimes with yellow or reddish lateral stripe.

8 Pronotum with rear margin (may be narrow). 4.0-6.0 mm ... Key G6: Genus *Prasocuris* (p. 59)

Confirmatory characters: Elongate, parallel-sided with pronotum only a little narrower than elytra.

- Pronotum without a rear margin. 4.0-5.0 mm .... Key G5: Genus *Hydrothassa* (p. 59)

Confirmatory characters: Fairly elongate, metallic blue with yellowish edges to elytra and/or pronotum.
Distribution: Generally in or around wet habitats.

9 Yellow, orange or reddish, with or without dark lines or spots. Middle and hind tibiae with a large thorn-like tooth on upper side near apex (Fig. 139). There may be a similar, but often smaller, tooth on the front tibia. 3.7-7.5 mm .... Key G8: Genus *Gonioctena* (p. 60)

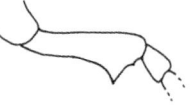

Fig. 139

- Metallic but variable in colour. Legs and antennae brown or dark brown, with femora and apical antennal segments more likely to be dark. No tibial teeth. 3.7-5.0 mm .... Key G9: Genus *Phratora* (p. 62)

Key G1: Genus *Timarcha*

1 At least slightly shiny violet/blue-black with random, dense moderately-sized punctures. Pronotum constricts less sharply after rounded side-angles (Fig. 140). 8.0-13.0 mm ....
.... *goettingensis* (lesser bloody-nosed beetle)

Fig. 140

Distribution: Widespread though may have declined outside southern England. In various open habitats on bedstraws (*Galium*), crosswort (*Cruciata laevipes*) and woodruffs (*Asperula*).

- Entirely blue-black; random, dense, tiny punctures; duller than *T. goettingensis*. Pronotum constricts more sharply after rounded side-angles (Fig. 141). 11.0-18.0 mm (the largest British chrysomelid) ....
.... *tenebricosa* (bloody-nosed beetle)

Fig. 141

Distribution: Widespread in the southern half of Britain. In various open habitats (especially with freely-draining soils) on bedstraws (*Galium*), crosswort (*Cruciata laevipes*), woodruffs (*Asperula*) and madders (*Rubia*).

Key G2: Genus *Chrysolina*

1 Upper surface dark blue or black; elytra with reddish lateral margins. 6.5-11.0 mm 2

> Note that, at the time of going to press, the large 'blue mint beetle' *C. coerulans* had recently been recorded as breeding in Britain for the first time, having been collected in east Kent in July 2011 (Salisbury *et al.*, 2012). It had previously been recorded in Britain in 2003, 2008 and 2009 but was not known to have become established (Sage, 2009a, 2009b). The elytral margins are not reddish; also, unlike *sanguinolenta*, the front edge of the pronotum is straight to slightly convex. It is the only British mint-feeding *Chrysolina* that is commonly blue, although there is an uncommon deep blue colour form of *herbacea*. The pronotal disc of *coerulans* has entirely fine punctures, while those of *herbacea* and *graminis* have a mixture of fine and coarse punctures; *coerulans* differs from other blue to purple *Chrysolina* in Britain by having unicolorous blue elytra and a parallel-sided thorax. It may become widely established in Britain on mints *Mentha*, although the current assessment predicts it is most likely to be associated with private gardens than commercial premises (Malumphy *et al.*, 2011).

- Not as above; may be dark but without reddish elytral margins. 4.5-11.0 mm 3

2 Elytra black and coarsely punctured, rarely with dull leaden reflection. Front edge of pronotum between the eyes straight or slightly convex. 7.0-11.0 mm .... *intermedia*

Distribution: Vulnerable (RDB2) at Loch Etive (western Argyll), Shetlands and Orkneys. On various herbaceous plants on or near cliff-tops, also a quarry and a saltmarsh (Loch Etive).

- Elytra blue-black and less coarsely punctured, sometimes with violet reflection. Front edge of pronotum between the eyes slightly concave. 6.5-8.4 mm .... *sanguinolenta*

Distribution: Scarce (Na) and scattered in various habitats, on toadflaxes (*Linaria*) (usually common toadflax (*L. vulgaris*)), sometimes on snapdragon (*Antirrhinum majus*).

> Note that *C. intermedia* and *C. sanguinolenta* are superficially similar to genus *Hydrothassa* (Key G5, p. 59) which shares dark coloration with lateral elytral stripe but punctures very different.

3 Green pronotum, head, legs and underside (very rarely blue, occasionally pronotum red-purple). Red-brown or orange-brown elytra with random punctures. 5.9-8.6 mm .... *polita*

Distribution: Widespread and common in various habitats, usually on mints (*Mentha*) and other Lamiaceae, also on common nettle (*Urtica dioica*), sometimes on ivy (*Hedera helix*).

- Not as above; colours vary, but not the combination of green pronotum, head, legs and underside with red-brown or orange-brown elytra. 4.5-11.0 mm 4

4 Colourful with multiple regular longitudinal stripes. 6.7-8.1 mm 5

- Not as above; often (though not always) colourful, but where stripes are present, not the dense regular arrangement above. 4.5-11.0 mm 6

5 Dark metallic green with metallic red (which can appear golden at certain angles and lighting conditions) on pronotum and elytra. Elytra with fine distinct punctures in double rows with smooth intervals between each series. Pronotum not punctured. 6.7-8.1 mm .... *americana* (rosemary beetle)

Distribution: Scattered in gardens and parks, on Lamiaceae, especially rosemary (*Rosemarinus officinalis*) and lavenders (*Lavendula*), also sage (*Salvia officinalis*) and garden thyme (*Thymus vulgaris*).

- Stripes metallic green, blue and golden-red. 7.0-8.0 mm .... *cerealis* (rainbow leaf beetle)

Distribution: Endangered (RDB1) on wild thyme (*Thymus polytrichus*). Only on Snowdon and nearby montane grassland.

6 Oval with rear of elytra rounded and sides slightly flattened. Head, pronotum, elytra and underside metallic purple or purplish-blue. Elytral punctures largely confused, but forming some indistinct rows and/or double rows. 5.8-9.4 mm .... *violacea*

Distribution: Scarce (Nb) and locally distributed on ground-ivy (*Glechoma hederacea*) on chalk grassland, heaths, scrub or disturbed ground.

Superficially similar to *Timarcha goettingensis* but tarsi and palps orange-brown, and paler than the rest of the legs.

- Not as above; may have some of the characters above but not all. 4.5-11.0 mm 7

7 Elytra metallic green (sometimes bronze) with a blue suture, blue lateral longitudinal stripe and red or gold longitudinal stripe nearer centre of each elytron. 4.8-7.0 mm .... *fastuosa*

Confirmatory characters: Clawed tarsal segment with two small teeth under the tip (Fig. 142).

Distribution: Widespread on Lamiaceae (especially hemp-nettles (*Galeopsis*) and dead-nettles (*Lamium*)) and common nettle (*Urtica dioica*) in various habitats.

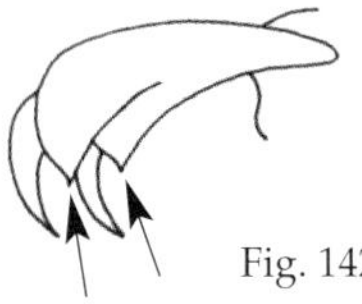

Fig. 142

- Not as above; no longitudinal stripes as above, though other colour combinations may be the same. 4.5-11.0 mm 8

8 Metallic bright green dorsally. 7.0-11.0 mm 9

- Colours vary and may be metallic dark green, but not bright green. 4.5-10.7 mm 10

9 Metallic bright green, sometimes with gold-purple reflection; varies to golden-red or deep blue. Elytral suture golden-green or brassy; this may vary but in any case is the same colour as the rest of the elytra. 7.0-11.0 mm .... *herbacea*

Distribution: Scattered though mainly in central southern England. On various Lamiaceae, especially mints (*Mentha*), in a wide range of wet habitats.

- Metallic bright green. Suture metallic blue or blue-green and darker than elytra. 7.7-10.5 mm .... *graminis* (tansy leaf beetle)

Distribution: Scarce (Na), though a designation of Vulnerable (RDB2) would be more accurate, and listed as a UK BAP species. Scattered on tansy (*Tanacetum vulgare*) and water mint (*Mentha aquatica*) in fens and the banks of rivers with broad floodplains.

10 Rounded. Head, pronotum and elytra the same colour, though may be metallic blue, purple, green, brass, bronze, or almost black. Elytra densely randomly punctured. 4.5-6.0 mm .... *varians*

Distribution: Widespread on St John's worts (*Hypericum*) in various habitats.

- May have some of the characters above but not all. Elytral punctures striate or sparsely random, or if dense and random, dorsally red-brown in colour. 5.0-10.7 mm 11

11 Dark in colour, though may be blue-black, dark violet, very dark green, deep bronze or black with a bronze reflection. If green, then punctures forming elytral striae are coarse and sparse (within a stria, punctures separated by about 2 diameters from each other), otherwise punctures may form sparse striae or be finer, more densely packed and largely random. 5.0-9.1 mm 12

- Not as above; colour may be coppery-red, red-brown, brassy, metallic green or metallic bronze but not conspicuously dark. Elytral punctures vary widely in coarseness, density and randomness or arrangement. 5.0-10.7 mm 14

Take care here e.g. *C. hyperici* may vary in the depth and darkness of green colour but elytral punctures are distinctive.

12 Oval. Dark metallic green or bronze, sometimes reddish, blue-black or almost black. Pronotum and elytral interstices dull and very finely punctured. Striae formed of sparse punctures. 5.0-7.3 mm .... *hyperici*

Distribution: Widespread on St John's worts (*Hypericum*) in various habitats.

Distinguished from *C. brunsvicensis* below by overall depth of colour and features of pronotum.

- Distinctly rounded. May have some of the characters above but not all. 5.0-9.1 mm ... 13

13 Blue-black, dull, no metallic reflection. Pronotum without a lateral longitudinal furrow; it is straight laterally and narrows, cone-like towards the front (Fig. 143). Elytral punctures largely confused, forming irregular double-rows in part. 5.0-9.0 mm .... *haemoptera*

Fig. 143

Distribution: Scarce (Nb) in coastal habitats (sometimes inland e.g. on chalk downs) on plantains (*Plantago*), especially buck's-horn plantain (*P. coronopus*).

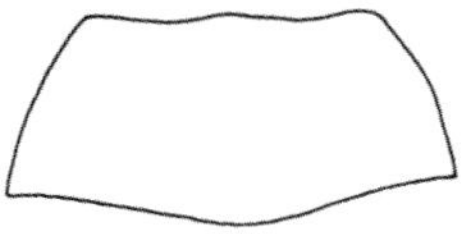

- Usually dark blue, sometimes dark violet, very dark green, deep bronze or black with a bronze reflection. Distinguished from *C. haemoptera* by trapezoidal pronotum with lateral longitudinal furrows (Fig. 144). Elytra striate with sparse punctures. 6.5-9.1 mm .... *oricalcia*

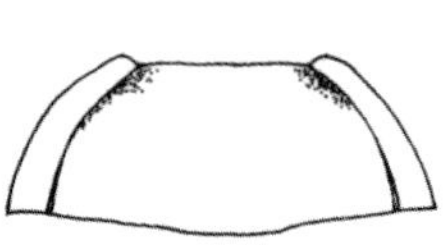

Fig. 144

Distribution: Scarce (Nb) but widespread on various umbellifers in a range of habitats.

14 Coppery-red with a brassy reflection, sometimes golden green. Pronotum and elytral interstices coarsely punctured and shiny. Elytral punctures form somewhat faint, partly irregular, striae among the smaller interstitial punctures. 5.3-6.3 mm .... *brunsvicensis*

Distribution: Widespread on St John's worts (*Hypericum*) in various habitats.

> Distinguished from *C. hyperici* above by overall depth of colour and features of pronotum.

- Red-brown, brassy, metallic bronze or metallic dark green. Not coppery-red or golden green. Elytral punctures either random or clearly striate, not forming faint irregular striae. 5.0-10.7 mm 15

15 Oval. Head, pronotum, legs and underside brassy or metallic dark green. Legs may be dark brown. Elytra red-bronze with orange or yellowish lateral margins; striate. 5.0-6.8 mm .... *marginata*

Distribution: Scarce (Na) and scattered on yarrow (*Achillea millefolium*) in open grasslands and heaths. Nocturnal.

- Dorsally bronze or red-brown, but without orange or yellowish lateral margins to elytra. 5.2-10.7 mm 16

16 Rounded; widest just behind midpoint of elytra. Dorsally red-brown, usually with a weak metallic reflection. Elytral punctures dense and random, sometimes forming a partial row along the suture, especially in the rear half. 5.2-8.7 mm .... *staphylaea*

Distribution: Widespread and common on various plants in a wide range of habitats.

- Round to the rear, and squat with sides somewhat straight. Metallic bronze to blackish with appendages usually orange-brown to dark brown and without metallic reflection. Elytral punctures sparse and random. 8.0-10.7 mm .... *banksi*

Distribution: Locally common on various plants, usually in open coastal habitats but also in valley woodland.

Key G3: Genus *Gastrophysa*

1 Usually metallic golden-green or green, sometimes brassy/bronze, rarely blue. Antennae entirely dark metallic. 4.0-6.0 mm .... *viridula* (green dock beetle)

Distribution: Widespread and common in various habitats, usually on docks (*Rumex*), especially broad-leaved dock (*Rumex obtusifolius*), other Polygonaceae and buttercups (*Ranunculus*).

- Pronotum, legs (mainly) and base of antennae red; head and elytra metallic blue or violet, rarely green. 3.9-5.0 mm .... *polygoni*

Distribution: Widespread and common in various habitats, usually on knotgrass (*Polygonum aviculare*) and other Polygonaceae.

Key G4: Genus *Phaedon*

1 Bright metallic green to greenish-blue, sometimes coppery, rarely metallic blue. Elytra sometimes with a golden, purplish or violet reflection. 3.2-4.1 mm .... *concinnus*

Distribution: Scarce (Nb) on sea plantain (*Plantago maritima*) and sea arrowgrass (*Triglochin maritimum*) in various coastal habitats.

> The rare metallic blue form can be confused with *P. cochleariae* but can they can be separated by antennal and aedeagal characters. In *P. concinnus*, the antennae are entirely black, whereas in *P. cochleariae*, the underside of the 2nd and 3rd antennal segments are reddish (or at least with a reddish spot). The aedeagi are very similar in lateral view, but can be distinguished in dorsal view (Figs 145, 146).

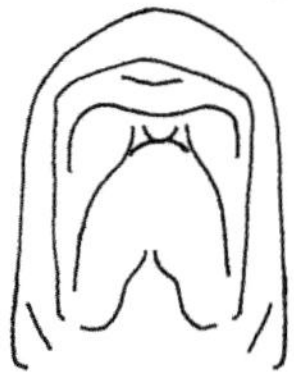

Fig. 145

Fig. 146

- Colours not as above. 3.0-4.7 mm 2

2 Pronotal disc very finely punctured (may appear not to have punctures). Colour normally dark green or brassy, occasionally dark blue. 3.5-4.0 mm .... *tumidulus* (celery leaf beetle)

Distribution: Widespread and common on umbellifers in various habitats.

- Pronotal disc distinctly punctured. Colours various, usually bluish. 3.0-4.7 mm 3

3 Constant deep blue in colour. 5th elytral striae deepened at the base with distinctly swollen shoulder to the outside usually partially obscuring the outline of the elytral margin as seen from above. Antennae entirely dark. Aedeagus as in Fig. 147. 3.5-4.7 mm ....
.... *armoraciae*

Distribution: Widespread and common on a range of water plants in various habitats.

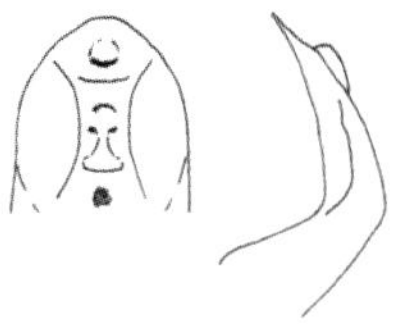

Fig. 147

- Usually bright metallic blue, may also be purplish, rarely bronze-brown or brassy. Strial deepening and shoulder swelling of *P. armoraciae* usually absent, sometimes present but reduced. Antennal segments 1 and 2 usually yellowish or orange ventrally, the orange or yellow colour sometimes spreading dorsally. 3.0-4.0 mm ....
.... *cochleariae* (water-cress beetle)

Distribution: Widespread and common in various habitats, usually on brassicas, sometimes on other plants including gorse (*Ulex europaeus*).

Key G5: Genus *Hydrothassa*

Note that *Chrysolina intermedia* and *C. sanguinolenta* (Key G2, p. 54) share dark coloration with lateral elytral stripe with *Hydrothassa* but punctures are very different.

1 Pronotum entirely metallic blue, without a broad yellow lateral margin visible from above. 3.0-4.0 mm .... *glabra*

Distribution: Widely scattered on Ranunculaceae, especially creeping buttercup (*Ranunculus repens*) and meadow buttercup (*R. acris*), in various habitats.

- Pronotum with a yellow lateral margin. 3.4-5.0 mm 2

2 Elytra with a yellowish or reddish discal stripe and broad yellow lateral margin. The discal stripe may be broken or absent. Where the stripe is absent, separation from *H. marginella* requires examination of the aedeagus; in lateral view the tip has a small angled bend (Fig. 148). 3.5-5.0 mm .... *hannoveriana*

Distribution: Rare (RDB3) and very locally distributed, usually on marsh-marigold (*Caltha palustris*) in tarns, marshes and peat bogs (sometimes in forests).

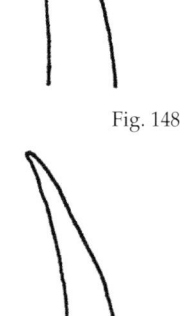

Fig. 148

- Similar to *H. hannoveriana* but elytra without discal stripe. Tip of aedeagus in lateral view is more-or-less straight or slightly curved, but not angled (Fig. 149). 3.4-4.5 mm .... *marginella*

Distribution: Widespread and common in various habitats, usually on buttercups (*Ranunculus*).

Fig. 149

Key G6: Genus *Prasocuris*

1 Dark metallic blue (rarely green) without coloured stripes. 4.0-5.0 mm ....
.... *junci* (brooklime leaf beetle)

Distribution: Widespread and locally common on various water plants in a range of habitats.

- Pronotum with broad yellowish or reddish margins; elytra with yellowish longitudinal stripes close to suture joining apically with yellow stripes that run from the shoulder along each elytral margin; background colour dark metallic (generally green, blue or brassy. 5.0-6.0 mm .... *phellandrii*

Distribution: Widespread on various plants in a range of wetland habitats.

Key G7: Genus *Chrysomela*

1 Usually entirely metallic green, sometimes blue or brassy; occasionally pronotum and elytra are different colours. 6.3-8.0 mm .... *aenea*

Distribution: Widespread, especially in the north and west. Usually in dense, shaded stands of alder *Alnus* on the banks of watercourses and in woodland. Sometimes on elms (*Ulmus*) and white willow (*Salix alba*); sometimes in alder carr and sphagnum bogs by heaths.

- Head, pronotum, antennae, legs and underside metallic blue or greenish and elytra reddish-brown. 7.5-12.0 mm 2

2 Small dark apical spot on elytra. Sides of pronotum more or less rounded or with a very rounded angle (Fig. 150). 10.0-12.0 mm .... *populi* (red poplar leaf beetle)

Distribution: Widespread but scattered in various habitats (possibly absent from Scotland), usually on willows (*Salix*) and poplar (*Populus*) saplings.

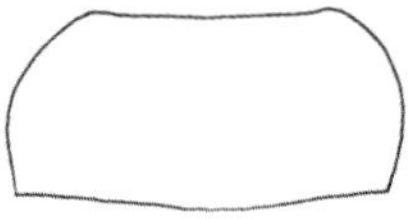

Fig. 150

- No dark apical spot on elytra. Sides of pronotum usually more or less straight or slightly emarginate (Fig. 151), at least in the rear half. 7.5-10.0 mm .... *tremula*

Distribution: Endangered (RDB1) and may be extinct. Usually on poplar (*Populus*) saplings and willows (*Salix*) in broad-leaved woodlands and commons.

Fig. 151

Key G8: Genus *Gonioctena*

1 Broadly oval, highly convex. Elytra weakly shouldered. Aedeagus asymmetric in dorsal view, somewhat hooked in lateral view (Figs 152, 153). 3.7-5.2 mm .... *olivacea* (broom leaf beetle)

Confirmatory characters: Yellowish or brownish with black marks, though colour variable and pale forms may be entirely yellowish dorsally. Pronotum yellow, brown or black; scutellum black, dark brown or yellow. Elytral suture usually dark brown (it can be yellowish in pale forms), elytra strongly punctured and sometimes with longitudinal brown lines. Underside unicolorous with, or darker than, dorsal surface.

Distribution: Widespread in various habitats, usually on brooms (*Cytisus*), sometimes on Dyer's greenweed (*Genista tinctoria*), laburnum (*Laburnum anagyroides*), gorse (*Ulex europaeus*) and lupins (*Lupinus*).

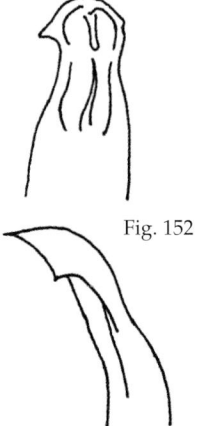

Fig. 152

- Relatively elongate, moderately convex. Elytra usually distinctly shouldered. Aedeagus as in Figs 154 to 159. 4.6-7.5 mm 2

Fig. 153

2 Front tibia without a thorn-like tooth on the outer edge. In males there
may be a small blunt wedge-like tooth; in females there may be a
rounded bump. Aedeagus blunt-ended as in Figs 154, 155. 4.6-7.0 mm
.... *pallida*

Confirmatory characters: Uniformly yellow, orange or reddish. No darkened suture,
or other dark lines or spots.

Distribution: Widespread in various habitats, usually on hazel (*Corylus*), sometimes on
other (usually small) trees.

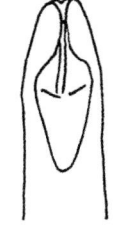

Fig. 154

- Front tibia with a clear, sharp thorn-like tooth on the outer edge near,
but before, the apex. Aedeagus as in Figs 156 to 159. 5.5-7.5mm 3

Fig. 155

3 Legs black or dark brown, rarely with reddish tibiae. Aedeagus constricted into a 'bottle-
neck' shape near the apex (Figs 156, 157). 5.5-7.0 mm .... *viminalis*

Confirmatory characters: Head entirely black, legs with yellowish claws. Orange or yellow with two black
marks on pronotum and five on each elytron, but pattern variable with marks merging, missing, or sometimes
dorsally all black.

Distribution: Widespread, especially in southern England in broad-leaved woodland, parkland, commons and
moors. Usually on willows (*Salix*) and poplars (*Populus*), rarely on hazel (*Corylus avellana*), alders (*Alnus*),
blackthorn (*Prunus spinosa*) and apples (*Malus*).

- Legs yellow, orange-red or pale brown. Aedeagus drawn out and narrowed at the apex,
not constricted (Figs 158, 159). 5.5-7.5mm .... *decemnotata*

Confirmatory characters: Head not entirely black (clypeus and labrum are yellow or reddish-brown). Markings
broadly similar to *G. viminalis*, never all black, rarely some or all markings absent.

Distribution: Scarce (Nb) but widely scattered in central and southern England (not the south-west). Usually
on aspen (*Populus tremula*); sometimes black poplar (*P. nigra*), goat willow (*Salix caprea*), hazels (*Corylus*) and
oaks (*Quercus*). In glades and rides in broad-leaved woodland, fields bordering woodland, and commons.

Fig. 156   Fig. 157   Fig. 158   Fig. 159

Key G9: Genus *Phratora*

1   2nd antennal segment equal to or slightly longer than 3rd 2

     2nd antennal segment shorter than 3rd 3

2   Usually metallic blue, sometimes greenish, blue-green or nearly black (take care with very dark specimens, use confirmatory characters). 4.0-5.5 mm .... *vulgatissima*

Confirmatory characters: Pronotum with a fine rear margin (this can be very difficult to see unless the light is coming from just the right direction). Elytral punctures somewhat irregular; elytra may appear somewhat wrinkled particularly in outer third where the elytral convexity becomes distinctly uneven halfway along the length of the beetle; shoulder bulge especially noticeable just behind the pronotum. Ventral surface of antennal segments 4-6 with tufts of hairs in males. Aedeagus as in Fig. 160.

Distribution: Widespread and common on willows (*Salix*), rarely on poplars (*Populus*) and birches (*Betula*), in a range of habitats.

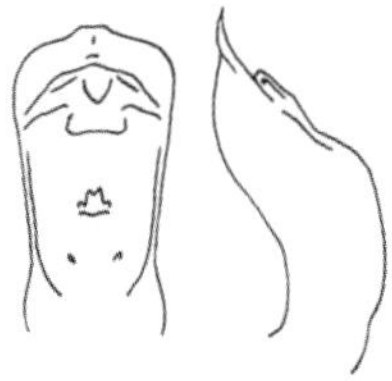

Fig. 160

-   Shiny bronze to bronze-black (as above take care with very dark specimens). 3.8-4.6 mm .... *polaris*

Confirmatory characters: Pronotum without a rear margin. Somewhat elongate but tends to be less parallel-sided and more oval than *P. vulgatissima*. Pronotum strongly arched. Aedeagus shaped like the nib of a fountain pen (Fig. 161).

Distribution: Rare (RDB3) under stones among dwarf willow (*Salix herbacea*) or associated with *Racomitrium lanuginosum* moss. Restricted to mountains between 700 m and 1100 m in north and west Scotland in grassland on dolomitic limestone outcrops where shoots of *S. herbacea* wind through the *Racomitrium* moss. Likely to be under-recorded.

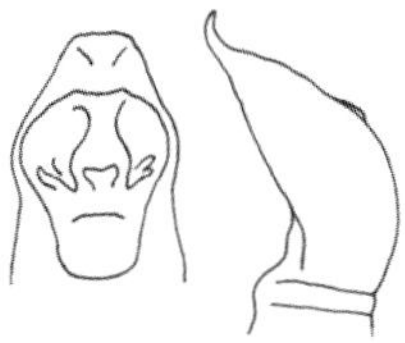

Fig. 161

3   Longitudinal groove or depression on front of head between antennae, with small prominence on either side, the groove widening towards the front to become more or less triangular (Fig. 162). Usually metallic blue, sometimes greenish-blue. Aedeagus as in Fig. 163 in lateral view. In males, antennae more than half as long as the body. 3.7-5.0 mm .... *laticollis*

Fig. 162

Distribution: Widespread on poplars (*Populus*), rarely willows (*Salix*), crab apple (*Malus sylvestris*) and English elm (*Ulmus procera*), in a range of habitats.

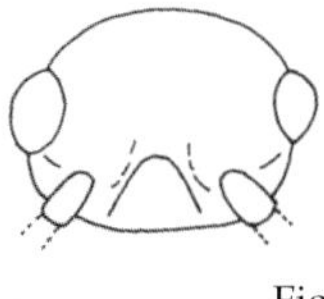

-   Front of head without depression between antennae. Variable in colour; usually metallic brassy or bronze, but sometimes greenish, blue, greenish-blue or (rarely) almost black. Aedeagus as in Fig. 164 in lateral view. Antennae less than, or just equal to, the body length, including in males. 3.8-5.0 mm .... *vitellinae*

Fig. 163

Confirmatory characters: Less elongate; more parallel-sided and squarer. Pronotum weakly arched.

Distribution: Widespread and common on willows (*Salix*) and poplars (*Populus*) in a wide range of habitats.

For an alternative separation of *Phratora* species (at that time known as genus *Phyllodecta*), including the initial descripton of *P. polaris*, see Morris (1970).

Fig. 164

KEY H: SUBFAMILY GALERUCINAE

In many cases within this subfamily, dissection of males is required in order to allow accurate identification to species. Features useful for separating males and females are given for genera and species where present. However, in some cases, clear features may not be easy to see, or may be absent. In such cases, the shape of the rear abdominal segment may prove useful as this tends to be smoothly rounded in females, but often exhibits some lateral sinuosity, incision, indentation or other interruption of smoothness in males.

1   Hind femora not thickened; unable to jump. Pronotum without impression or furrow on or just in front of the rear edge. Bulges at/above bases of antennae stretch forwards and between bases (Fig. 165a), though their shape is variable .... **Key Ha: Tribe Galerucini** (Fig. 169) (p. 64)

-   Hind femora thickened; able to jump and so known as the 'flea beetles'. In species with hind femora only slightly thickened, the pronotum has an impression or groove on or just in front of the rear edge (Figs 166, 167), sometimes only lateral longitudinal furrows (Fig. 168). Bulges at/above bases of antennae do not stretch forwards, although they vary in shape and there may be a longitudinal keel between the bases (Fig 165b) .... **Key Hb: Tribe Alticini** (Fig. 170) (p. 69)

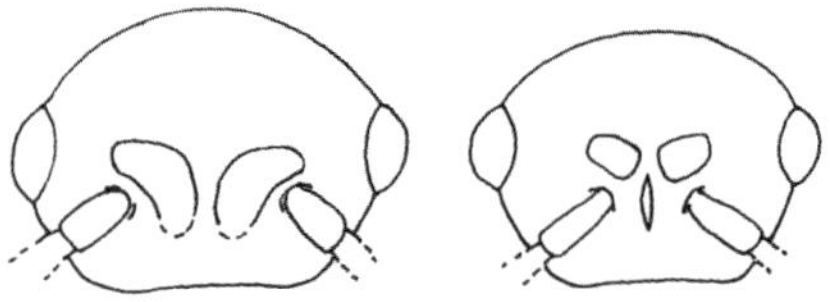

Fig. 165

a. Galerucini   b. Alticini

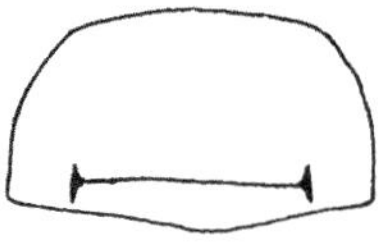

Fig. 166 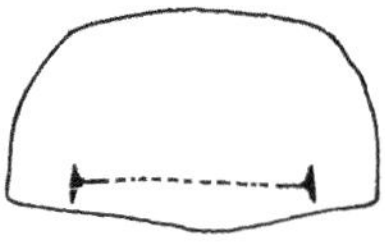   Fig. 167 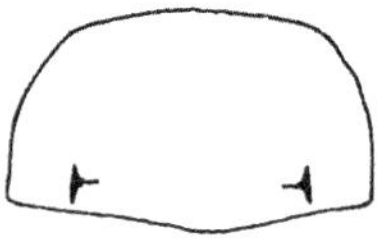   Fig. 168

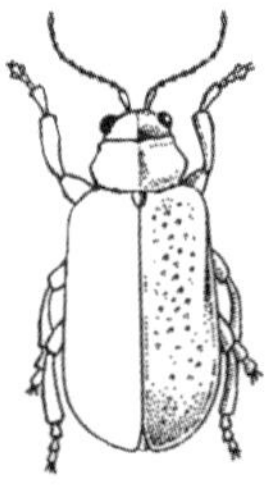

Fig. 169. Galerucini

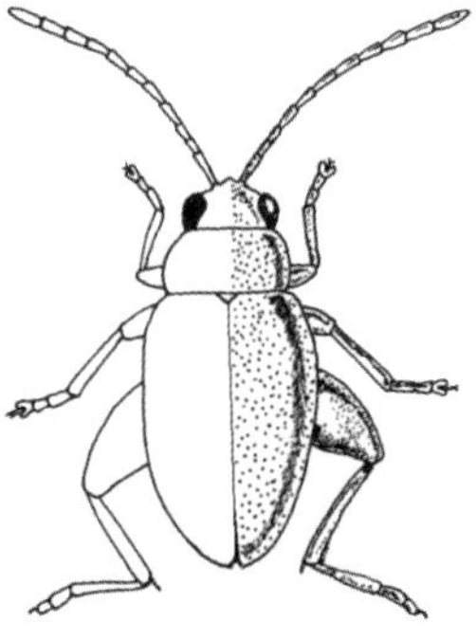

Fig. 170. Alticini

Key Ha: Tribe Galerucini

1 Elytra metallic green, blue, purple, bronze or copper. 5.0-7.0 mm 2

- Various colours, shiny or dull, but not metallic. 3.0-10.0 mm 3

2 Elytra metallic green or blue (rarely coppery). Head and pronotum yellow-brown (dark green to blackish spot on the top of the head). Antennae, tarsi and tips of tibiae usually dark brown to blackish; rest of legs yellow-brown (occasionally legs and antennae entirely reddish-brown. Elytra densely and moderately coarsely punctured, pronotum smooth and shiny. Pronotum approximately rectangular and twice as wide as long. 5.0-7.0 mm .... *Sermylassa halensis*

Distribution: Widespread on bedstraws (*Galium*), sometimes calamints (*Clinopodium*), in a wide range of habitats.

- Dorsal surface, legs and antennae deep metallic blue with violet reflection (sometimes purple or bronze), though specimens may lose their colour and appear dull black. Elytra widened towards the rear and with fairly distinct shoulders. Dorsal surface finely and densely punctured. Pronotum narrower than elytra and very short. 6.0-7.0 mm .... *Agelastica alni* (alder leaf beetle)

Distribution: Very rare, previously considered extinct but found in the Manchester area in 2004 and since in Cheshire (Stenhouse, 2006), so is considered RDBK. In open sunny locations in wetlands, especially alder carr; also river banks and wet woodland flushes. On young alder (*Alnus*), sometimes hazel (*Corylus avellana*), hybrid black-poplars (*Populus* x *canadensis*) and goat willow (*Salix caprea*); also a recent record (Ramsay, 2009) of feeding damage on silver birch (*Betula pendula*).

3 4th hind tarsal segment no longer than the first. 6.0-10.0 mm .... Key Ha1: Genus *Galeruca* (p. 66)

Confirmatory characters: Pronotum and elytra black or buff. Elytra with more or less distinct longitudinal ridges.

- 4th hind tarsal segment longer than the first. 3.0-7.0 mm 4

4 Long antennae and slender legs (Fig. 171). 3.8-5.0 mm 5

- Without especially long antennae or slender legs (Fig. 172). 3.0-7.0 mm 6

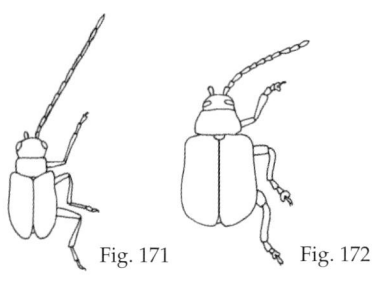

Fig. 171   Fig. 172

5 Pronotum black or very dark, yellow or reddish-brown, never yellow with a black band at the rear. Elytra dark (usually black or blackish). 3rd antennal segment usually twice as long as 2nd. 3.5-5.0 mm .... Key Ha2: Genus *Luperus* (p. 67)

Confirmatory characters: Elytra hairless, though care is needed to see the hairs on *Calomicrus* below. Legs at least partly orange.

- Pronotum yellow with black band at the rear. Elytra yellow with black border along outer margin continuing along inner margin next to suture. 3rd antennal segment about as long as 2nd. 3.0-4.5 mm.. *Calomicrus circumfusus*

Confirmatory characters: Rear half of elytra sparsely hairy, though this can be very difficult to see. Legs black.

Distribution: Scarce (Na) and widely scattered in various habitats on Fabaceae, especially gorse (*Ulex europaeus*), possibly also greenweeds (*Genista*), brooms (*Cytisus*) and Spanish broom (*Spartium junceum*).

6 Elytra yellowish with bold dark spots or lines (not only a dark suture). 5.0-7.0 mm 7

- Yellowish, brownish or greyish. No dark spots or lines, though the suture may be dark. 3.0-7.0 mm 8

7 Upper surface and appendages orange-yellow. Two black spots on each elytron (the front one may be missing). Top of head black. 5.0-7.0 mm .... *Phyllobrotica quadrimaculata*

Distribution: Widespread, but not common, in various damp, mainly open, habitats on skullcaps (*Scutellaria*).

- Elytra shiny yellow with wide dark suture (may not reach the rear) and lateral longitudinal bands (Fig. 173). Bands may be joined by a broad transverse band. Pronotum yellow, occasionally with small brown marks. Distinct shoulders. Head, legs and antennae dark (femora yellow beneath). 5.0-6.0 mm .... *Diabrotica virgifera* (western corn rootworm)

Distribution: Introduced pest of maize (*Zea mays*) found mainly near major airports.

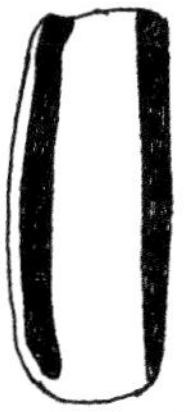

Fig. 173

8 Elytra hairless, smooth, irregularly punctured. Legs orange or yellowish, usually with at least femora darkened, sometimes black; if entirely orange, then elytra orange to red-brown with one or two black stripes or elongated spots. 3.7-6.0 mm .... Key Ha3: Genus *Lochmaea* (p. 67)

Confirmatory characters: Elytra yellow-brown with lateral bump extending along the entire length, although this may be vague and hard to determine.

- Elytra finely or densely pubescent with hairs laid flat. Legs entirely orange or yellowish (except in *Pyrrhalta* which often has a blackened dorsal ridge along the length of the tibia, or other dark marks). 3.0-7.0 mm 9

Confirmatory characters: Elytra with no lateral bump; at most a weak central bump.

9 Underside entirely reddish-brown. Head not especially small or short. 4.5-6.5 mm .... *Pyrrhalta viburni* (viburnum leaf beetle)

Confirmatory characters: Pronotum and elytra yellow-brown, dull. Three dark longitudinal lines on pronotum. Pronotum only a little wider than head. Scutellum and elytral shoulders at least slightly darkened. Elytra dull with dense silky pubescence; punctures fine and dense. Head relatively large, narrowing slightly in front of and behind eyes; width across eyes only slightly less than pronotum.

Distribution: Widespread and fairly common on viburnums (*Viburnum*) in various habitats, including scattered records in Scotland not included in Cox's 2007 Atlas (Alexander, 2011) which may indicate a northward range expansion although this is uncertain.

- Underside at least partly black. Head relatively small, narrowing slightly in front of and behind eyes; width across eyes considerably less than width of pronotum (Fig. 174). 3.0-7.0 mm 10

Fig. 174

10 3rd antennal segment longer than 4th. 3.0-6.0 mm ....
.... Key Ha4: Genus *Galerucella* (p. 68)

Confirmatory characters: Brownish- or greyish-yellow. Elytra with fairly coarse punctures (usually with finer ones between); varies from entirely yellowish to mostly darkened, sometimes with dark longitudinal bands. Distinctly punctured pronotum much wider than head (shape of pronotum may vary). Front of head entirely yellow or orange.

Fig. 175

- 3rd and 4th antennal segments approximately equal in length. 5.5-7.0 mm .... *Xanthogaleruca luteola* (elm leaf beetle)

Fig. 176

Confirmatory characters: Antennae blackish above. Pronotum yellow with three dark marks (can be variable) or a dark triangular spot. Head yellow with a dark spot in the female and transverse band in the male (Figs 175, 176). Elytra orange-yellow (sometimes yellow-brown or yellow-grey) with long dark longitudinal band from the shoulder (Fig. 177).

Distribution: Occasional specimens but not yet established. A major pest of elms (*Ulmus*).

More detail on the separation of *X. luteola* from *Galerucella* is given in Buckland & Skidmore (1999).

Fig. 177

Key Ha1: Genus *Galeruca*

In males, the tip of the last abdominal sternite is deeply indented; in females it is smoothly rounded (females may also exhibit a swollen abdomen when gravid).

1 Pronotum and elytra brownish. Antennae black, except basal segments 1-3 which are at least partly brownish. 6.0-9.0 mm .... *laticollis*

Distribution: Endangered (RDB1) on thistles (*Cirsium*) in fens and coppices. Recent records from a single site in the Norfolk Broads.

- Pronotum and elytra black. Antennae black, or with segment 2 brownish. 6.0-10.8 mm
.... *tanaceti*

Distribution: Widespread on a range of plants in open habitats.

Key Ha2: Genus *Luperus*

In males, the antennae are at least as long as the body and the last antennal segment is at least twice as long as the first. In females, the antennae are clearly shorter than the body and the last antennal segment is no more than slightly longer than the first. Males also have larger, more prominent eyes and the head is wider than the pronotum; in females it is narrower.

1 Pronotum black or very dark with sides moderately to strongly curved. 3.5-5.0 mm .... *longicornis*

> Distribution: Widespread and locally common, usually on young bushes and trees in a range of mainly damp habitats.

- Pronotum yellow or reddish-brown with the sides almost straight. 3.6-5.0 mm .... *flavipes*

> Distribution: Scarce (Nb), though may be locally common, on alder (*Alnus glutinosa*), birches (*Betula*) and sometimes other trees in a variety of habitats.

Key Ha3: Genus *Lochmaea*

In males, the mid-tibiae have a short spur which is absent in females. Males usually have the first segment of the hind tarsus dilated (not the case in females) and the hind tibiae are stouter and more sinuous than in females.

1 Head orange or reddish with darker markings. Elytra usually orange or red-brown with one or two black stripes or elongated spots. 3.7-5.5 mm .... *crataegi*

> Distribution: Widespread and common in a range of habitats on hawthorn (*Crataegus monogyna*), sometimes on cockspur-thorn (*C. crus-galli*), blackthorn (*Prunus spinosa*), rowan (*Sorbus aucuparia*) and gorse (*Ulex europaeus*).

- Head black with or without other markings, pronotum and elytra yellow-brown. Elytra without clear black elongated marks (sometimes with smaller, less distinct marks) 2

2 Head black with yellowish or brownish spot in front of eyes, although this can be difficult to see. Pronotum relatively shiny. Elytra variably coloured, dark ochraceous or occasionally dark brown-black; suture usually narrowly darkened. 4.3-6.0 mm .... *suturalis* (heather beetle)

> Distribution: Widespread and may be abundant on heather (*Calluna vulgaris*) and rarely heaths (*Erica*), anywhere that the host plants are present. Breeding requires a damp moss or litter layer for egg-laying and pupation.

- Head entirely black without paler spot in front of eyes. Pronotum relatively dull. Elytra always ochraceous; suture not narrowly darkened. 4.0-6.0 mm .... *caprea*

> Distribution: Widespread and common in a range of mainly wet/damp habitats, usually on willows (*Salix*) and birches (*Betula*), sometimes other trees and shrubs.

Key Ha4: Genus *Galerucella*

In males of *G. lineola*, *G. pusilla* and *G. tenella*, the mid-tibiae have a short spur which is absent in females. In *G. calmariensis* males, this spur is on the hind tibiae.

1 Pronotum with disc and depressions shiny, depressions with hairs; strong sparse punctures. Pronotum laterally curved with angular projection at about the mid-point (Fig. 178). Yellowish, brownish or brick-red. Elytra usually with two indistinct longitudinal ridges, and yellowish, brownish or dark brown with a paler margin. 4.0-8.0 mm .... *nymphaeae/sagittariae* complex

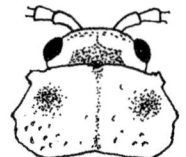

Fig. 178

Distribution: Widespread and common in a range of wetland habitats. Larger, darker forms (may be *nymphaeae*) usually on water-lilies (*Nuphar* and *Nymphaea*); smaller, paler forms (may be *sagittariae*) on a range of plants especially docks (*Rumex*) with later instar larvae also sometimes on water-lilies.

> There are few, if any, reliable morphological features available to separate these species and their taxonomic status is unclear. At 6.0-8.0 mm, *nymphaeae* may simply be a larger, darker form of the 4.0-5.5 mm *sagittariae* as separated in Hincks (1950). Beyond this, no attempt is made to separate them here. Further information on *nymphaeae* can also be found in Manguin *et al.* (1993).

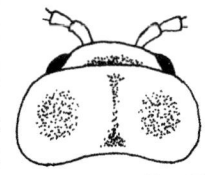

- Not as above, pronotum rounded at the sides or with an indistinct angulation at its widest point (Fig. 179). 3.5-6.0 mm 2

Fig. 179

2 Yellowish, brownish or brick-red. Dark spot on top of head (often all dark on top except for a narrow pale margin), one on pronotum and one on elytral shoulder. Elytra with short, close, shiny pubescence. 5.0-6.0 mm .... *lineola*

Distribution: Widespread and often common on alder (*Alnus glutinosa*), hazel (*Corylus avellana*) and willows (*Salix*) in various habitats.

- Not as above (some but not all dark spots may be present). Pubescence inconspicuous ... 3

3 Elytra usually with dark shoulder spot extending into a longitudinal band along the side; may be somewhat diffuse (Fig. 180). Aedeagus sinuously curved and narrow (Fig. 181) with a blunt tip. In female, 5th abdominal sternite with a deep dent at the tip. 3.6-5.6 mm .... *calmariensis*

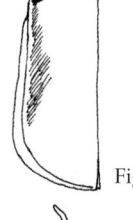

Confirmatory characters: Yellowish, brownish or brick-red with a large dark spot on the pronotum. Following features usually black: top of head, scutellum, mesosternum, metasternum, front coxae and abdominal sternites (apart from the last 1-3).

Distribution: Widespread and locally common on purple-loosestrife (*Lythrum salicaria*) in a range of habitats, usually near water.

Fig. 180

Fig. 181

- Elytra without dark shoulder spot extending into a longitudinal band. Aedeagus evenly curved and thick (Fig. 182) with the tip a rounded point. In female, 5th abdominal sternite without a deep dent at the tip; at most a shallow dent. 3.0-4.6 mm 4

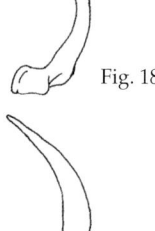

Fig. 182

4 Yellowish, brownish or brick-red. Pronotum sometimes with dark central spot (Fig. 183); rarely a dark spot on elytral shoulder. Front and side edges of pronotum (and sometimes rear edge) bare and shiny. Female pronotum may have a bare central area, possibly indented (Fig. 184). In male, 5th abdominal sternite with a small to moderate impression and a shallow dent at the tip (Fig. 185). In female, 5th abdominal sternite without a dent at the tip. 3.0-4.0 mm .... *tenella*

Fig. 183

Fig. 184

Confirmatory characters: Yellowish, brownish or brick-red with a large dark spot on the pronotum. Following features usually black: top of head, scutellum (except the tip), mesosternum, metasternum and abdominal sternites 1-4. More convex overall.

Distribution: Widespread and common on various Rosaceae in a range of wetland habitats.

Fig. 185

- Yellow-brown usually without a distinct pronotal spot. Front edge of pronotum bare and shiny. Elytra less strongly punctured, usually with small dark shoulder spot very rarely extending into a longitudinal band along the side. In male, 5th abdominal sternite with a large triangular impression and a deep dent at the tip (Fig. 186). In female, 5th abdominal sternite with a shallow dent at the tip (Fig. 187). 3.5-4.6 mm .... *pusilla*

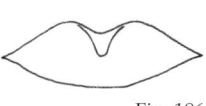

Fig. 186

Fig. 187

Confirmatory characters: Yellowish, brownish or brick-red with a large dark spot on the pronotum. Following features usually black: top of head, scutellum (sometimes except the tip), mesosternum, metasternum and abdominal sternites 1-2 or 1-3. Less convex overall.

Distribution: Scattered on purple-loosestrife (*Lythrum salicaria*), sometimes on other water plants and willows (*Salix*), in and around a range of wetland habitats.

> There is considerable variation and overlap in the sizes, colours and markings of *Galerucella* and species may be difficult to separate. For more information, see Hincks (1950).

Key Hb: Tribe Alticini

1 Hind tarsus joins tibia before the end, leaving a distinct overlap (Fig. 188). Antennae with 10 segments (see Fig. 3). 2.0-4.5 mm .... Key Hb1: Genus *Psylliodes* (p. 74)

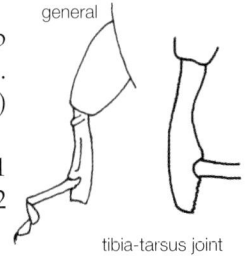

general

tibia-tarsus joint

Fig. 188

- Hind tibia without an overlap at the tarsal joint. Antennae with 11 segments. 1.0-6.0 mm 2

2 Tiny (1.0-1.5 mm), very convex (almost hemispherical) with head concealed from above. Black (usually with vague metallic sheen), antennae and legs reddish-brown. Last 3 antennal segments thickened .... *Mniophila muscorum*

Distribution: Scarce (Nb) and widely scattered among mosses in woodland, parkland or moorland. Probably under-recorded.

- Not as above 3

3 Spurs at end of hind tibiae wide and forked (Fig. 189). 2.4-3.0 mm
.... *Dibolia cynoglossi*

> Confirmatory characters: Metallic bronze or dark green, tibiae yellow-reddish, apical
> half of antennae dark brown. Hind femora greatly swollen-even more so than other
> flea beetles.

> Distribution: Endangered (RDB1) on Lamiaceae in woodland rides, clearings and
> margins, on chalk hillsides and on coastal shingle. Recent records from only two sites
> in south-east England though may be under-recorded.

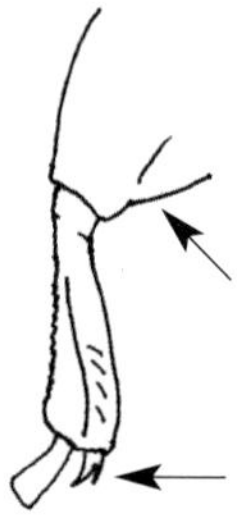

- Terminal spurs on hind tibiae with a single point. 1.0-6.0 mm 4

Fig. 189

4 Distinct dent on middle and hind tibiae (Fig. 190), with hairy upper
margin (hairs may be difficult to see). 1.5-2.5 mm ....
.... Key Hb2: Genus *Chaetocnema* (p. 78)

- Middle and hind tibiae without such a dent. 1.2-6.0 mm 5

Fig. 190

5 Pronotum without a groove parallel to the rear edge; at most, weak traces of short
longitudinal furrow at the rear edge. If the pronotum has a pair of short furrows near the
rear edge, then the dorsal body surface may vary in colour, but not entirely reddish-
brownish. 1.0-6.0 mm 6

> Take care with *Hippuriphila modeeri* (couplet 10 below) as it can incorrectly key out here because the pronotal
> groove is very poorly defined. *H. modeeri* has a red-brown to bronze dorsal surface with paler elytral tips
> and is generally found on horsetails (*Equisetum*).

- Pronotum with a more or less distinct groove parallel to, and a little in front of, the rear
edge, and/or a pair of short longitudinal furrows at the rear edge. If the groove is very
shallow or faint, then either the elytra is densely pubescent, or the dorsal surface is
entirely reddish-brownish and the groove ends with short furrows at right-angles to it.
1.2-5.5 mm 13

6 First segment of hind tarsus at least half as long as hind tibia (Fig.
191). In side view, apical spur of hind tibia as in Fig. 191; when viewed
from the rear, the spur is at the middle of lower edge. Wide range of
colours. 1.0-4.0 mm .... Key Hb10: Genus *Longitarsus* (p. 86)

- First segment of hind tarsus less than half as long as hind tibia. Apical
spur of hind tibia absent, small or variably placed. 1.4-5.0 mm 7

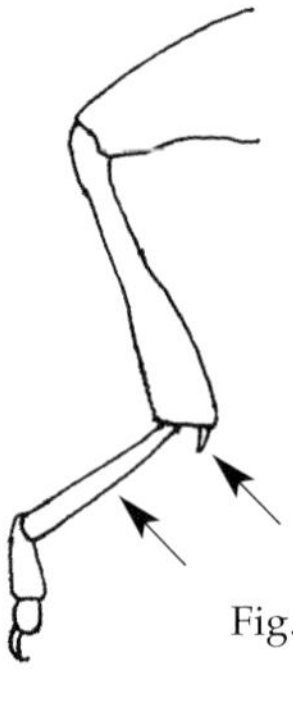

Fig. 191

7 Elytra randomly punctured or in irregular rows. 1.0-5.0 mm 8

- Elytral punctures regularly striate, at least at the sides. 1.0-2.0 mm 11

8 Round to oval, very convex, often almost hemispherical. Upper surface brick-red to orange-red, sometimes yellowish or brownish. Antennae slender without thickened segments. 2.3-4.5 mm .... Key Hb14: Genus *Sphaeroderma* (p. 110)

- Oval, no more than moderately convex, may be slightly flattened 9

9 Pronotum orange-red; elytra, head, legs and antennae black or dark brown. 5.0 mm ....
.... *Luperomorpha xanthodera* (rose flea beetle)

Distribution: Introduced on garden plants (larvae are root-feeding) with occasional records from garden centres. Originally from China.

- Not this combination of colours 10

10 Bulges above antennal bases weakly convex, indistinct and not separated from front of the head by deep furrows. Front of the head above these weak bulges usually punctured. Hind tibiae without a longitudinal groove or 'gutter' on the dorsal side. Body dorsally dark or metallic, elytra sometimes with longitudinal yellow bands or other yellow markings. Apical spur of hind tibia at middle of lower edge (Fig. 192). 1.4-3.5 mm .... Key Hb11: Genus *Phyllotreta* (p. 101)

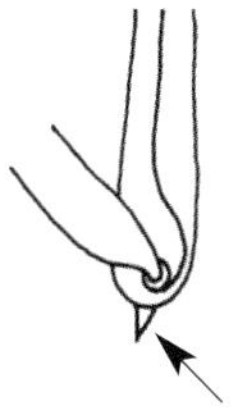

Fig. 192

- Bulges above antennal bases usually well developed and separated from front of the head by deep furrows. Front of head above these bulges not punctured. Hind tibiae with a longitudinal groove or 'gutter' on the apical half of the dorsal side. Body dorsally yellow, brown, black, dark metallic blue or green. No yellow marks or bands on elytra. Apical spur of hind tibia at outer side of lower edge (Fig. 193). 1.5-3.0 mm .... Key Hb12: Genus *Aphthona* (p. 106)

Take care with the the separation of *Phyllotreta* and *Aphthona*; some of the features may be difficult to see and differences can be subtle. However, careful observation and use of the range of features given should permit separation of these genera.

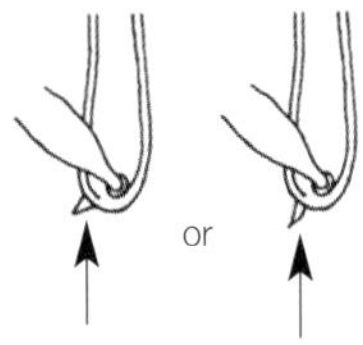

or

Fig. 193

11 Short-oval, very convex, almost hemispherical. 2.2-3.0 mm ....
.... Key Hb13: Genus *Apteropeda* (p. 109)

- Body oval, not especially shortened, clearly not hemispherical 12

12 Brownish, yellowish or reddish-yellow; not metallic. Head and pronotum rarely dark. Striae becoming faint towards tips of elytra. 1.8-2.0 mm .... *Lythraria salicariae*

Confirmatory characters: Dark suture not reaching scutellum; where the darkening stops, diagonal lines sometimes run forward to shoulders forming faintly darkened triangles forward of this point.

Distribution: Scarce (Nb) on loosestrifes (*Lysimachia*) and purple-loosestrife (*Lythrum salicaria*), sometimes chickweed-wintergreen (*Trientalis europaea*), in various habitats.

- Metallic dark bronze-green, dark brown or black. Striae formed of large punctures, not becoming faint towards tips. 1.0-2.0 mm .... Key Hb9: Genus *Batophila* (p. 86)

13 Rear edge of pronotum with two short longitudinal furrows but no transverse groove (Fig. 168) 14

- Rear edge of pronotum with a transverse groove (e.g. Figs 166, 167, 195) 15

14 Scutellar row of punctures reaches no more than one third the length of the suture. Head and pronotum red or reddish-brown. Elytra dark blue, green or violet, more-or-less metallic; punctures at least partly confused. Base of pronotum curves inward to become narrower than front of elytra (Fig. 194). 3.0-6.0 mm .... Key Hb7: Genus *Podagrica* (p. 84)

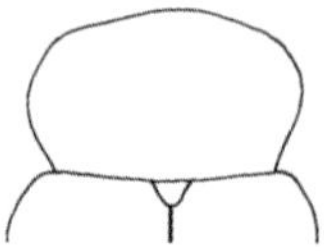

Fig. 194

- Scutellar row of punctures reaches more than half the length of the suture. Dorsally dark brown or blackish (tips of elytra sometimes black and brown) with metallic tinge. Elytral punctures striate. Base of pronotum as wide as front of elytra. 1.8-2.8 mm .... Key Hb8: Genus *Mantura* (p. 85)

15 Pronotal groove extends almost to the sides of the pronotum; no short furrows at its ends (Fig. 195). 2.8-5.5 mm .... Key Hb3: Genus *Altica* (p. 80)

Confirmatory characters: Metallic green, blue-green or blue. Body fairly flat. Elytra randomly punctured.

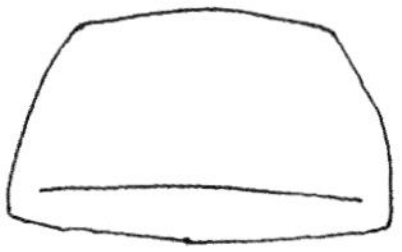

Fig. 195

- Pronotal groove ends well before sides with short furrows joining base at right-angles (Figs 166, 167). 1.2-5.5 mm 16

16 Elytra randomly punctured. Front coxal cavities open at the rear (Fig. 7). 2.3-3.0 mm .... *Hermaeophaga mercurialis*

Confirmatory characters: Blue-black; antennae and legs black except reddish-brown tarsi and antennal bases. Pronotum wide and convex; groove ends with short grooves joining base at right-angles, sometimes with a dent at each end (Fig. 196). Body short-oval and very convex.

Distribution: Widespread and fairly common in southern Britain, occasionally further north. On dog's mercury (*Mercurialis perennis*) in sunny woodland glades, hedgerows, chalk grassland, meadows, commons, heaths and quarries.

Fig. 196

- Elytral punctures striate, at least at the sides. Front coxal cavities closed at the rear (see Fig. 8). 1.2-5.5 mm 17

17 Elytra hairy, elytral hairs erect and in rows. 1.2-2.0 mm ... Key Hb4: Genus *Epitrix* (p. 82)

Confirmatory characters: Oval. Dark brown, black, sometimes yellow, rarely metallic. Pronotum hairy though this is often difficult to see.

- Elytra hairless, or if there is some pubescence it is confined to the near-vertical sides. 1.8-5.5 mm 18

18 Rear margin of bulges above antennal bases weakly separated from the remainder of the front of the head by a faint groove. 3.0-5.5 mm .... Key Hb6: Genus *Neocrepidodera* (p. 84)

Confirmatory characters: Pale or reddish-brown, sometimes partly or wholly darker. Strong, unbroken transverse pronotal furrow (e.g. Fig. 166). Top of head smooth or finely wrinkled, without coarse, dense punctures. 9th and 10th antennal segments elongate (2-3 times as long as wide).

- Rear margin of bulges above antennal bases clearly separated from the remainder of the front of the head by a deep groove. 2.3-4.2 mm 19

Take care with the the separation of *Neocrepidodera* from the remaining genera; the depth of the groove on the head may be difficult to determine. However, careful observation and use of the range of features given, including those of the remaining genera, should permit separation.

19 Dorsally unicolorous yellow or pale brown, head and prothorax rarely darkened; pronotum and elytra sometimes with a fine dark border. 2.1-2.5 mm .... *Ochrosis ventralis*

Fig. 197

Confirmatory characters: Transverse pronotal furrow weak with a central break (Fig. 197). Elytral punctures becoming faint in the rear half. Bulges above antennal bases triangular with their rear edges separated from the remainder of the front of the head by a transverse furrow (Fig. 198).

Distribution: Rare (RDB3), scattered and very local on various plants in lakesides, downland leys, coastal bays, cliffs and (probably) on disturbed ground, especially with free-draining soils.

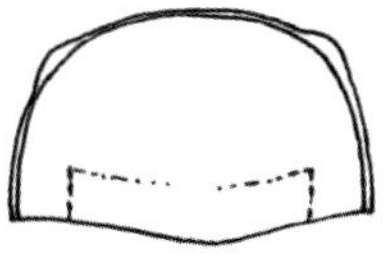

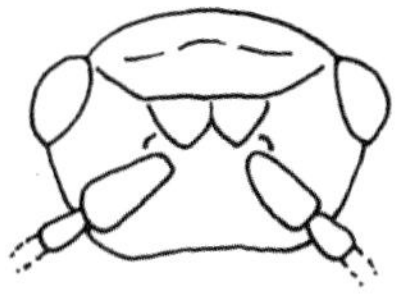

Fig. 198

- Dorsally bicolorous or with a metallic reflection 20

Confirmatory characters: Elytral punctures not becoming faint in the rear half. Bulges above antennal bases roundish or transverse, surrounded by a deep furrow (Fig. 199). Take care as the surrounding furrows join above the bulges, and may appear superficially similar to the transverse furrow in Fig. 198. Also, the bulges may be more or less triangular in *Derocrepis rufipes* but still partly rounded and transverse on the inner and lower corners as in Fig. 200.

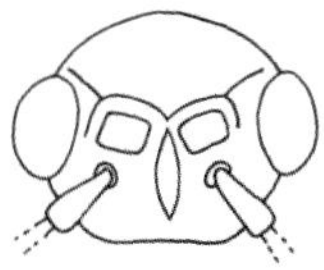

Fig. 199

20 Head, pronotum, antennae and legs red or rusty. Elytra blackish to distinctly metallic blue, blue-green, bronze-green or blackish-green. 2.3-3.8 mm .... *Derocrepis rufipes*

Confirmatory characters: Bulges above antennal bases large and rounded to triangular (Fig. 200).

Distribution: Widespread and locally common on various Fabaceae in a range of habitats.

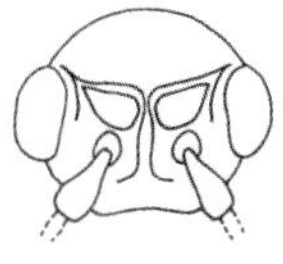

Fig. 200

- Not this combination of colours 21

21 Dorsal surface entirely metallic blue, green or bronze. Legs orange with hind femora darkened. 2.5-4.2 mm .... Key Hb5: Genus *Crepidodera* (p. 82)

Confirmatory characters: Bulges above antennal bases short and broad (Fig. 199).

- Dorsally pitchy dark brown or black with weak bronze reflection; tips of elytra paler reddish-brownish. 1.8-2.5 mm .... *Hippuriphila modeeri*

Distribution: Widespread on horsetails (*Equisetum*) in various habitats.

Key Hb1: Genus *Psylliodes*

1 Dark bronze, sometimes with greenish (rarely bluish) tinge. Head concealed from above by the pronotum (*P. picina* (qv) sometimes has the head partly covered). Lacks distinct shoulders. 2.1-2.4 mm .... *cucullata*

Distribution: New to Britain in 1991 and known only from a few sites in S. Wales. In woodlands and arable fields, possibly associated with corn spurrey (*Spergula arvensis*).

- Head not completely covered from above. 2.0-4.5 mm 2

2 Pronotum with a mixture of coarse and fine punctures (take care to ensure that apparent fine punctures are not simply shagreening between the coarser punctures as this can give the appearance of fine puncturation). 2.6-4.0 mm 3

- Pronotal punctures either all fine or all coarse. 2.0-4.5 mm 5

3 Dark metallic blue. Front angles of pronotum large and distinct with a sharp tooth/angle at the position of the bristled pore (Fig. 201). Head with frontal lines usually indistinct, often obscured by punctures .... *dulcamarae*

Fig. 201

Confirmatory characters: Majority of femora, tibiae and tarsi dark brown or black, rarely with tibiae reddish. 3.1-4.0 mm

Distribution: Locally common south of a line from the Humber to the Severn, on bittersweet (*Solanum dulcamara*) in various habitats.

- Pronotum without distinct front angles. Frontal lines usually distinct. 2.6-3.5 mm 4

4 Short-oval. Dorsally blue-black, rarely black with green or bronze reflection; may appear metallic blue or greenish-blue, sometimes bronze. Head usually shiny. Front femora usually mostly brownish. Final ventrite entirely dark, not pale in the apical half. In lateral view, aedeagus with a clear raised flange at the tip (Fig. 202). 2.6-3.4 mm .... *chalcomera*

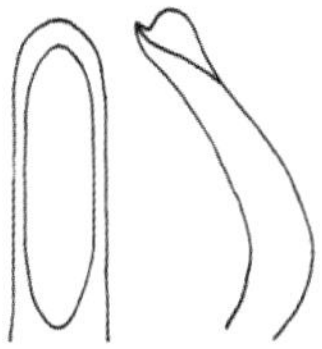

Fig. 202

Distribution: Scarce (Nb) and scattered in various habitats on thistles (*Carduus* and *Cirsium*) as well as other Asteraceae.

- Oval. Dorsally blackish with blue-green or dark bronze reflection; may appear metallic green or bronze, sometimes coppery or blue-green. Head usually dull, with distinct frontal lines. Front femora usually mostly yellowish. Apical half of final ventrite pale. In lateral view, aedeagus without a flange at the tip (Fig. 203). 2.9-3.5 mm .... *hyoscyami* (henbane flea beetle)

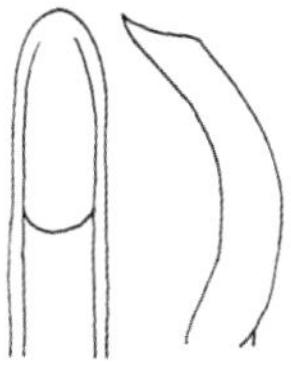

Fig. 203

Distribution: Endangered (RDB1) and possibly extinct with no records since 1930. On Solanaceae, especially henbane (*Hyoscyamus niger*), in areas of disturbed ground, particularly where sandy.

5 Narrow. Metallic green or bronze, usually with ends of elytra reddish-brown, but elytra may be entirely green or bronze. Frontal lines form an X between the eyes (Fig. 204) though note they don't actually cross. Top of head dull, without punctues. Pronotum coarsely punctured, dull. Elytra coarsely punctured; interstices shiny. Hind tibiae with outer margin bearing 3-6 small spines before the tarsus joins (Fig. 205). 2.0-2.8 mm .... *attenuata* (hop flea beetle)

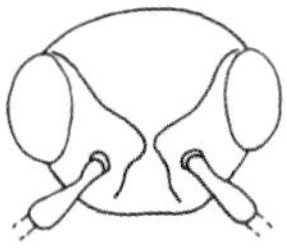

Distribution: Endangered (RDB1) and very widely scattered; mainly in south-east England. On Cannabaceae, especially hop (*Humulus lupulus*), on and around cultivated land and in woodland.

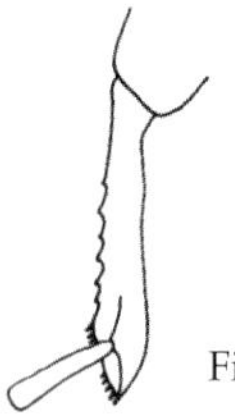

Fig. 204

Fig. 205

- Frontal lines behind antennae usually indistinct; if clearly present, then hind tibiae without 4-6 small lateral spines (may be fewer or absent). 2.0-4.5 mm 6

6 Hind tibia with outer edge distinctly and evenly curved (Fig. 206). 2.0-3.1 mm 7

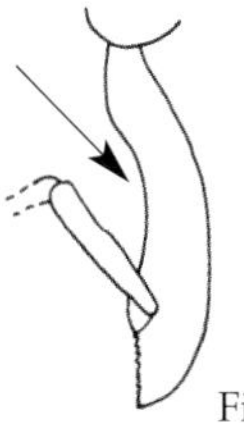

Fig. 206

- Hind tibia with outer edge more or less straight or slightly curved (Fig. 207). 2.2-4.5 mm 8

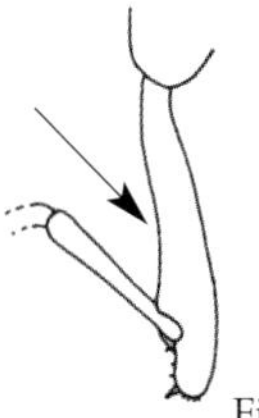

Fig. 207

7 Dorsally brown-yellowish to reddish. Front of head with sparse, medium-coarse punctures. Frontal lines usually partly missing. 2.2-3.1 mm .... *luteola*

Distribution: Very local in southern and central England, but poorly known (RDBK), on various plants in a range of habitats.

Similar to pale teneral specimens of *P. picina*.

- Dark chestnut brown, sometimes rusty-red or with pronotum red and elytra very dark brown. Front of head usually without punctures, or with a few very fine punctures. Frontal lines usually distinct, complete. 2.0-2.9 mm .... *picina*

Distribution: Widely scattered on various plants in a range of habitats.

8 Elytra yellowish to reddish-brown with narrow pitchy-black sutural band. Head pitchy brown without metallic reflection, top without punctures, darker than pronotum. 2.2-2.9 mm .... *affinis* (potato flea beetle)

Confirmatory characters: Underside and hind femora (entirely or apically) blackish.

Distribution: Widespread and common on wild and cultivated Solanaceae in a range of habitats.

- Elytra variously coloured, metallic, with vague metallic reflection. If yellowish with a darkened suture, head not pitchy-brown nor darker than pronotum, and length 3.0-4.5 mm (otherwise range 2.3-4.5 mm) 9

9 Front third of epipleura almost hairless. 2.3-3.6 mm 10

- Front third of epipleura with short pubescence. 2.3-4.5 mm 11

10 Dark blue, sometimes with greenish tinge, rarely bronze or brassy. Head usually brown with metallic reflection, sometimes coloured as elytra and pronotum. Pronotum with distinct front angles and a clear lateral margin (Fig. 208). 2.3-3.3 mm .... *napi*
Confirmatory characters: Front and middle legs yellow (femora rarely darkened). Aedeagus as in Fig. 210.
Distribution: Widespread and common on Brassicaceae in various habitats.

- Deep blue, sometimes with purple tinge. Pronotum usually with rounded front angles, slightly protruding at front of margin (Fig. 209). 2.8-3.6 mm .... *laticollis*
Confirmatory character: Aedeagus as in Fig. 211.

Distribution: Widely scattered in various habitats, usually on watercress (*Nasturtium officinale*), sometimes garlic mustard (*Alliaria petiolata*), possibly also brooklime (*Veronica beccabunga*).

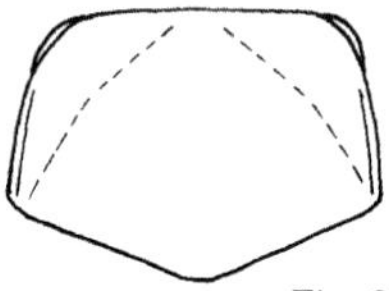

Fig. 208 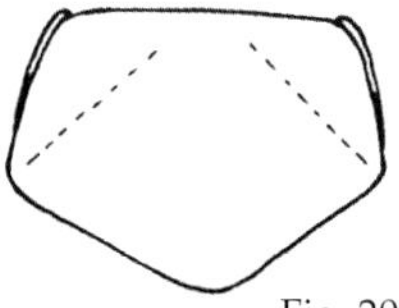   Fig. 209

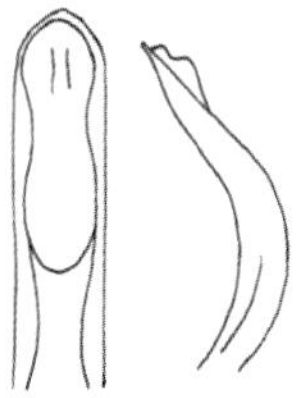

Fig. 210

Fig. 211

11 Front and/or top of head at least partly reddish or brownish. 2.8-4.5 mm 12

- Front and top of head entirely metallic green or bronze, sometimes blue. 2.3-3.7 mm 14

12 Middle of upperside of hind tibiae usually darkened. In males, 1st front tarsal segment clearly wider than 3rd. 2.8-3.7 mm .... *sophiae*
Confirmatory characters: Pronotum usually reddish, sometimes very dark brown. Elytra metallic blue with coarse punctures between striae. Pronotum usually with distinct front angles. Colour of hind tibiae, and pronotal angles separate this from the similar *P. chrysocephala*. Aedeagus as in Fig. 212.

Distribution: Rare (RDB3) and very local on flixweed (*Descurainia sophia*), and possibly woad (*Isatis tinctoria*). In disturbed or waste areas, arable fields and margins, grassland and roadside verges (especially on sandy or chalky-sandy Breckland soils), also in fens. Recent records from west Suffolk and west Norfolk only.

Fig. 212

- Hind tibiae entirely yellowish or pale brown. In males, 1st front tarsal segment approximately equal in width to, or narrower than, 3rd. 3.0-4.5 mm 13

13 Pronotum and elytra usually concolourous yellowish or brownish. Pronotum usually with distinct front angles. Punctures on top of head usually coarser than those between elytral striae. In males, 1st front tarsal segment slightly narrower than 3rd. 3.2-3.8 mm .... *marcida*

Distribution: Coastal on sea rocket (*Cakile maritima*) and other Brassicaceae, mainly on sand dunes, sometimes roadside verges. Distinct front pronotal angles separate it from the similar *P. chrysocephala* var. *anglica*.

- Variably-coloured, usually with pronotum and elytra concolourous metallic blue; in var. *anglica* elytra yellowish to pale brown. Pronotum usually without distinct anterior angles. Punctures on top of head equally as coarse as, or finer than, those between elytral striae. In males, 1st front tarsal segment approximately equal in width to 3rd. 3.0-4.5 mm .... *chrysocephala* (cabbage-stem flea beetle)

Distribution: Widespread and common on wild and cultivated Brassicaceae in various habitats.

14 Metallic green, bronze or blue. Front of head entirely green, bronze or blue. Pronotum with distinct front angles. 2.3-4.0 mm. Aedeagus as in Fig. 213 .... *cuprea*

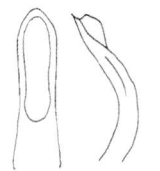
Fig. 213

Confirmatory characters: The partly pubescent epipleura separate it from the similar *P. napi* as do the more strongly reticulate head and pronotum, and the narrower and less convex shape.

Distribution: Widely scattered on Brassicaceae, in autumn also on ash (*Fraxinus excelsior*) and oaks (*Quercus*), in various habitats.

- Variably-coloured; head and pronotum usually metallic bronze, or greenish or bluish; elytra varying from brownish-yellow, usually with darkened suture, through to concolorous with the head and pronotum. Pronotum usually lacking distinct front angles. 3.1-3.7 mm. Aedeagus as in Fig. 214 .... *luridipennis*

Fig. 214

Distribution: Endangered (RDB1); also listed as Vulnerable (RDB2) and Endemic. Only on Lundy cabbage (*Coincya wrightii*) on Lundy Island.

For more on *Psylliodes* species in the UK, including further features of genitalia, see Cox (1998). For more about *luteola*, including comparison with teneral *picina*, see Cox (2000a). Covering species found in Russia and neighbouring countries, which encompasses much of the British fauna, this genus was reviewed by Nadein (2007), including keys to species and numerous figures of legs, heads, pronota and both male and female genitalia.

Key Hb2: Genus *Chaetocnema*

1 Head with distinct keel between antennae and 7 or 8 coarse punctures above each eye, some of which may be obscured by the pronotum depending on angle of view (Fig. 215). Elytral striae regular. Femora dark, rest of legs at least partly yellowish-brownish. Overall colour bronze, coppery or dark green. 1.7-2.4 mm 2

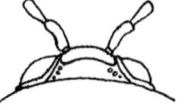

Fig. 215

- Not as above. Striae may be regular or irregular, at least in part. Keel between the antennae absent, or there may be very fine (not distinct as in Fig. 215) keel running towards the eyes; if so, the end may almost reach the eyes or may stop, leaving a clear gap before the edge of the eyes. 1.5-2.5 mm 3

2 Last antennal segment more broadly rounded and slightly asymmetrical (Fig. 216). First antennal segment usually slightly darkened, 2nd and 3rd pale, others gradually darkened. 1.8-2.4 mm. Aedeagus as in Fig. 218 .... *concinna* (mangold flea beetle)

Distribution: Widespread and common in various habitats on Polygonaceae, Chenopodiaceae, lesser periwinkle (*Vinca minor*), yew (*Taxus baccata*), birches (*Betula*) and possibly other plants where they may feed on pollen.

- Last antennal segment somewhat pointed and more or less symmetrical (Fig. 217). Antennal colour as *C. concinna* or darker (first, second and third antennal segments are usually dark dorsally). 1.7-2.3 mm. Aedeagus as in Fig. 219 .... *picipes*

Distribution: Scattered in various habitats on Polygonaceae, oraches (*Atriplex*) and possibly other plants.

See Cox (2007) regarding confusion between *C. concinna* and *C. picipes*, with further detail given in Booth & Owen (1997).

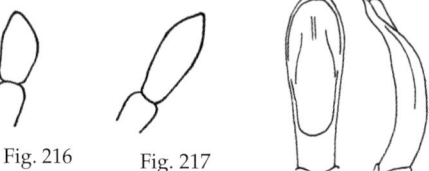

Fig. 216   Fig. 217   Fig. 218   Fig. 219

3 Broad. Black with leaden reflection, sometimes bluish or dark bronze. Elytral striae coarse, and regular away from the front half of the suture. Femora darkened, tibiae and tarsi yellowish to reddish-brown. Pronotum hood-like and smooth with fine, dense punctures. 1st to 4th antennal segments reddish-brown. 1.8-2.5 mm. Aedeagus as in Fig. 220 .... *confusa*

Distribution: Widespread but local on sedges (*Carex*), purple moor-grass (*Molinia caerulea*) and possibly rushes (*Juncus*) in various, usually wet, habitats.

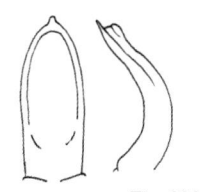

Fig. 220

- Not as above (may have some of these features, but not all). 1.5-2.3 mm 4

4 Punctures regular, except for abbreviated scutellar striae, with striae 1 and 2 forming irregular double rows at the front. Pronotum and elytra coarsely and densely punctured. 1.6-2.2 mm. Aedeagus as in Fig. 221 .... *aerosa*

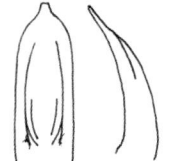

Fig. 221

Confirmatory characters: Short-oval. Brassy-bronze or dark green, almost black. Head slightly less coarsely punctured than pronotum. Elytral shoulders distinct.

Distribution: Rare but poorly known (RDBK) on spike-rushes (*Eleocharis*), especially common spike-rush (*E. palustris*), in wet habitats in south and east England. May be extinct, but searches should be made in areas where the host plant grows.

- Not as above. Punctures more widely irregular. 1.5-2.3 mm 5

5 Pronotal punctures fine or moderately fine, sometimes a little coarser in the rear half (Fig. 222). 1.5-2.2 mm 6

Fig. 222

- Pronotal punctures moderately coarse (Fig. 223). 1.5-2.3 mm 7

  The judgement regarding coarseness of pronotal puncturation can be difficult, though it eases with experience. If in doubt regarding an identification, bear in mind the various features of the species in question and consider returning to this couplet.

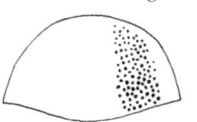

Fig. 223

6 Short-oval. Bronze-brown, often with greenish reflection, sometimes very dark blue or almost black. Tibiae and tarsi usually brownish; sometimes front tibiae partly bronze. Head and pronotum finely punctured. Elytral punctures regular except along suture and/or front edge. 1.5-2.0 mm. Aedeagus as in Fig. 224 .... *arida*

Distribution: Scattered on sedges (*Carex*), rushes (*Juncus*) and galingales (*Cyperus*) in various habitats in southern England and Wales.

- Dark blue, rarely greenish or black. Elytra elongate-oval and only slightly broader than pronotum. Femora black with vague metallic reflection. Tibiae, tarsi and antennal segments 2-4 usually brownish; sometimes front tibiae partly black. Sides of pronotum with a rounded angle (Fig. 225). Elytral punctures usually random on top, regular around rear and sides. 1.8-2.2 mm. Aedeagus as in Fig. 226 .... *subcoerulea*

Distribution: Scarce (Nb) on sedges (*Carex*) and rushes (*Juncus*) in wet habitats, mostly in the southern most counties of England.

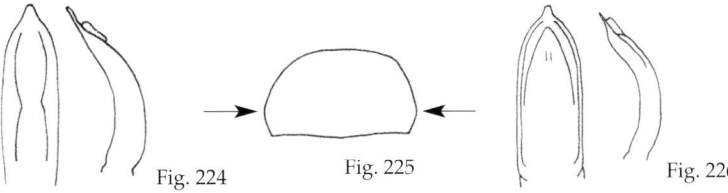

Fig. 224   Fig. 225   Fig. 226

7 Unicolorous bronze, coppery, coppery-bronze, sometimes metallic green. Head with a fine keel ending well before the eyes. Moderately coarsely punctured. 1st antennal segment reddish-brownish, often also several following this. 1.5-2.3 mm. Aedeagus as in Fig. 227 .... *hortensis*

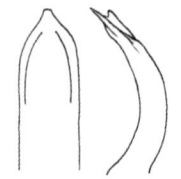

Fig. 227

Distribution: Widespread and common on wild and cultivated grasses (Poaceae), possibly also on galingales (*Cyperus*) and sheep's sorrel (*Rumex acetosella*), in various habitats.

- Metallic blue, sometimes blue-black or violet; also sometimes greenish-brassy, or with pronotum greenish or bronze and elytra blue. Head with a fine keel from behind the antennal sockets almost to the eyes or up to the bristled pore above the eyes. Coarsely punctured; those at rear of pronotum almost as large as those at the front of elytra. Tibiae, tarsi and 1st to 5th antennal segments reddish-brownish; 1st darkened above, 4th darkened apically. 1.8-2.3 mm. Aedeagus as in Fig. 228 .... *sahlbergii*

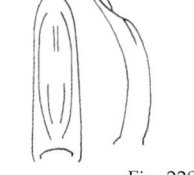

Fig. 228

Distribution: Scarce (Na) and very local in a range of usually coastal habitats (especially estuaries and saltmarshes) on sedges (*Carex*), rushes (*Juncus*) and sea-milkwort (*Glaux maritima*).

Key Hb3: Genus *Altica*

Note that reliable identification of *Altica* species requires dissection of males and careful examination of the aedeagus; a key previous work on this is Kevan (1962), though take care to note changes in nomenclature. In males the first segment of the front tarsus is usually expanded with curved sides and wider than the 2nd segment; in females it is straight-sided and narrower than the 3rd (bilobed) segment (Fig. 229). Also, in males the hind margin of the rear abdominal sternite is laterally incised; in females the margin is smooth without such incisions (Fig. 230).

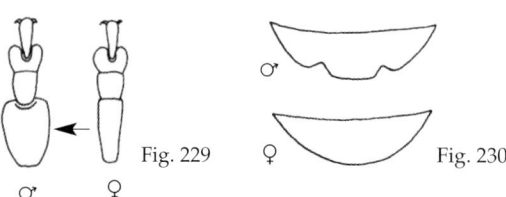

Fig. 229   Fig. 230

♂   ♀

1 Elytra parallel-sided (or at most very slightly curved) for front two-thirds. Metallic green or blue. Aedeagus as in Fig. 231. 2.8-4.2 mm .... *ericeti (=longicollis)*

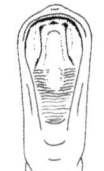

Fig. 231

Distribution: Scarce (Nb) on heather (*Calluna vulgaris*) and heaths (*Erica*), sometimes accidentally on other plants, in various habitats.

> Note that *A. ericeti* is a continental species not found in the UK and British specimens may be more accurately considered as *A. longicollis* with which it is now synonymised (e.g. Denton 2009). However, *A. ericeti* is given in Duff (2008) and retained here to ensure consistency with the 2008 checklist. The synonym *A. britteni* may also be found e.g. in Kevan (1962) which keys out British species using features of genitalia.

- Elytra not parallel-sided. 2.8-5.5 mm 2

2 Rear of elytra highly rounded and at least slightly widened, possibly almost bulbous (Figs 232, 233). 3.5-5.5 mm 3

- Rear of elytra may be evenly rounded, but not widened. 2.8-4.5 mm 4

3 Shiny metallic green, sometimes blue, rarely brassy. Elytra densely punctured on top, more sparsely to the sides; pronotum with fine, sparse punctures. Rear of elytra widened and highly rounded; with various small bumps and bulges (Fig. 232). Dorsal surface of aedeagus with relatively short longitudinal structures near the tip (Fig. 234). 3.5-4.5 mm (males occasionally as small as 3 mm).. *brevicollis*
   Distribution: Scarce (Na) on hazel (*Corylus avellana*) in broad-leaved woodland (especially glades and clearings), heathland and roadside verges in southern England.

- Usually not very shiny, metallic purplish-blue or blue, sometimes greenish, rarely black. Top of head dull. Elytra and top of pronotum with dense punctures. Rear of elytra less widened and rounded; with fewer bumps and bulges (Fig. 233). Dorsal surface of aedeagus with relatively elongate longitudinal structures near the tip (Fig. 235). 4.5-5.5 mm .... *lythri*
   Distribution: Widespread and fairly common on Onagraceae and various other plants in a wide range of mainly damp habitats.

  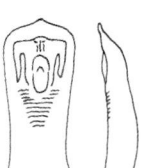 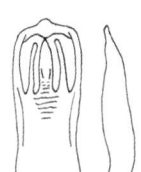

Fig. 232   Fig. 233   Fig. 234   Fig. 235

4 Clear small depressions by suture at tips of elytra (Fig. 236). Tip of aedeagus rounded (Fig. 237). 3.0-4.2 mm .... *oleracea*
   Confirmatory characters: Dull metallic green, sometimes bright blue. Strong punctures.
   Distribution: Widespread on a wide range of plants in various habitats.

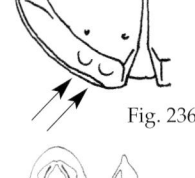

Fig. 236

- No clear depressions by suture at tips of elytra. Tip of aedeagus with a (more or less blunt) point, not rounded. 2.8-4.5 mm 5

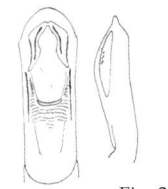

Fig. 237

5 Very fine, shallow elytral punctures. Tip of aedeagus with a very broad, blunt point (Fig. 238). 2.8-3.8 mm .... *helianthemi*
   Confirmatory characters: Very dark blue or blackish. Top of head dull.
   Distribution: Widespread on Cistaceae, Rosaceae and enchanter's-nightshade (*Circaea lutetiana*) in woodland, parkland, calcareous grassland, commons and roadside verges.

- Punctures not fine and shallow, though may be more or less distinct. Tip of aedeagus with a narrower blunt point. 3.5-4.5 mm 6

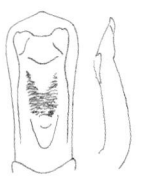

Fig. 238

6 Usually dull metallic bluish, greenish or greenish-blue (colour variable). Pronotal punctures distinct. Elytra with distinct shoulders. Relatively more elongate. Males with first front tarsal segment more elongate. Aedeagus usually orange with a blunt triangular tip (Fig. 239). 2.8-4.1 mm .... *palustris*

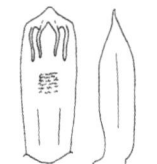

Fig. 239

Distribution: Widespread and common on a wide range of plants in various habitats.

- Deep metallic blue, tending towards violet-blue. Pronotal punctures and elytral shoulders less distinct. Relatively more squat. Males with shorter first front tarsal segment. Aedeagus usually brown with a small blunt point (Fig. 240). 3.0-4.0 mm .... *carinthiaca*

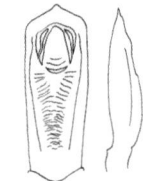

Distribution: Only recognised as British in 2000 (Cox, 2000b). On meadow vetchling (*Lathyrus pratensis*) in fens, marshes, parkland, meadows and heathland in the southern half of England.

Fig. 240

Key Hb4: Genus *Epitrix*

1 Pronotum shiny. Elytra dark brown or black with yellow tip (approximately the rear third) and usually some yellow at shoulders, occasionally extensive, even meeting the apical yellow mark in some aberrant specimens. 1.5-2.1 mm .... *atropae* (belladonna flea beetle)

Distribution: Scarce (Nb) and scattered in various habitats in southern and eastern England on Solanaceae, especially deadly nightshade (*Atropa belladonna*), also known from *Daldinia* fungus on dead wood.

- Pronotum relatively dull (due to reticulation between punctures). Entirely black or dark brown, rarely red-brown with dark sides and/or suture. 1.5-2.0 mm .... *pubescens*

Distribution: Widespread, mainly in southern England (some records north to the Humber and from Wales) on Solanaceae, especially bittersweet (*Solanum dulcamara*), in various habitats.

Key Hb5: Genus *Crepidodera*

Note that a detailed key to Palaearctic species of *Crepidodera* is given in Konstantinov (1996).

1 Rear angles of elytra sometimes with a small tooth. Elytral striae confused near the suture; interstices with incomplete lines of punctures often equal in size to those of striae. 3.0-4.2 mm .... *nitidula*

Confirmatory characters: Moderately shiny. Pronotum golden or golden-green. Elytra usually blue or bluish-green. Pronotal punctuation is equally coarse throughout. Aedeagus as in Fig. 241.

Distribution: Scarce (Nb) and widely scattered in southern England. On poplars (*Populus*), especially aspen (*P. tremula*) saplings, sometimes oaks (*Quercus*); in woodlands and other habitats such as commons with young aspen (*P. tremula*).

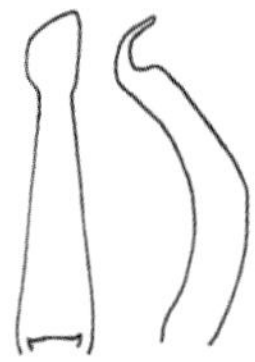

Fig. 241

Rear angles always without tooth, striae all regular (may be slightly wavy). 2.5-3.8 mm 2

2 Antennal segments 1-4 yellowish or orange with remaining segments black or dark brown. Relatively elongate, narrow and parallel-sided, only slightly convex. Unicolorous coppery-green, brassy, bronze, coppery, blue or bluish-green; elytra sometimes very dark green, or bronze. Front and middle femora yellow, hind femora black. 2.5-3.2 mm. Aedeagus as in Fig. 242 .... *plutus*

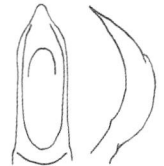

Fig. 242

Distribution: Fairly widespread; locally common in southern England, rare in Wales. In various habitats, usually near water, mainly on willows (*Salix*), rarely on poplars (*Populus*) and blackthorn (*Prunus spinosa*); possibly also feeding on pollen from other plants including dandelion (*Taraxacum officinale*).

- Not as above, especially antennal colour. 2.5-3.8 mm 3

3 Very shiny. Pronotum usually reddish, sometimes golden-green or brassy. Elytra bright metallic green, sometimes dark green or bronze/brassy/coppery, rarely bluish; thus appears bicolorous. 2.5-3.3 mm .... *aurata*

Confirmatory characters: Pronotum not transverse, narrowing towards the rear but sides rounded. Striae entirely regular and interstriae very finely punctured. Pronotal puncturation coarse and very unequal. Hind femora black. Apical antennal segments variably darkened, usually from about the midpoint of the antennae. Aedeagus as in Fig. 243.

Distribution: Widespread and common on willows (*Salix*), occasionally other trees, in a range of habitats where willows *Salix* are found.

Fig. 243

- Head, pronotum and elytra unicolorous. 2.5-3.8 mm 4

4 Broad, unicolorous golden-green to coppery red, brassy, bronze, sometimes bright green or blue. Pronotum distinctly transverse, punctures usually coarse but shallow and sparse such that pronotum remains clearly domed and shiny. Front of head dull with large punctures, some irregular in shape. 2.5-3.8 mm. Aedeagus as in Fig. 244 .... *aurea*

Distribution: Widespread in England and Wales, rare in Ireland. On poplars (*Populus*), sometimes willows (*Salix*), occasionally other trees, in a range of habitats.

Fig. 244

- Moderately narrow, unicolorous pale brilliant green, bordered with blue, golden green or coppery bronze, sometimes dark blue; sometimes with the pronotum blue or bluish green or with the elytra blue. Pronotum slightly transverse, punctures coarse, deep and dense. 2.5-3.5 mm. Aedeagus as in Fig. 245 .... *fulvicornis*

Distribution: Widespread and common on willows (*Salix*), sometimes poplars (*Populus*), occasionally other trees, in a range of habitats.

Fig. 245

Key Hb6: Genus *Neocrepidodera*

1 Smaller (3.0-3.6 mm). 2nd and 3rd elytral striae entirely regular in the front third of the elytra (Fig. 246a) .... *ferruginea* (wheat stem flea beetle)

Confirmatory characters: Stout, rusty red, sometimes pale or orange-brown. Pronotum usually distinctly punctured level with and behind furrow. Pronotal furrow flat and shallow; front edge straight or slightly curved, ends not extended forwards (Figs 247, 248).

Distribution: Widespread and common on a wide range of plants in many habitats.

- Larger (4.0-5.5 mm). 2nd and 3rd elytral striae irregular or doubled in the front third of the elytra (Fig. 246b) 2

Confirmatory character: Ends of furrow extended forwards as points; surface not flat (Fig. 249).

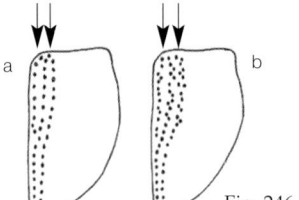 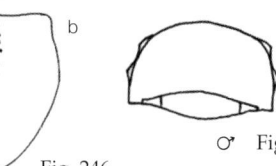 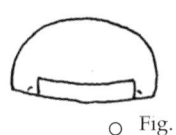 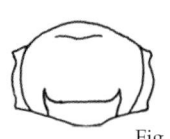

a   b   ♂ Fig. 247   ♀ Fig. 248   Fig. 249

Fig. 246

2 Dark yellowish red. Elytral striae more finely punctured; in males, 1st and 2nd striae formed of double rows of punctures. Pronotum smooth with punctures very fine, sometimes almost absent. Tip of aedeagus broadened and leaf-shaped (Fig. 250). 4.0-5.5 mm .... *impressa*

Distribution: Scarce (Na) on common sea-lavender (*Limonium vulgare*), possibly also cabbage thistle (*Cirsium oleraceum*) and creeping thistle (*C. arvense*), in coastal habitats, mainly saltmarshes and dunes.

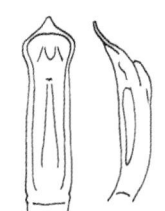

Fig. 250

- Pale reddish-yellow. Sometimes dark with pitchy-brown head, black pronotum, dark brown elytra (with large dark scutellar spot) and dark brown legs with red-brown femora. Elytral striae more coarsely punctured; in males, 1st and 2nd striae formed of irregular, but not double, rows of punctures. Pronotal punctures moderately coarse and dense. Tip of aedeagus spear-shaped (Fig. 251). 4.0-5.0 mm ... *transversa*

Distribution: Widespread and common on a wide range of plants in many habitats.

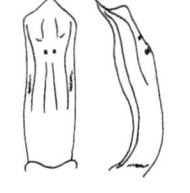

Fig. 251

Key Hb7: Genus *Podagrica*

1 Legs yellowish to pale brown; occasionally reddish-brown with dark femora. Elytra usually dark blue or bluish-green, rarely slightly metallic; finely, densely and irregularly punctured. 3.0-6.0 mm .... *fuscicornis*

Distribution: Fairly widespread though scarce (Nb) and local, mainly in southern and eastern England. On Malvaceae in various habitats.

- Legs black or dark brown. Elytra blue or bluish-green, sometimes bronze; coarsely, quite (but not entirely) regularly punctured. 3.0-6.0 mm .... *fuscipes*

Distribution: Scarce (Na) and very local, mostly around the Thames Estuary, with scattered records elsewhere in southern and eastern England. On Malvaceae in various habitats.

Key Hb8: Genus *Mantura*

1 Metallic blue, bronze-green, or coppery; sometimes bicolorous with pronotum blue or blackish and elytra green, bronze or coppery, or pronotum green and elytra blue. Pronotum shiny and hood-like, projecting forwards over the head. 2.0-2.7 mm .... *matthewsi*

Distribution: Widespread but local on rock-roses (*Helianthemum*) in various habitats.

- Not as above, pronotum not hood-like. 1.8-2.8 mm 2

2 Head and pronotum metallic green or bluish. Elytra dark reddish-brown, usually with the apical third, except the suture, yellowish; sometimes entirely dark reddish-brown, rarely dark blue or blue-green with yellow tips. 2.0-2.8 mm .... *rustica*

Distribution: Widespread but scarce (Nb) on docks and sorrels (*Rumex*), especially broad-leaved dock (*R. obtusifolius*), also knotgrass (*Polygonum aviculare*) and rhubarb (*Rheum* x *hybridum*), in various habitats.

- Not as above; head and pronotum not green or bluish. 1.8-2.7 mm 3

3 Dark brown with metallic bronze reflection, sometimes reddish-brown with a weaker reflection; shiny. Overall shape relatively rounded-oval. Pronotum with two short grooves (sometimes faint) running forwards from the base (Fig. 252). 1.8-2.7 mm ..... *chrysanthemi*

Fig. 252

Distribution: Scarce (Na) and very local in various habitats on sheep's sorrel (*Rumex acetosella*), common sorrel (*R. acetosa*) and beet (*Beta vulgaris*), often found at the roots.

- Black with dark green or blue reflection. Overall shape relatively elongate, though rear still rounded. Pronotum without grooves. 1.8-2.6 mm .... *obtusata*

Distribution: Widespread but scarce (Nb) and local on common sorrel (*Rumex acetosa*) and sheep's sorrel (*R. acetosella*) in various habitats.

Key Hb9: Genus *Batophila*

1 Elongate, metallic dark bronze-green. Punctures of elytral striae slightly coarser than those on pronotum. Pronotum more or less quadrate (approx. 1.3 times as wide as long). Tip of aedeagus slightly spatulate (Fig. 253) 1.0-1.8 mm .... *aerata*

Fig. 253

Distribution: Widespread in southern England with scattered records in Wales and central England. On Rosaceae, especially brambles (*Rubus*), also wild strawberry (*Fragaria vesca*), hawthorns (*Crataegus*), roses (*Rosa*), creeping cinquefoil (*Potentilla reptans*), possibly on vetches (*Vicia*) and gorse (*Ulex europaeus*), in various habitats.

- Oval, dark brown or black, rarely with an indistinct metallic reflection. Punctures of elytral striae considerably coarser than those on pronotum. Pronotum broad, slightly transverse (approx. 1.5 times as wide as long). Tip of aedeagus comes to a very blunt, rounded point, but not spatulate (Fig. 254). 1.4-2.0 mm .... *rubi* (raspberry flea beetle)

Fig. 254

Distribution: Widespread on Rosaceae, especially brambles (*Rubus*) and raspberry (*R. idaeus*), also wild strawberry (*Fragaria vesca*), hawthorns (*Crataegus*), salad burnet (*Sanguisorba minor*), dog-rose (*Rosa canina*), possibly on creeping thistle (*Cirsium arvense*) and bog-myrtle (*Myrica gale*), in various habitats.

Key Hb10: Genus *Longitarsus*

Note that many *Longitarsus* species are variable, and may be difficult to separate without dissection. All are small. Where possible, surface features are used, but in many cases dissection of males is required. The first segment of the front tarsi is more dilated in males, but this is not always clear, particularly for *succineus*, *ochroleucus*, *membranaceus* and *parvulus*; similarly in some species the males' antennae are longer. This tarsal dilation is not seen in females. The shoulders of the elytra are often less strongly marked than in females. Note however, that these are comparative features and determination of the sex of a specimen may not always be possible with certainty prior to dissection. Therefore, for species where this is considered most likely, the aedeagus is figured. Colour variation means that some species key out in more than one place.

Teneral specimens may also be problematic as they are typically lighter in colour than mature specimens and often do not have the full extent of darker markings. To confirm if a specimen is teneral, gently put pressure on the elytra and if the elytra yields and depresses, then the specimen is undoubtedly teneral.

As with other potentially problematic genera, to help with identification, it is important to note the food-plant that the beetle was obtained from as well as the habitat. Sweeping or beating one particular stand of the host plant will often produce a given species in some numbers, though avoid repeatedly sampling the same stand in order to avoid depleting populations locally through disturbance and over-collection.

1 Sloping sides of elytra with a definite fold and more-or-less vertical outer section (when viewed from the rear). Tips of elytra truncated and blunt to flattened, not rounded. 1.5-2.4 mm .... *anchusae*

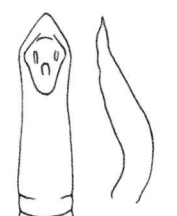

Confirmatory characters: Dorsally shiny black, sometimes with a very weak metallic reflection. Pronotum nearly quadrate, with very fine (sometimes almost absent) punctures. Legs brownish, yellowish or reddish with femora and tarsi darker (hind femora black). Aedeagus as in Fig. 255.

Distribution: Scarce (Nb) and scattered on various Boraginaceae in a range of habitats.

Fig. 255

- Sloping sides of elytra without a definite fold or vertical outer section (when viewed from the rear). Tips of elytra rounded (may be separated or together). 1.1-4.0 mm 2

2 Small tooth at the base of tarsal claws (Fig. 256). 1.6-2.2 mm ..... *ballotae*

Confirmatory characters: Head reddish-brown, sometimes pitchy. Pronotum and elytra dull yellowish (pronotum may be reddish). Legs pale yellowish, reddish or brownish. Apical half of hind femora dark. Upper surface of hind tibiae with one longitudinal border at the outer margin (in addition to the inner margin), the border at the outer margin usually without fine teeth or spines. Elytra without clearly developed shoulders. Underside of body usually dark. Aedeagus as in Fig. 257.

Fig. 256

Distribution: Scarce (Nb) and widely scattered on Lamiaceae (especially black horehound (*Ballota nigra*)) in various habitats in Wales and southern England.

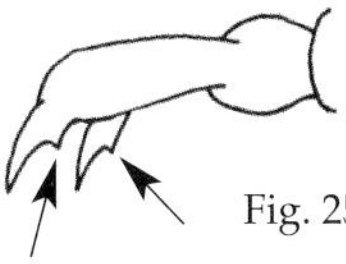

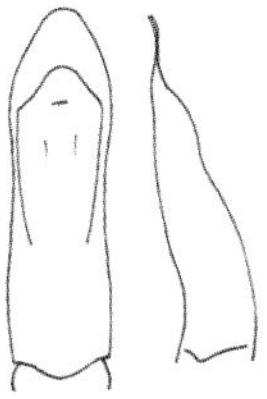

- Tarsal claws simple without a basal tooth 3

Fig. 257

3 Elytra dark with paler spots or stripes 4

- Elytra either all dark, all pale or pale with darker marks 6

4 Elytra black with yellowish to reddish-yellow bands along the full length of the sides. Legs entirely dark brown or black. 2.0-3.0 mm .... *dorsalis*

Confirmatory characters: Yellow or yellow-brown pronotum, sometimes yellow with brownish spot.

Distribution: Scarce (Nb) but widespread in England south of the Humber. On ragworts (*Senecio*) and other Asteraceae (also on rock-roses (*Helianthemum*)) in various habitats, especially with free-draining soils.

- Elytra dark with paler spots rather than bands 5

5 Dorsally shiny black. Large yellow, orange or red spot on rear half of elytra, not reaching the tip (Fig. 258a); even if covering the rear half, does not reach the tip itself (Fig. 258b). 1.5-2.0 mm .... *holsaticus*

Distribution: Widespread but scattered on marsh lousewort (*Pedicularis palustris*) and sometimes speedwells (*Veronica*) in various, usually damp, habitats.

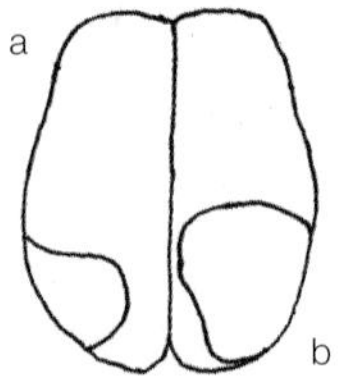

a

b

Fig. 258

- Dorsally dull black, sometimes with weak metallic tinge. Elytra with two large yellow, orange or red spots, one at the front, one towards rear; spots may be indistinct (var. *binotatus*) or missing (var. *immaculatus*), the latter keying out elsewhere. 2.5-3.0 mm .... *quadriguttatus*

Confirmatory characters: Hind femora black, rest of legs usually brownish. Antennae largely dark, at least the apical half. Pronotum less than 1.5 times as wide as long.

Distribution: Scarce (Na) and very local in south-east England on hound's-tongue (*Cynoglossum officinale*), and possibly viper's-bugloss (*Echium vulgare*), in various open habitats.

6 Elytra entirely black or dark brown (includes dark *quadriguttatus*) 7

- Elytra entirely yellowish, pale brown or reddish. May have dark sutural line or dark markings along the rim or side margins of elytra (includes pale *luridus* and pale *plantagomaritimus*) 14

7 Antennae and legs entirely black to pitchy or dark brown. Hind tibial apical spur distinctively long (Fig. 259); take care with *obliteratus* and *obliteratoides* where the spur may be almost as long but is more strongly curved (Fig. 266) .... *nigerrimus* (very black flea beetle)

Confirmatory characters: Elytra with clearly developed shoulders. Broad oval, convex. Elytra notably wider than pronotum. 1.5-2.3 mm.

Distribution: Endangered (RDB1) in boggy areas with bladderworts (*Utricularia*) in the New Forest and east Dorset. May be on purple moor-grass (*Molinia caerulea*) and cottongrasses (*Eriophorum*) by boggy pools.

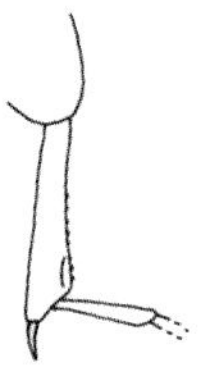

Fig. 259

- Antennae black or dark, with basal joints yellowish or pale. Front and mid-femora and tibiae usually yellowish (except often pitchy in *absynthii*). Hind tibial spur shorter 8

8 Larger, 2.3-3.0 mm 9

- Smaller, less than 2.3 mm 10

9 Elytra finely punctured. Shoulders prominent with impression inside shoulder bump .... *quadriguttatus* var. *immaculatus*

Confirmatory characters: Hind femora black, rest of legs usually brownish. Antennae largely dark, at least the apical half. Pronotum less than 1.5 times as wide as long. 2.5-3.0 mm. Aedeagus as in Fig. 260 (also use this for the typical form of this species).

Distribution: Scarce (Na) and very local in south-east England on hound's-tongue (*Cynoglossum officinale*), and possibly viper's-bugloss (*Echium vulgare*), in various open habitats.

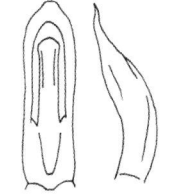

Fig. 260

- Elytra strongly punctured. Shoulders relatively rounded without impression ….. *plantagomaritimus*

Confirmatory characters: In males, 1st tarsal segment on front and middle leg short, 1.4-1.5 times as long as wide. Head usually blackish. Aedeagus as in Fig. 261. 2.4-2.7 mm.

Distribution: Scarce (Nb) on sea plantain (*Plantago maritima*) in saltmarshes, estuaries, coastal dunes and possibly sea cliffs and coastal shingles.

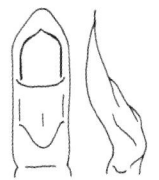

Fig. 261

10 Pronotum and elytra about equally and very finely punctured. Pronotum very finely shagreened and may be slightly more finely punctured than elytra. Elytra more or less shiny. Shoulders prominent. 1.3-1.5 mm .... *parvulus* (flax and linseed flea beetle)

Confirmatory characters: Distinctly convex. Hind tibiae pale or slightly darker than other tibiae. Upper surface shiny, usually black elytra occasionally dark red-brown with area around scutellum black (this may occur in preserved specimens). Hind femora dark brown to black (occasionally less darkened), rest of legs yellow, sometimes partly darkened to brownish or reddish-brown (front and mid femora and/or the apical part of the hind tibiae). Aedeagus as in Fig. 262.

Distribution: Widespread and fairly common in various habitats on cultivated linseed (*Linum usitatissimum*) as well as wild pale flax (*L. bienne*) and fairy flax (*L. catharticum*). After harvesting, in late summer and autumn, they may be on a wide range of plants including woody species.

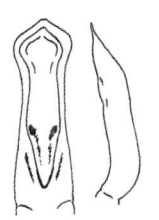

Fig. 262

- Pronotum less strongly punctured than elytra or if not, both strongly punctured in proportion to size. 1.1-4.0 mm 11

11 Pronotum distinctly shagreened and relatively dull. Front and mid-femora generally pitchy. 1.4-1.8 mm .... *absynthii*

Confirmatory characters: Weakly convex. Pronotum and hind femora pitchy-red, elytra usually darker and are relatively long and narrow. Aedeagus as in Fig. 263.

Distribution: Scarce (Na) on sea wormwood (*Seriphidium maritimum*) and mugworts (*Artemisia*), sometimes yarrow (*Achillea millefolium*) and tansy (*Tanacetum vulgare*), in coastal habitats in south-east England-river banks, estuaries, saltmarshes, cliffs and rough ground. May be under-recorded.

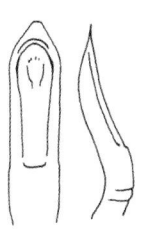

Fig. 263

- Pronotum not, or not distinctly, shagreened and usually shining (except occasionally in *luridus*). Front and mid-femora usually pale. 1.1-4.0 mm 12

12 Spur on hind tibia relatively short (Fig. 264). Dorsal surface at its darkest is pitchy rather than intense black and without a metallic reflection. Orbital lines (vertical along the inner edge of the eye) clear and deep. Bulge above each antennal base not usually separated from the top of the head by a sharp groove. Larger, 1.5-2.2 mm .... *luridus* (dark var.)

Confirmatory characters: Rear margin of elytra may have short bristles (often missing). In males (also use this feature for typical colour forms), aedeagus with sides constricted below the tip (Fig. 265). The paler colour form keys out at couplet 41.

Distribution: Widespread and common on many plants in almost any habitat.

- Spur on hind tibia usually relatively long (Fig. 266), especially in *obliteratus*; in *obliteratoides* it tends to be intermediate in length between *luridus* and *obliteratus* and angled towards the 1st tarsal segment (this should be seen as a helpful 'rule of thumb' rather than a strict method of separating these three species). Dorsal surface intense black with a weak or strong metallic reflection. Orbital lines (vertical along the inner edge of the eye) very shallow, faint or absent. Bulge above each antennal base clearly separated from top of head by a sharp groove. Smaller, 1.1-1.5 mm 13

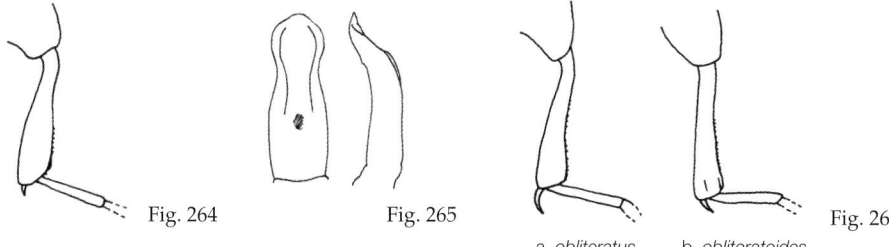

Fig. 264   Fig. 265   Fig. 266

a. *obliteratus*   b. *obliteratoides*

13 Blackish (usually with a weak metallic reflection). Elytra with coarse punctures. Hind femora close to dorsal coloration (may be slightly paler). Aedeagus as in Fig. 267 .... *obliteratus*

Distribution: Scattered on various Lamiaceae, also on rock-roses (*Helianthemum*), in a range of habitats.

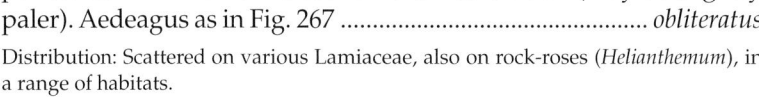

Fig. 267

- Dark bronze or green-bronze (may be almost blackish), pronotum sometimes with coppery tinge. with punctures no more than moderately coarse. Hind femora dark reddish-brownish. Aedeagus as in Fig. 268 .... *obliteratoides*

Distribution: Very local; first described in 1973 and first recognised in Britain in 1992. Usually on Breckland thyme (*Thymus serpyllum*) on sea cliffs, limestone grassland and sandy beaches. Only recorded from a few coastal sites in the far south-west of England, Pembrokeshire and north Wales.

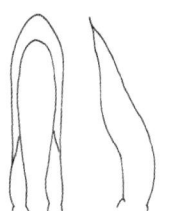

Fig. 268

14 Tibial spur long (Fig. 269) 15

Confirmatory characters: Upper surface of hind tibiae with two longitudinal borders (take care not to confuse these with the inner margin which is also present). The border on the inside of the joint with the 1st tarsal segment has fine teeth or spines as in many *Longitarsus*; the other (indicated by an arrow) does not, and is usually shortened and/or faint (Fig. 269). These margins can be a difficult feature to see clearly, but may be useful if spur length does not provide a definitive split at this couplet.

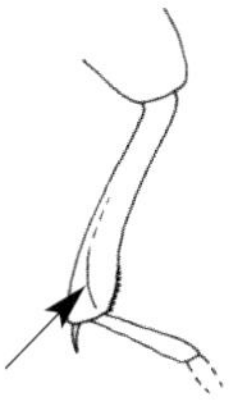

Fig. 269

- Tibial spur shorter (e.g. Fig. 264) 16

Confirmatory characters: Second (unspined) tibial border absent or nearly so.

15 Shiny. Head and pronotum brown, (pronotum sometimes reddish or darkened to an uneven pitchy-red) and usually darker than yellowish elytra. Elytra usually all one colour; may have dark streaks but not always with dark suture. Head usually darker than pronotum. Punctures equally coarse and dense on elytra and pronotum. Spaces between elytral punctures distinctly dulled or roughened. Aedeagus with a long thin projection at the tip which is sinuous when viewed from the side (Fig. 270). 2.0-3.0 mm ....
.... *nigrofasciatus*

Distribution: Scarce (Na) and very local on Scrophulariaceae in calcareous and unimproved grasslands and on sea cliffs.

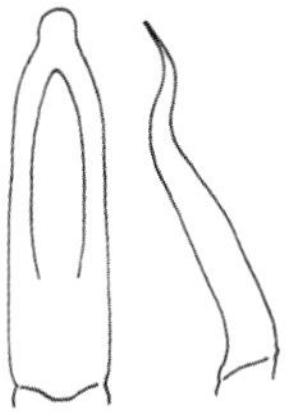

Fig. 270

- Head and pronotum pale yellow to orange. Elytra yellowish, sometimes with a dark sutural stripe in var. *thapsi* which also has darker antennae. Punctures random. Elytral punctures coarser and denser than on pronotum. Spaces between elytral punctures smooth. Aedeagus without a long thin projection at the tip which is weakly curved when viewed from the side (Fig. 271). 3.5-4.0 mm .... *tabidus*

Distribution: Scarce (Nb), very local and scattered on mulleins (*Verbascum*) in chalk grassland, woodland clearings, heathland, roadside verges, sand pits and sand dunes.

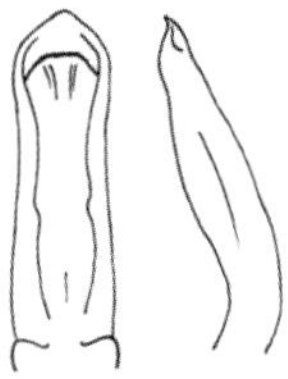

Fig. 271

16 Elytra with clearly defined but often narrow, dark sutural stripe 17

- Elytra uniformly coloured, without a clearly defined and contrasting sutural stripe 29

17 Sutural line incomplete, being absent from the basal and/or apical sections of the elytra (e.g. Fig. 272). Note that *gracilis* var. *poweri* may also key out here) 18

- Sutural line complete or nearly so 19

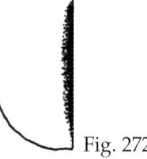

Fig. 272

18 Smaller, 1.6-2.0mm. Pronotal punctures coarse and dense at rear, finer and sparser towards the front. Pair of long bristles on tips of elytra, though these are often lost .... *longiseta* (heath speedwell flea beetle)

Confirmatory characters: Head and hind femora black. Elytra shiny with coarse punctures. Dark suture absent from front of elytra and fainter or absent from the tip (Fig. 272), also often fading after death. Aedeagus as in Fig. 273.

Distribution: Rare but poorly known (RDBK) in south-east England on speedwells (*Veronica*), possibly preferring heath speedwell (*V. officinalis*), in woodland clearings, shady grassland and fallow fields, especially bordering woodland.

See Cox (2007) for taxonomic issues regarding this species.

- Larger, 2.5-3.0mm. Pronotal punctures fine throughout. Bristles absent .... *agilis*

Confirmatory characters: Hind femora black, sometimes brown. Dorsally pale yellow-brown. Antennae long, reddish-brownish. Elytral suture sometimes partly narrowly reddened (especially towards the rear), sometimes with a bold black stripe (broad or narrow). Elytra sometimes vaguely darkened with weakly linear marks near the front and sides. Colour of femora also separates this from the similar *rutilis* (qv). Aedeagus as in Fig. 274.

Distribution: Scarce (Na) and scattered in various habitats in southern England as far north as the Wash, usually on figworts (*Scrophularia*), sometimes on mulleins (*Verbascum*).

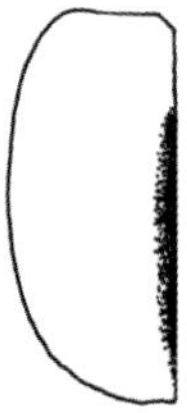

Fig. 272 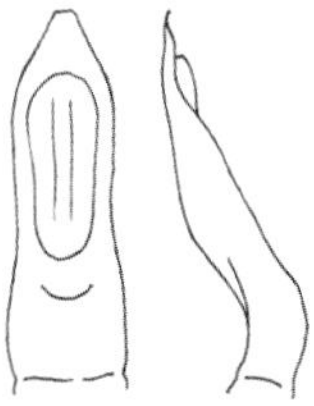   Fig. 273 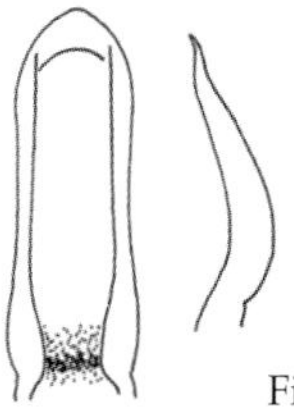   Fig. 274

19 Pronotum finely to very finely punctured 20

- Pronotum more strongly punctured 23

20 Aedeagus with lateral folds relatively broad and the space between them relatively narrow in ventral view (Fig. 275) .... *reichei*

Confirmatory characters: Head dark reddish or pitchy-yellow, blackish on top. Pronotum pale yellowish, sometimes reddish or brownish. Elytra slightly elongate, overall shape elongate-oval. Hind femora slightly darkened to a reddish-brown. Antennae at least two thirds the length of the body. In females, last abdominal sternite with two distinct impressions. 1.5-2.0 mm.

Distribution: Widely scattered on plantains (*Plantago*), and other plants accidentally, in various habitats.

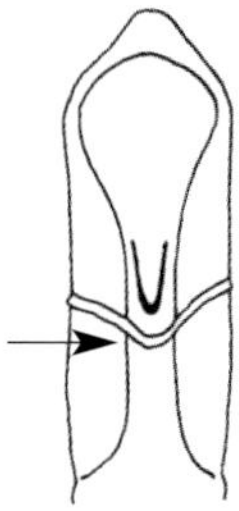

Fig. 275

- Aedeagus with lateral folds relatively narrow and the space between them relatively wide in ventral view (Fig. 276) 21

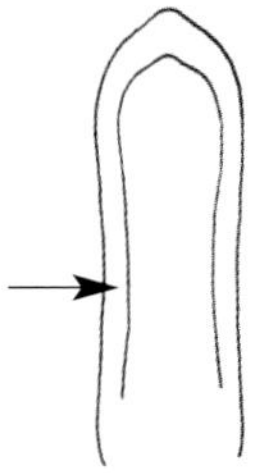

Fig. 276

21 Elytra more convex and rounded at the sides; broader and relatively shorter, elytral shoulders rounded, not prominent .... *suturellus*

Confirmatory characters: Head dark brown or black, usually darker than pronotum. Pronotum dull orange-brown, red-brown or dark brown. Elytra yellowish; suture darkened along its length, though width varies; doesn't reach tip (except in darker forms). Aedeagus as in Fig. 277. 1.8-2.2 mm.

Distribution: Widespread and common, usually on Asteraceae, in various habitats.

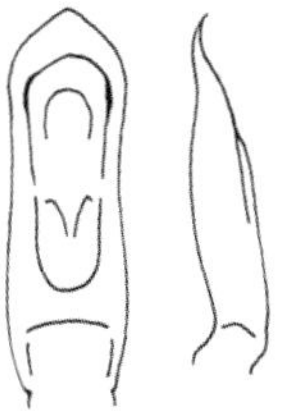

Fig. 277

Elytra less convex and less rounded at the sides; overall a longer oval shape 22

22 Moderately convex, elytra elongate with sides less rounded. Dorsally brownish, sometimes yellow-brown; elytral suture darkened (variably in extent and depth of colour). 2.0-2.5 mm. Aedeagus as in Fig. 278 .... *gracilis* var. *poweri*

Confirmatory characters: Hind femora yellowish to yellow-brown, separating it from the similar *ochroleucus* (qv). Pronotum brown-black in var. *nigrothorax*. Var. *poweri* is similar to *ganglbaueri* but head brownish and dark sutural stripe usually ends well before the tip. Typical specimens of *gracilis* do not have a darkened elytral suture.

Distribution: Widespread and locally common on Asteraceae, especially ragworts (*Senecio*) and a range of non-host plants in various habitats.

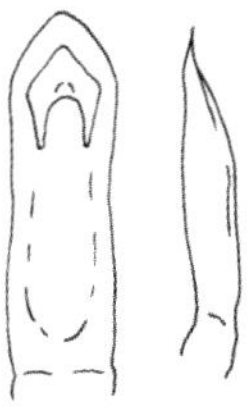

Fig. 278

- Somewhat flattened, sides of elytra more rounded. Head dark brown or black. Pronotum and elytra yellowish to orange-brown. Wide sutural stripe (often somewhat diffuse). 1.8-2.5 mm. Aedeagus as in Fig. 279 .... *ganglbaueri*

Distribution: Scarce (Na), usually on ragworts (*Senecio*), in various habitats.

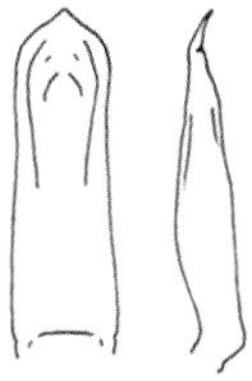

Fig. 279

23 Pronotum non-metallic, reddish. Elytral tips prominent with coarse dense punctures similar to those on the upper surface. 1.7-3.1 mm 24

- Pronotum reddish or pitchy to black, but with a distinct metallic reflection. Elytral tips not prominent with weak or almost absent punctures, finer and/or shallower than those on the upper surface. 1.5-2.5 mm 27

24 Elytral punctures form more or less regular rows on the disc between the suture and the shoulders. Dorsal side of hind tibia with two ridges; (a) outer margin with a row of minute teeth, (b) inner ridge which is smooth, usually shortened and often weak and thus indistinct (Fig. 269). 1.5-1.9 mm .... *lycopi*

Confirmatory characters: Pronotum yellowish, reddish or brownish. Elytra yellowish. Hind femora darkened slightly (orange-red) to deeply (dark red-brown). Dark suture complete but may be narrow and unclear. Head usually black.

Distribution: Scarce (Nb) on various Lamiaceae in marshes, calcareous grasslands, woodlands (including clearings), commons, pondsides, ditches and watercourses, mostly in England south of the Wash.

Elytral punctures do not form regular rows. Dorsal side of hind tibia with the external ridge only. Usually 2.0-2.7 mm (*kutscherae* can be as small as 1.7 mm but is usually around 2.0 mm) 25

Separation of *kutscherae*, *melanocephalus* and *plantagomaritimus*

These three species, *L. kutscherae*, *melanocephalus* and *plantagomaritimus* can only be separated reliably by fairly subtle features of the genitalia and male tarsi, and are also keyed in Bienkowski (1997), with *L. kutscherae* and *melanocephalus* covered by Doguet (1994). An alternative and somewhat outdated key to British species is given in Kevan (1967). *L. plantagomaritimus* is strictly littoral in habitat being associated with sea plantain (*Plantago maritima*), while *melanocephalus* may be separated partially by colour as it is rarely entirely dark reddish-brown. The elytra of *plantagomaritimus* are less elongate and usually more coarsely punctured than those of *melanocephalus*.

25 Aedeagus 5.2-5.8 times as long as wide (Fig. 280). 2.3-3.1 mm .... *melanocephalus*

Confirmatory characters: Head usually dark brownish to blackish, rarely pale.

Distribution: Widespread and common on plantains (*Plantago*), sometimes common hemp-nettle (*Galeopsis tetrahit*), wood sage (*Teucrium scorodonia*) and speedwells (*Veronica*), in a range of habitats.

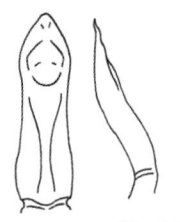

Fig. 280

- Aedeagus 4.2-4.7 times as long as wide. 1.7-2.7 mm 26

26 In males, 1st tarsal segment on front and middle leg long, 1.8-1.9 times as long as wide. 1.7-2.4 mm. Aedeagus as in Fig. 281 .... *kutscherae*

Distribution: Widespread and locally common on plantains (*Plantago*), sometimes oaks (*Quercus*) and common hemp-nettle (*Galeopsis tetrahit*), in various, mainly damp, habitats.

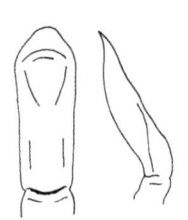

Fig. 281

- In males, 1st tarsal segment on front and middle leg short, 1.4-1.5 times as long as wide. 2.4-2.7 mm. Aedeagus as in Fig. 282 .... *plantagomaritimus*

Confirmatory characters: Head usually blackish.

Distribution: Scarce (Nb) on sea plantain (*Plantago maritima*) in saltmarshes, estuaries, coastal dunes and possibly sea cliffs and coastal shingles.

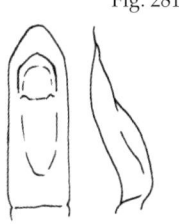

Fig. 282

27 Elytra with dark sutural stripe; side and rear margins not darkened. 2.0-2.5 mm ....
.... *atricillus*

> Confirmatory characters: Weak metallic reflection on head, pronotum and apices of hind femora. Coarse punctures on pronotum. Elytra randomly punctured with dark suture; each may have a small pale orange-brown lateral mark towards the front.

> Distribution: Widespread and common on a wide range of plants in many habitats.

- Elytra with dark sutural stripe as well as darkened side or rear margins. 1.5-2.0 mm ... 28

28 Side margins of elytra usually slightly darkened in the front third. If so, the dark sutural band may reach the tip, but only narrowly and does not extend to the sides. Usually only apical half of hind femora darkened. Larger, 1.8-2.0 mm. Aedeagus as in Fig. 283 .... *aenicollis*

> Distribution: Scarce (Nb) and very scattered on several Boraginaceae, mulleins (*Verbascum*) and various Asteraceae in woodland, dry open habitats, quarries, hedgebanks, field margins and disturbed ground.

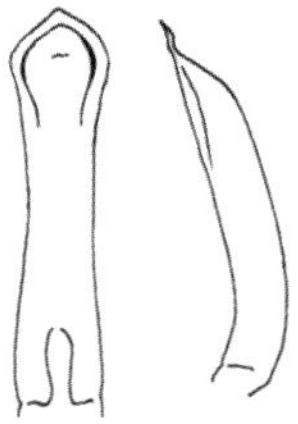

Fig. 283

- Entirely darkened side rims of elytra with broad dark suture which may occasionally form a dark patch near the tip; if the band reaches the tip it may extend round to the sides. Hind femora usually entirely dark. Pronotum distinctly punctured, often with vague brassy reflection. Smaller, 1.5-1.8 mm. Aedeagus as in Fig. 284 .... *nasturtii*

> Distribution: Scarce (Nb) in England and south Wales on Boraginaceae in woodland and on calcareous grassland, chalky hedgerows, sand, shingle and riverbanks.

Fig. 284

29 Puncturation of dorsal surface fine to very fine 30

- Puncturation of dorsal surface strong to moderately strong 40

30 Body length 2.5-3.0 mm 31

- Body length less than 2.5 mm (exceptionally to 2.8 mm in *symphyti* (qv), in which case the cuticle is translucent making the dark gut contents visible) 34

31 Tip of aedeagus comes to a bluntly rounded point; not broadened at the tip (see Fig. 274) .... *agilis*

> Confirmatory characters: Pronotal punctures fine throughout. Hind femora black, sometimes brown. Dorsally pale yellow-brown. Antennae long, reddish-brownish. Elytral suture sometimes partly narrowly reddened (especially towards the rear), sometimes with a bold black stripe (broad or narrow). Elytra sometimes vaguely darkened with weakly linear marks near the front and sides. Colour of femora also separates this from the similar *rutilis* (qv).

> Distribution: Scarce (Na) and scattered in various habitats in southern England as far north as the Wash, usually on figworts (*Scrophularia*), sometimes on mulleins (*Verbascum*).

- Tip of aedeagus either broadened or comes to a small blunt point (not broadened) 32

32 First two front tarsal segments relatively slender (Fig. 285), the first segment often with a slight expansion towards the tip in males .... *aeruginosus*

Confirmatory characters: Pronotum transverse and strongly narrowed at base (Fig. 286), especially in males (in females, this narrowing may be reduced or not present). Elytral punctures moderately coarse; elytra not especially smooth in appearance. Antennae as long as the body with elongate segments. Long bristle at tip of elytra (often lost).

Distribution: Endangered (RDB1) and extremely local on hemp-agrimony (*Eupatorium cannabinum*) and common comfrey (*Symphytum officinale*) in coastal and riverbank habitats in southern England.

First two front tarsal segments widen evenly towards the apex in both sexes (Fig. 287) 33

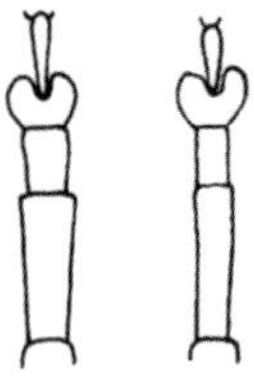

Fig. 285 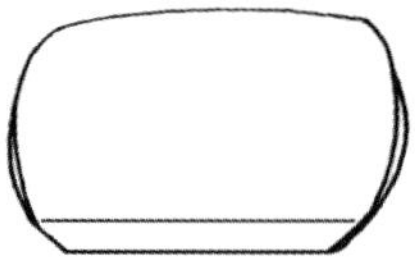   Fig. 286 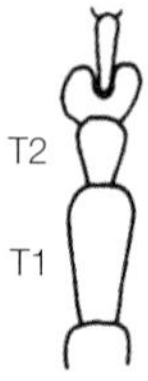   Fig. 287

33 Aedeagus with sides more or less parallel (there may be a very slight constriction or sinuosity) and not (or barely) broadened at the tip which is relatively pointed and bears a small prominence (Fig. 288) .... *jacobaeae*

Distribution: Widespread and locally common all over Britain on ragworts (*Senecio*).

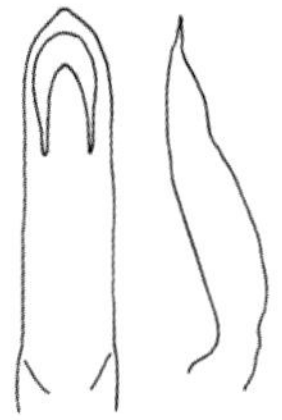

Fig. 288

- Aedeagus with sides clearly constricted, tip broadened and rounded, also with a small blunt prominence (Fig. 289) ...... *flavicornis*

Distribution: Widespread and common south of the Humber on ragworts (*Senecio*) in various habitats.

Details of prior confusion between *flavicornis* and *jacobaeae* are given in Shute (1975).

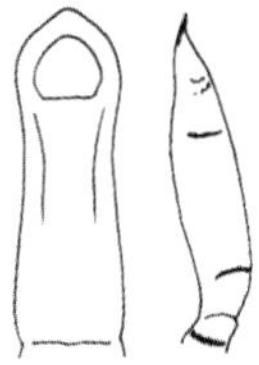

Fig. 289

34 Pronotum short and broad. Head brown to blackish, clearly darker than pronotum. Head and pronotum slightly shiny (sometimes clearly and deeply reticulated). Elytra sometimes with brownish sutural stripe (can be blurred). Antennae approximately two thirds body length 35

- May have some but not all of these characters 36

35 Aedeagus with sides almost parallel (slightly concave), tip blunt and triangular (see Fig. 275) .... *reichei*

Confirmatory characters: Head dark reddish or pitchy-yellow, blackish on top. Pronotum pale yellowish, sometimes reddish or brownish. Elytra slightly elongate, overall shape elongate-oval. Hind femora slightly darkened to a reddish-brown. In females, last abdominal sternite with two distinct impressions. 1.5-2.0 mm.

Distribution: Widely scattered on plantains (*Plantago*), and other plants accidentally, in various habitats.

- Aedeagus with sides concave, tip expanded and rounded, coming to a blunt leaf-shaped triangular point (Fig. 290) .... *pratensis*

Confirmatory characters: Head brown or blackish, sometimes pitchy. Pronotum pale yellowish, sometimes reddish or brownish, sometimes pitchy. Elytra not elongate, overall shape oval. Hind femora clearly darkened to a deep red-brown. 1.2-1.8 mm.

Distribution: Widespread and common, usually on plantains (*Plantago*), in various habitats.

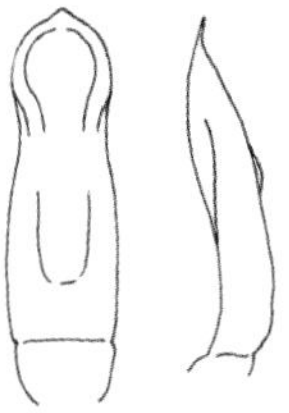

Fig. 290

36 Aedeagus clearly constricted, tip broadly rounded with a small blunt point (Fig. 291) .... *ochroleucus*

Confirmatory characters: Flattish. Dorsally pale dusky yellow. Hind femora black, sometimes pitchy, at least apically. Colour of femora also separates this from the similar *gracilis* (qv). 2.0-2.5 mm.

Distribution: Scarce (Nb) and widely scattered in various habitats usually on ragworts (*Senecio*), sometimes on mayweeds (*Matricaria*), scentless mayweed (*Tripleurospermum inodorum*), wormwood (*Artemisia absinthium*), tansies (*Tanacetum*), yarrow (*Achillea millefolium*) and alisons (*Alyssum*).

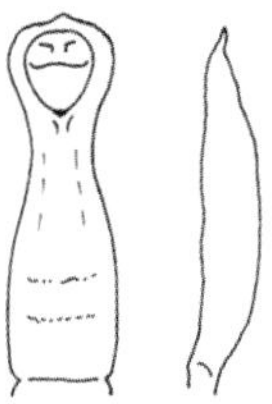

Fig. 291

- Aedeagus without this clear constriction, although the sides may be somewhat concave and the tip somewhat rounded (especially in *pellucidus*) 37

37 Apical half of antennae considerably darker than the basal half .... *gracilis*

Confirmatory characters: Moderately convex. Dorsally pale yellowish (sometimes very pale, appearing whitish-yellow) to yellow-brown. Elytral punctures fine and shallow. Abdomen brown to blackish. Hind femora yellowish to yellow-brown, separating it from the similar *ochroleucus* (qv). Pronotum brown-black in var. *nigrothorax* which may also have a distinct broad, dark sutural stripe. Var. *poweri* is similar to *ganglbaueri* but head brownish and with a dark sutural stripe that usually ends well before the tip. 2.0-2.5 mm. Aedeagus as in Fig. 278.

Distribution: Widespread and locally common on Asteraceae, especially ragworts (*Senecio*) and a range of non-host plants in various habitats.

- Apical half of antennae may be more or less the same colour as the basal half, or darker but not clearly contrasting with it 38

38 Cuticle transparent with dark gut contents visible, especially in live females .... *symphyti*

Confirmatory characters: Dorsally pale yellow. Antennae of males clearly longer than body length. 4th to 11th antennal segments 5-6 times as long as wide, segment 11 more or less the same colour as the rest of the antenna. 1.5-2.8 mm. Aedeagus as in Fig. 292.

Distribution: First recorded in Britain in Berkshire in 2009 on riverside comfrey (*Symphytum officinale*) among *Phragmites* reeds and *Urtica* nettles; specimens were wingless and thus dispersal may be slow (Harrison, 2010). The species is restricted to *S. officinale* across its broad European range (Kippenberg, 1994)

Fig. 292

- Cuticle opaque 39

39 4th to 11th antennal segments 3 times as long as wide, segment 11 the same colour as segment 10. In males, antennae no more than as long as body length. Tip of aedeagus slightly broadened and rounded with a small blunt point (Fig. 293). Elytral shoulders relatively distinct and prominent. 2.0-2.5 mm .... *pellucidus*

Distribution: Widespread on Convolvulaceae (*Convolvulus* and *Calystegia*) in various habitats.

Fig. 293

- 4th to 11th antennal segments 4 times as long as wide, segment 11 slightly but distinctly darker than segment 10. In males, antennae at least as long as body length. Tip of aedeagus rounded with a small blunt point, but less clearly broadened (Fig. 294). Elytral shoulders relatively weakly developed. 1.5-2.4 mm .... *succineus*

Distribution: Widespread and common, mainly on Asteraceae (especially *Achillea*), in various habitats.

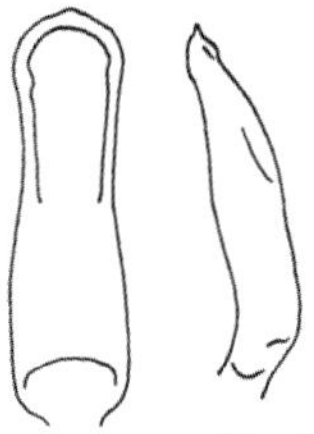

Fig. 294

40 Hind femora at least partly pitchy or black 41

- Hind femora pale, reddish or yellowish 47

41 Aedeagus with sides strongly constricted in apical half, the tip rounded with a broad, blunt point (Fig. 265) .... *luridus*

Confirmatory characters: Dorsal surface entirely yellow-orange, brownish or (occasionally, take care) pitchy brown, the darker colour form keying out at couplet 12; suture not clearly darkened (may be very narrowly darker than elytra). Rear margin of elytra may have short bristles (often missing). 1.5-2.2 mm.

Distribution: Widespread and common on many plants in almost any habitat.

> Take care here, *luridus* is especially variable in colour and may overlap with *brunneus*. Atypically coloured specimens in particular require dissection to confirm identification.

- Aedeagus with sides more or less parallel or at most weakly constricted; the tip not so clearly rounded, though take care with *fowleri* and *membranaceus* which show some constriction and rounding of the aedeagus 42

42 Elytral punctures form more or less regular rows on the disc between the suture and shoulders .... *lycopi*

Confirmatory characters: Pronotum yellowish, reddish or brownish. Elytra yellowish. Hind femora darkened slightly (orange-red) to deeply (dark red-brown). Dark suture complete but may be narrow and unclear. Head usually black. Dorsal side of hind tibia with two ridges: external margin with a row of minute teeth; and internal ridge which is smooth, usually shortened and often weak and thus indistinct (see Fig. 269). 1.5-1.9 mm.

Distribution: Scarce (Nb) on various Lamiaceae in marshes, calcareous grasslands, woodlands (including clearings), commons, pondsides, ditches and watercourses, mostly in England south of the Wash.

- Elytral punctures random, not forming regular rows 43

43 Aedeagus parallel-sided with a sharp triangular tip (Fig. 295) .... *brunneus*

Confirmatory characters: Dorsal surface all red-brown, sometimes with narrowly but clearly darkened elytral suture. Rear margin of elytra may have long bristles (often missing). 2.0-2.5 mm.

Distribution: Scarce (Nb) and sparsely scattered on Asteraceae, especially common meadow-rue (*Thalictrum flavum*), French meadow-rue (*T. aquilegiifolium*) and sea aster (*Aster tripolium*), on both inland and littoral habitats, usually in wetlands.

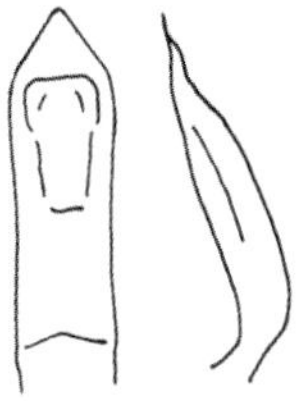

Fig. 295

- Aedeagus without a sharp triangular tip 44

44 Sides of aedeagus slightly constricted, tip slightly widened and rounded with a small point (may be blunt or sharp) 45

- Sides of aedeagus more or less parallel, tip rounded-triangular without a point 46

45 Abdominal sternites yellow to yellow-brown or brown. Aedeagus with a small sharp point (Fig. 296). Head with a broad longitudinal keel between the eyes; this keel narrows from the rear of the head but is more or less parallel between the eyes and has a narrow blunt process continuing forward between the antennal bases (Fig. 297). Very fine, shallow groove on the head behind the bumps above the antennae (note that this feature may be difficult to see and is also found in *ferrugineus*) ....
.... *membranaceus* (wood sage flea beetle)

Confirmatory characters: Antennae pale, often slightly darkened in apical half. Front corners of elytra with rounded angles, not prominent shoulders. Head and pronotum pale orange (head sometimes darker red-brown), slightly darker than yellow elytra (though this difference can be hard to determine). Elytra finely punctured. Apical spurs of hind tibiae less than one third the length of the first hind tarsal segment. 1.6-1.8 mm.

Distribution: Widespread on Lamiaceae, and sometimes oaks (*Quercus*), in various habitats.

-      Abdominal sternites blackish. Aedeagus with a small blunt point (Fig. 298). Longitudinal keel on the head narrows towards the front without a parallel-sided section between the eyes; the small process continuing between the antennal bases is short and does not continue forwards (Fig. 299). Head not grooved as above .... *fowleri*

Confirmatory characters: Head and pronotum yellowish (head dull), elytra somewhat shiny, pale yellow-brown. Antennal tips (usually) blackish. 1.4-1.7 mm.

Distribution: Scarce (Na) and sparsely scattered on dry soils in southern England as far north as the Wash, usually on young teasel (*Dipsacus fullonum*), sometimes accidentally on other plants.

Note that work is ongoing to determine whether *L. fowleri* is identical to the widespread continental species *L. strigicollis*.

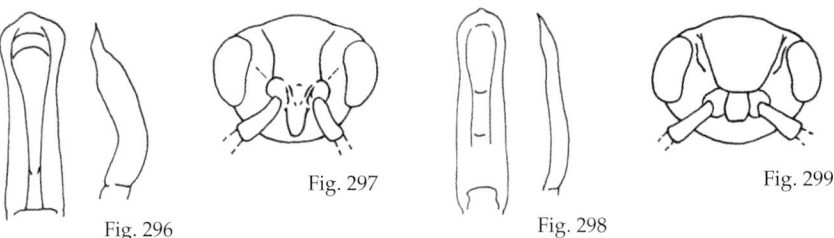

Fig. 296   Fig. 297   Fig. 298   Fig. 299

46 Smaller, 1.7-2.0 mm. Elytra with a narrow sutural stripe (dark to reddish-brownish) ....
.... *curtus*

Confirmatory characters: Very convex. Head dark brown or black. Pronotum and elytra more or less unicolorous yellowish, reddish or brownish (occasionally the pronotum is slightly darker).

Distribution: Scarce (Na) and widely but sparsely scattered on Boraginaceae, usually in grasslands.

-      Larger, 2.3-3.2 mm. Elytra without a darkened sutural stripe .... *exoletus*

Confirmatory characters: Head reddish-brown. Pronotum pale yellowish-orange and elytra paler still. Pronotum less than 1.3 times as wide as long. Punctures fine. Hind femora dark above in apical half. Apical 5 or 6 antennal segments black or brown.

Distribution: Widespread and locally common on Boraginaceae in various habitats.

47 Aedeagus clearly constricted and darkened in the basal half (Fig. 300) .... *ferrugineus* (mint flea beetle)

Confirmatory characters: Head reddish to orange, pronotum orange, elytra yellowish. Abdominal sternites brown, blacker towards the sides. Apical half of antennae darkened. 1.7-2.4 mm. Front corners of elytra more or less sharply angled.

Distribution: Endangered (RDB1) and sparsely scattered in various, usually damp, habitats in southern England as far north as the Wash, usually on mints (*Mentha*), sometimes on gypsyworts (*Lycopus*) and germanders (*Teucrium*).

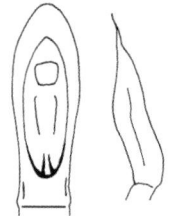

Fig. 300

- Aedeagus not as above; may be more or less parallel-sided, weakly constricted (e.g. in *rutilus*) or with a constriction in the apical half (e.g. *membranaceus*), but not with the strong basal darkening 48

48 Larger, 2.5-3.0 mm. Aedeagus elongate with sides weakly concave and long blunt triangular tip (Fig. 301) .... *rutilus*

Confirmatory characters: Dorsally reddish or yellow-brown. Hind femora and underside yellowish, reddish or brownish. Elytra broad and at least moderately coarsely punctured. Colour of femora also separates this from the similar *agilis* (qv). Large hind tibial spur (usually longer than width of base of tibia).

Distribution: Vulnerable (RDB2; also designated Scarce, Na) in southern England on figworts (*Scrophularia*), usually near stream and pond margins, in marshes and woodland clearings; sometimes around clay pits and on chalky slopes.

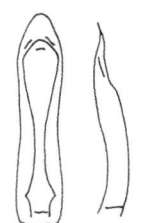

Fig. 301

- Smaller, 2.0-2.5 mm. Aedeagus with a slightly broadened and rounded tip bearing a small, wide, blunt point (Fig. 302) .... *rubiginosus*

Confirmatory characters: Dusky yellow to orange or reddish, sometimes darker, even pitchy. Antennae usually darker towards the tip. Pronotal punctures very coarse and dense, with interspaces slightly wrinkled and rough. Elytral punctures also coarse.

Distribution: Widespread and fairly common on Convolvulaceae especially hedge bindweed (*Calystegia sepium*) and field bindweed (*Convolvulus arvensis*), sometimes accidentally on other plants, in various habitats.

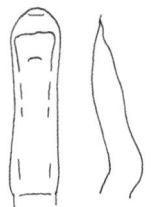

Fig. 302

Key Hb11: Genus *Phyllotreta*

Note that this key aims to separate all species using external characters. However, for atypically coloured specimens (e.g. strongly bronze-tinged *cruciferae*), dissection of males may be required, therefore aedeagus figures are also given.

Several species of *Phyllotreta* show modifications to the antennae in males as follows, with the modifications absent in females (see species accounts for figures):

P. exclamationis, 5th segment strongly dilated.

P. ochripes. 5th segment moderately dilated.

P. nemorum. 4th (and to a lesser extent 5th) segment moderately dilated.

P. nodicornis. 4th segment strongly dilated.

P. consobrina. 4th and 5th segments moderately dilated.

1 Elytra with yellow markings on a dark background. 1.5-3.5 mm 2

- Elytra uniformly dark, with or without metallic reflection. 1.6-3.0 mm 9

2 Elytra black with outer edge of longitudinal yellow band clearly indented in the middle and usually reaching to, or close to the outer edge towards the rear (Fig. 303). 1.5-3.5 mm 3

- Not as above; may have a yellow band without a clear indent, or a small, shallow indent, but usually not reaching as close to the outer edge. 1.8-3.5 mm 7

Fig. 303

3 Front part of yellow elytral band curved no more than slightly towards suture. 2.5-3.0 mm .... *flexuosa*

Confirmatory characters: Dark sutural band no more than slightly widest in the middle, may be parallel-sided (Fig. 304). Smaller than *tetrastigma* (*flexuosa* averages nearer 2.5 mm), with pronotum more finely punctured and less transverse. Aedeagus as in Fig. 305.

Distribution: Widespread but local on Brassicaceae, especially great yellow-cress (*Rorippa amphibia*), large bitter-cress (*Cardamine amara*), winter-cress (*Barbarea vulgaris*), and sometimes radishes (*Raphanus*), in various wet habitats or those near water.

- Front part of yellow elytral band clearly curved towards suture. 1.5-3.5 mm 4

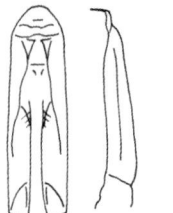

Fig. 304

Fig. 305

4 Tibiae, and front and middle femora reddish-brownish; hind femora black. 5th antennal segment elongate in both sexes, may be at least slightly thickened; males with 5th antennal segment very elongate, slightly thickened and darkened (Fig. 306); in females, it is less elongate, but still nearly as long as segment 1 (Fig. 307). 2.0-3.0 mm .... *ochripes*

Distribution: Widespread in England (except the north-west) and S. Wales, on Brassicaceae, and possibly brooklime (*Veronica beccabunga*), in various habitats.

- Tibiae black, at least in the apical half; femora black, sometimes reddish-brownish apically. In males, 5th antennal segment may be enlarged; in females it is close to the size of the 4th and 6th segments. 1.5-3.5 mm 5

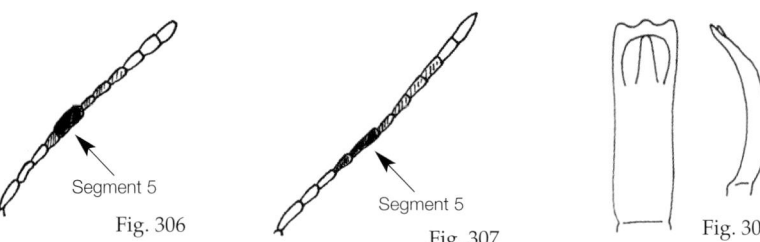

Segment 5

Fig. 306

Segment 5

Fig. 307

Fig. 308

5 Smaller, 1.5-1.8 mm and usually more strongly rounded in outline with rounded side angles (Fig. 309). Antennal segments 1-4 (sometimes 1-3 or 1-5, and sometimes 6) yellow-brown, sometimes reddish, others dark .... *exclamationis*

Confirmatory characters: In males the 5th antennal segment is very elongate and swollen towards the tip (Fig. 310); in females it is slightly elongate, but shorter than segment 1 (Fig. 311). Yellow markings can be a band or two separate elongate spots (Fig. 312), often thinly connected. Aedeagus as in Fig. 313.

Distribution: Widespread on Brassicaceae, especially water-cresses (*Rorippa*) and bitter-cresses (*Cardamine*), in various wet habitats or those near water.

- Larger, 1.9-3.5mm and usually more elongate in outline (Fig. 314). Antennal segments 1-3, 2-3 or only 2 yellow-brown, sometimes reddish, others dark 6

  Confirmatory characters: Dark sutural band clearly widest in the middle (Fig. 315); in *tetrastigma* males, there may a dark band across the middle of the elytra leaving 4 irregular pale spots.

  The judgement regarding overall shape can be difficult, especially given variation between individuals though it eases with experience. If in doubt regarding an identification, bear in mind the various features of the species in question and consider returning to this couplet.

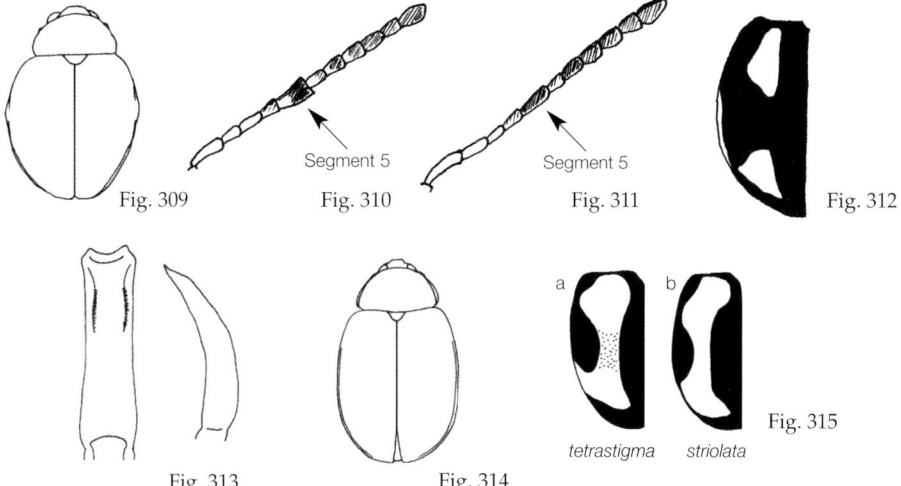

Fig. 309 Fig. 310 Segment 5 Fig. 311 Segment 5 Fig. 312

Fig. 313 Fig. 314 a b Fig. 315

tetrastigma *striolata*

6 Larger, 2.6-3.5 mm. Antennal segments 1-3 yellow-brown, sometimes reddish, others dark. Elytra oval; yellow stripe sometimes divided into two marks, often thinly connected (i.e. when the dotted area in Fig. 315a is pigmented black rather than yellow). 4th and 5th antennal segments the same size as adjacent ones .... *tetrastigma*

Confirmatory character: Aedeagus as in Fig. 316.

Distribution: Widespread but local on water-cresses (*Rorippa*), bitter-cresses (*Cardamine*), garden radish (*Raphanus sativus*) and sometimes mignonettes (*Reseda*), in wet areas, woodland, heathland and commons.

- Smaller, 1.9-2.5 mm. Antennal segments 1-3, 2-3 or only 2 yellow-brown, sometimes reddish, others dark. Elytra elongate; yellow stripe rarely divided into two marks. 5th antennal segment longer than adjacent ones in both sexes. In males, it is also slightly swollen, and the 4th segment may show these features to a lesser extent and be darker than 5th (Fig. 317). In females, the 5th segment is elongate but shorter than segment 1 (Fig. 318) .... *striolata* (striped turnip flea beetle)

Confirmatory character: Aedeagus as in Fig. 319.

Distribution: Scarce (Na) and very local on wild and cultivated Brassicaceae in various habitats.

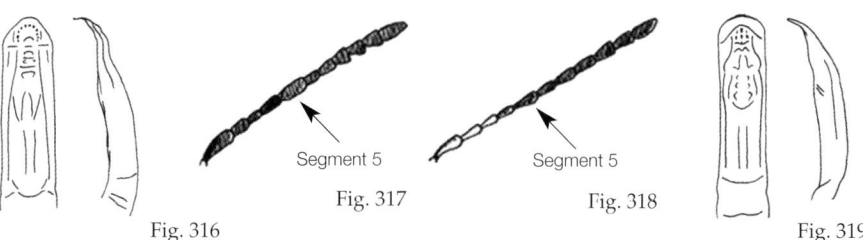

Fig. 316 Segment 5 Fig. 317 Segment 5 Fig. 318 Fig. 319

7 Tibiae entirely pale yellow to yellow-brown ....
.... *nemorum* (turnip flea beetle)

Fig. 320

Confirmatory characters: Yellow elytral band slightly sinuate and narrowing towards the rear where it clearly points towards the suture (Fig. 320). Head and pronotum black with weak metallic blue or green reflection. Antennae dark except for segments 2 and 3 (and sometimes the apex of the 1st segment) yellowish. 2.4-3.5 mm. Aedeagus as in Fig. 321.

Distribution: Widespread but local on Brassicaceae, sometimes also mignonettes (*Reseda*) and brooklime (*Veronica beccabunga*), in a wide range of habitats.

- Tibiae darkened brownish at least in the apical half 8

Fig. 321

8 Yellow elytral band relatively narrow, widening slightly towards the front and rear (Fig. 322). Top of head with a transverse band of punctures above the antennal bases, but no punctures behind the rear margin of eyes. Metallic reflection of pronotum vague or completely lacking .... *undulata* (small striped flea beetle)

Confirmatory characters: Head and pronotum black, sometimes with a weak metallic reflection. Antennae dark except for segments 2 and 3 yellowish. 2.0-2.8 mm. Aedeagus as in Fig. 323.

Distribution: Widespread and common in a wide range of habitats, on wild and cultivated Brassicaceae, sometimes also on wild mignonette (*Reseda lutea*), sea beet (*Beta vulgaris* ssp. *maritima*), nasturtium (*Tropaeolium majus*) and on trees.

- Yellow band usually narrowing towards the rear, especially in males (Fig. 324); in females the narrowing occurs, but may be less clear. Top of head punctured throughout. Pronotum with a strong bluish or greenish metallic reflection ..... *vittula* (barley flea beetle)

Confirmatory characters: Pronotum with metallic green or blue reflection. Antennal segments 1-4 (5th dark with pale base) or 1-6 yellowish, others black or brown. 1.8-2.3 mm. Aedeagus as in Fig. 325.

Distribution: Widespread but local (commonest in southern England) on Brassicaceae and Poaceae (wild and cultivated), sometimes also beet (*Beta vulgaris*), in various habitats.

 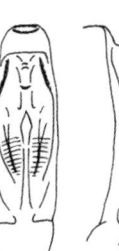  

Fig. 322   Fig. 323   Fig. 324   Fig. 325

9 Antennae entirely black (articulations between some basal pairs of segments may be pale). 1.8-2.8 mm 10

- Antennae with at least segments 2 and 3 paler, sometimes only slightly (e.g. in *atra* and *cruciferae*). 1.6-3.0 mm 11

10   Black or dark bluish. Dorsal punctures coarser than in *nigripes* and background shiny. Antennae robust, especially around the base; long, thick basal segment strongly curved outwards. 5th antennal segment elongate (clearly longer than 6th), in males segments 4 and 5 also dilated (Figs 326, 327). 1.8-2.8 mm .... *consobrina*

Confirmatory character: Aedeagus (Fig. 328) more or less evenly tapering towards the tip (in side view).

Distribution: Widely scattered, mainly in southern England on wild and cultivated Brassicaceae in various habitats.

-    Dark with metallic blue, blue-green or green reflection. Punctures on head, pronotum and elytra finer than in *consobrina*, and background dull/silky. Antennal segments 4 and 5 unmodified, segment 5 the same length as, or only marginally longer than, segment 6. 1.9-2.8 mm .... *nigripes*

Confirmatory character: Aedeagus (Fig. 329) with (in side view) a small up-curved process at the tip.

Distribution: Widespread and possibly increasing in range and abundance on wild and cultivated Brassicaceae (as well as other plants) in various habitats.

For more detail on *consobrina* and *cruciferae*, see Allen (1976). For alternative, detailed keys (in French), including features of genitalia, see Douget (1984, 1994) for North African and French species respectively, the latter giving by far the greater coverage of British species.

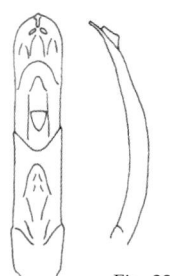

Fig. 326   Fig. 327   Fig. 328   Fig. 329

11   Dorsally metallic dark green or blue-green (rarely dark bronze); pronotum usually with a brassy tinge, rarely also the elytra. 1.8-2.5 mm .... *cruciferae* (cabbage flea beetle)

Confirmatory characters: Pronotum with coarse punctures. Elytral punctures striate. Aedeagus slender and parallel-sided, curving evenly to the tip which bears a small point and (in side view) a trapezoidal process (Fig. 330).

Distribution: Scarce (Nb) and scattered in southern and central England on wild and cultivated Brassicaceae, nasturtiums (*Tropaeolium*) and wild mignonette (*Reseda lutea*), in various habitats.

Fig. 330

-    Dorsally black, sometimes with bronze, brassy or coppery tinge. 1.6-3.0 mm 12

12   Top of head not punctured except for a band between the eyes. 1.8-2.5 mm .... *diademata*

Confirmatory character: Aedeagus (Fig. 331) with straight sides tapering slightly towards the tip which (in side view) has a thin, bent point.

Distribution: Widely scattered in southern Britain, on Brassicaceae in various habitats.

-    Top of head entirely covered in punctures. 1.6-3.0 mm 13

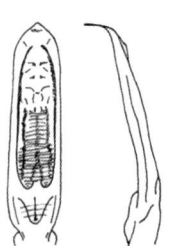

Fig. 331

13 Larger, 2.5-3.0 mm. Dorsal surface with a strong bronze reflection (rarely green-bronze); head and pronotum may be bronze while elytra black with bronze tinge. Pronotum distinctly less transverse (Fig. 332a). Males with 4th antennal segment very dilated, segments 3 and 5 less so (Fig. 333). Females with antennal segments 4 and 5 elongate, longer than segments 3 and 6 (Fig. 334). Aedeagus with an elongated point at the tip Fig. 335) .... *nodicornis*

Confirmatory characters: Elongate, narrow, nearly parallel-sided.

Distribution: Widespread but scattered on Resedaceae (sometimes various other plants) in a range of habitats.

- Smaller, 1.6-2.4 mm. Dorsally black, sometimes with a (usually weak) bronze tinge. Pronotum distinctly more transverse (Fig. 332b). Antennal segments not modified as in *nodicornis*. Aedeagus (Fig. 336) with a small point at the tip 14

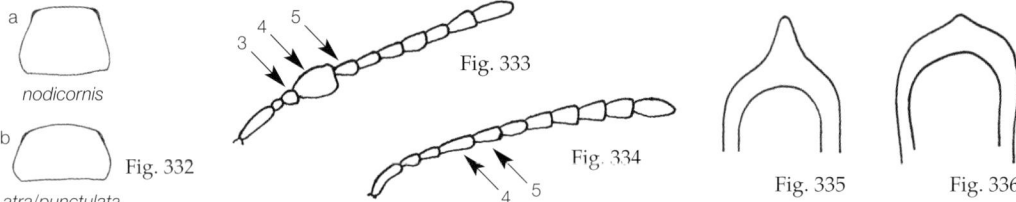

Fig. 333

Fig. 334

Fig. 332

Fig. 335   Fig. 336

14 Top of head coarsely punctured (punctures clearly larger than eye facets). 1.8-2.4 mm .... *atra*

Confirmatory characters: Elytral punctures may by striate, partly striate (especially away from the suture), or random. Aedeagus (in side view) thin at the tip, with a distinct thickening basally from this (Fig. 337).

Distribution: Widespread, especially in central and eastern England, on wild and cultivated Brassicaceae, sometimes on various other plants, in a wide range of habitats.

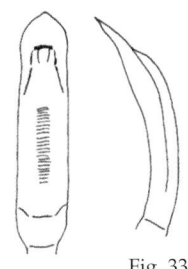

Fig. 337

- Top of head very finely punctured (punctures the same size as, or smaller than, eye facets). 1.6-2.0 mm .... *punctulata*

Confirmatory characters: Elytra finely, densely and randomly punctured. Aedeagus (in side view) thin at the tip, thickening gradually towards the base (Fig. 338).

Distribution: Scarce (Nb), scattered and very local in central and southern Britain, on Brassicaceae, sometimes also beet (*Beta vulgaris*) and weld (*Reseda luteola*), in saltmarshes, disturbed and cultivated land (including gardens and railway land) and woodland.

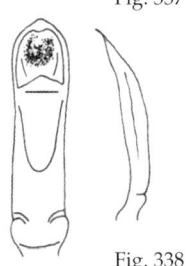

Fig. 338

Key Hb12: Genus *Aphthona*

Note that the small bluish/greenish metallic species (*atratula*, *atrocaerulea*, *euphorbiae* and *melancholica*) can be very difficult to separate without reference specimens and it is these that are most likely to require dissection of males. Of these, *euphorbiae* is the most frequently encountered. For more detailed keys of all Palaearctic species, including features of genitalia, see Konstantinov (1998).

1 Dorsally yellowish, head may be darker. Suture may be darkened (variably). 1.5-2.5 mm 2

- Dorsally black or blackish, or metallic blue, green or bronze. 1.5-2.8 mm 4

2 Head yellowish, pale brown or rusty red-brown. Rear half to two thirds of suture darkened, though this band often terminates before the tip. Hind femora, tarsi and antennae darkened apically. Transverse groove separating top of head from bulges above antennal bases vague or almost absent. 2.0-2.5 mm .... *lutescens*

Distribution: Widespread, though somewhat scattered (largely coastal in Wales) in wetland habitat on purple-loosestrife (*Lythrum salicaria*), also marsh cinquefoil (*Potentilla palustris*), meadowsweet (*Filipendula ulmaria*), cloudberry (*Rubus chamaemorus*) and woody nightshade (*Solanum dulcamara*).

- Head black. Suture may be darkened, narrowly to the front and rear, broadly in the centre. Hind femora red-brown without further apical darkening. Tarsi and antennae may be red-brown apically or may show apical darkening. Sharp transverse groove separating top of head from bulges above antennal bases. 1.5-1.8 mm 3

3 Aedeagus as in Fig. 339 .... *nigriceps*

Distribution: Scarce (Na), scattered and very local on several crane's-bills (*Geranium*) and stork's-bills (*Erodium*) in various habitats near water. However, note (as below) that some existing records may relate to *pallida*.

Fig. 339

- Aedeagus as in Fig. 340 .... *pallida*

Distribution: Recorded on meadow crane's-bill (*Geranium pratense*) in Scotland and Yorkshire, but wider range uncertain due to prior confusion with *nigriceps*.

Fig. 340

Sinclair & Hutchins (2009) added *A. pallida* to the British list based on Scottish specimens, and, with Jobe & Marsh (2012), note that some records of *A. nigriceps* are attributable to *A. pallida*; features of genitalia (Figs 339, 340) are given as well as noting that darker brown specimens of *pallida* may exist. Both species are usually considered to have pale elytra; *pallida* has, at most, a very narrowly darkened suture while *nigriceps* has a broader dark sutural band. However, at present due to the lack of *nigriceps* specimens, the aedeagus appears to be the only reliable method of separating these two species.

4 Larger, 2.6-2.8 mm (largest British *Aphthona*). Front and mid-femora darkened ... *nonstriata*

Confirmatory characters: Somewhat elongate. Metallic blue, sometimes dark green or dark brassy-bronze, rarely near black. Antennae dark brown except for segments 2-3 (sometimes 1-4) yellow. Underside dark brown. Hind femora red-brown to dark brownish, may be further darkened apically.

Distribution: Widespread and common near water, only on yellow iris (*Iris pseudacorus*).

- Smaller, 1.5-2.5 mm. Front and mid-femora pale, usually yellow 5

5 Weakly rounded elytral shoulders; not fully winged. 1.9-2.2 mm ....
.... *herbigrada*

Confirmatory characters: Slender. Pronotum sometimes wrinkled, mainly at the rear centre. Metallic green (rarely bluish) or black with blue reflection. Elytral punctures dense, very confused around the scutellum, slightly finer towards the front. Pronotal punctures may also show this dense confusion in front of the scutellum. Hind femora, last two tarsal segments (and sometimes hind tibiae) brown, slightly darker than rest of legs. Antennae yellowish or with apical half brown. Aedeagus as in Fig. 341.

Distribution: Widespread, though patchily so, on rock-roses (*Helianthemum*), also gorses (*Ulex*) and thymes (*Thymus*), in various habitats.

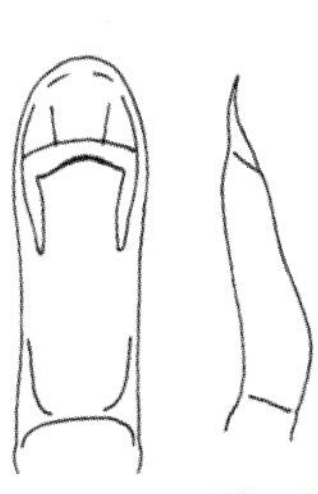

Fig. 341

- Strongly rounded elytral shoulders; fully winged. 1.5-2.5 mm 6

6 Larger, 2.3-2.5mm. Tip of aedeagus somewhat rounded with a small, blunt triangular point (Fig. 342) .... *melancholica*

Confirmatory characters: Shiny black or dark (usually metallic) blue. Pronotum with very fine punctures. Elytra more rounded in outline (Fig. 343), similar in shape to, but larger than, *atrocaerulea*

Distribution: Widespread but local on wood spurge (*Euphorbia amygdaloides*), Mediterranean spurge (*E. characias*), also hazels (*Corylus*) and oaks (*Quercus*), in various habitats.

- Smaller, 1.5-2.1 mm. Tip of aedeagus either bluntly pointed (*atrocaerulea*) or somewhat rounded but with a wide, blunt (rather than bluntly triangular) point (*atratula* and *euphorbiae*) (Figs 344, 346) 7

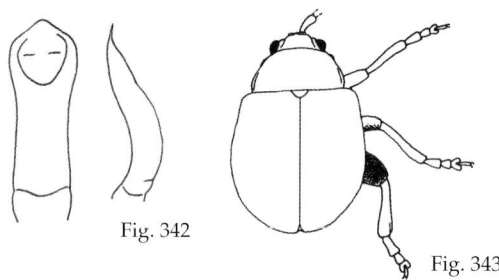

Fig. 342

Fig. 343

7 Black with dark violet or dark blue reflection (may appear more or less completely black). Elytra relatively more rounded in outline (Fig. 343). Aedeagus narrowing to a blunt triangular point and relatively elongate (Fig. 344) .... *atrocaerulea*

Confirmatory characters: Elytral punctures coarser in front half, more regular near the suture (note that this is somewhat variable and can be difficult to determine). 1.8-2.1 mm.

Distribution: Widespread but very local on spurges (*Euphorbia*), sometimes gorses (*Ulex*), in various habitats, but usually in gardens, allotments and arable situations.

- Dark, metallic greenish-black, sometimes black with a weak metallic blue or brassy reflection. Elytra relatively more elongate in outline (Fig. 345). Aedeagus relatively short and somewhat rounded at the tip which bears a small, broadly blunt point (Fig. 346) 8

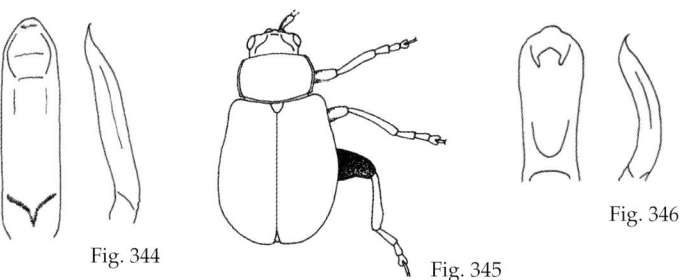

Fig. 344

Fig. 345

Fig. 346

8 Smaller, 1.5-1.7 mm. Black with weak metallic blue reflection. Poorly developed elytral shoulders, their outline more closely following that of the pronotum which is not distinctly narrower than the width of the elytra across the shoulders .... *atratula*

Distribution: Widespread but scattered on rock-roses (*Helianthemum*), Cypress spurge (*Euphorbia cyparissias*), wood sage (*Teucrium scorodonia*), wild marjoram (*Origanum vulgare*) and (especially in Wales) fairy flax (*Linum catharticum*). In forest rides, downland, chalky places and quarries (may appear rarely and sporadically at calcareous quarry sites on short turf).

- Larger, 1.8-2.0 mm. Metallic dark greenish-black to bronze, sometimes black with blue or brassy reflection. More strongly developed elytral shoulders such that the base of the pronotum is clearly narrower than the elytra across the shoulders ....
.... *euphorbiae* (large flax flea beetle)

Distribution: Widespread and common (effectively ubiquitous after a massive population expansion in the early 1990s), especially in southern, central and eastern England, on various plants in a very wide range of habitats, including gardens, although flax (linseed) (*Linum usitatissimum*) is its main host.

For notes on taxonomic confusion regarding *atratula*, *atrovirens* and *euphorbiae*, and the resulting taxonomic status of *atratula* in Britain, see Cox (2000b, 2007). This status remains somewhat uncertain, although note that in some continental publications (e.g. Warchałowski, 2003), *atrovirens* is given as a British species. This is not the case and it is likely that British '*atrovirens*' are actually *atratula*. Also note that Konstantinov (1998) considers *atratula* to be the same as *euphorbiae* and a formal taxonomic decision will be made following examination of a series of male and female genitalia from both species.

Key Hb13: Genus *Apteropeda*

1 Antennal segments 4 and 5 more or less equal in length.Variably metallic coloured and may have a green, bronze, coppery, blue or violet reflection. 2.2-2.6 mm. Aedeagus as in Fig. 347 .... *orbiculata*

Distribution: Locally common in various habitats on ribwort plantain (*Plantago lanceolata*), beneath buck's-horn plantain (*P. coronopus*), and on various other plants such as Lamiaceae, Scrophulariaceae, crosswort (*Cruciata laevipes*) and hazels (*Corylus*).

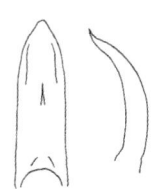

Fig. 347

- Antennal segment 5 longer than segment 4. Dark; may have a vague metallic reflection. 2.4-3.0 mm 2

2 Dark; vague metallic greenish, blue or bronze reflection. Top of head coarsely punctured (as coarse as pronotum). Elytral intervals with more diffuse punctures. 1st tarsal segment longer than 2nd. 2.5-3.0 mm. Aedeagus as in Fig. 348 .... *globosa*

Distribution: Scarce (Nb), scattered and very local on Lamiaceae and speedwells (*Veronica*) in various habitats, usually on calcareous soils.

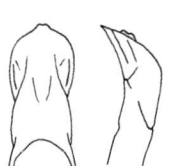

Fig. 348

- Shiny black without metallic reflection. Top of head finely punctured. Elytral intervals with less diffuse punctures. 1st tarsal segment only slightly longer than 2nd. 2.4-2.8 mm. Aedeagus as in Fig. 349 ... *splendida*

Distribution: Endangered (RDB1) and possibly extinct with no records in Great Britain since 1931 and one in Ireland in 1987. On bugle (*Ajuga reptans*), speedwells (*Veronica*) and plantains (*Plantago*) in wetlands, woodlands, grasslands and sand dunes.

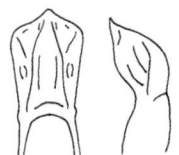

Fig. 349

Key Hb14: Genus *Sphaeroderma*

1 Convex, rounded, almost circular (Fig. 350a). Pronotal punctures uniform and fine (sometimes appearing almost absent). Pale rusty or orange-red. Pronotal front angles rounded and not prominent, sides not swollen hence lateral margin visible from above (Fig. 351a). 2.3-3.1 mm. Aedeagus as in Fig. 352 .... *rubidum*

Distribution: Widespread and common on Asteraceae, and sometimes the foliage of trees, in various habitats.

- Broadly oval (Fig. 350b). Pronotal punctures coarser at the rear, finer at the front. Yellowish, brownish or reddish. Pronotal front angles slightly more prominent (this can be quite subtle), sides swollen hence lateral margin usually not visible from above (Fig. 351b). 2.5-4.5 mm. Aedeagus as in Fig. 353 .... *testaceum*

Distribution: Widespread and common on Asteraceae in various habitats.

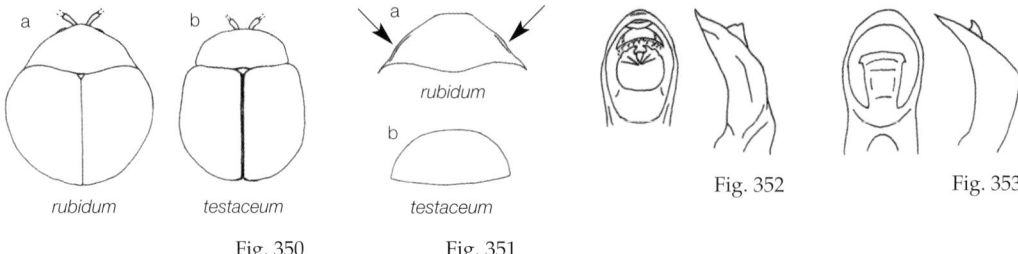

rubidum

testaceum

rubidum

testaceum

Fig. 350

Fig. 351

Fig. 352

Fig. 353

KEY I: SUBFAMILY CASSIDINAE

Males and females are difficult to separate but identification is possible using surface characters, so dissection is not required.

1 Elytra red with irregular black stripes and suture; sometimes black with a few red spots, or red with a few small black spots; newly emerged specimens sometimes greenish instead of red. Punctures in irregular lines. Pronotum no more than slightly narrower than elytra; shiny with black spots, and edges strongly raised (Fig. 354). Legs black. Deep antennal groove running alongside head on underside of pronotum. 4.5-6.5 mm .... *Pilemostoma fastuosa*

Distribution: Scarce (Na) in southern England and S. Wales on Asteraceae, especially ploughman's-spikenard (*Inula conyzae*) and common fleabane (*Pulicaria dysenterica*), sometimes common ragwort (*Senecio jacobaea*), possibly also on mints (*Mentha*), in various habitats.

Fig. 354

> There is some disagreement about whether *Pilemostoma* is a separate genus or a subgenus within *Cassida*. Here it is treated as a separate genus in order to follow the checklist in Duff (2008), and the matter is discussed in more detail in Sekerka (2008). Note also that as *Hypocassida subferruginea* is likely to be extinct (Cox, 2007), this is the only British member of the Cassidinae outside the genus *Cassida*.

- Colour and pattern not as above .... Key I1: Genus *Cassida* (p. 111)

> The Cassidinae are keyed in more detail in Bordy & Doguet (1987) and Bordy (2000), both of which cover the French fauna (in French).

Key I1: Genus *Cassida*

1 Elytra with dense, random punctures; without ridges, ribs, wrinkles or raised surface between punctures. Upper surface and legs greenish or yellow-green. 4.3-10.0 mm 2

- Not as above. Elytra with lines of punctures, though these may be partly (even largely) irregular. If more irregular, then surface raised between punctures. 4.0-9.0 mm 3

2 Convex. Green or yellowish-green, shiny (pale metallic golden green in life). Pronotum no more than slightly narrower than elytra, possibly with a dark central spot. Elytral punctures moderately coarse; splayed edges bounded by a line of coarse punctures on the inside (Fig. 355). Abdomen yellow, or black with yellow edges. 4.3-5.4 mm (possibly smaller) .... *hemisphaerica*

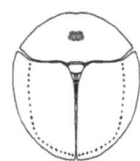
Fig. 355

Distribution: Scarce (Na) and widely scattered on Caryophyllaceae, including campions (*Silene*), also oaks (*Quercus*), in various habitats.

- Green (becomes brownish-green or yellow once dry). Pronotum narrower than elytra. Elytra with splayed edges not bounded by a line of coarse punctures. Underside black, abdomen with broad yellow edges. 7.0-10.0 mm .... *viridis* (green tortoise beetle)

Distribution: Widespread on Lamiaceae in wet habitats and their margins, woodland, heathland and moorland.

3 Green or reddish-orange (green in less mature specimens). Pronotum without spots. Elytra with small black spots, especially near suture (Fig. 356), sometimes mostly black or without spots. Underside black. Legs black. 6.5-9.0 mm .... *murraea* (fleabane tortoise beetle)

Fig. 356

Distribution: Recent records only from south and west of England and Wales. On common fleabane (*Pulicaria dysenterica*) and marsh thistle (*Cirsium palustre*) in various damp habitats, both inland and coastal.

- Not as above. Legs yellow, femora and tibiae (in *nebulosa*) sometimes partly darkened/black but not extensively so, and never completely dark. 4.0-8.0 mm 4

4 Dull, brownish-yellow or pale yellow (vaguely metallic gold in life). Elytra sometimes with dark spots; sometimes blackish-brown with pale spots. Underside mostly black. Pronotum narrower than elytra, rear angles broadly rounded. Splayed elytral edges very narrow, and of more or less even width along the entire length. Front of head with fine punctures, no larger than eye facets. 4.0-6.0 mm .... *flaveola* (pale tortoise beetle)

Distribution: Widespread and locally common on Caryophyllaceae (also a variety of other species) in a range of habitats.

- Combination of characters not as above. Usually greenish or yellow-green, may be yellowish (but not metallic gold) or reddish-brown. 5.5-8.0 mm 5

5 Rusty-red, brownish or green species, sometimes with a vague metallic green reflection. Elytra with numerous small black spots, sometimes merging to form irregular longitudinal bands more or less along striae (Fig. 357). Underside black, abdomen with yellow edge. Splayed elytral edges wider towards the front. Front edge of elytra notched, making front angles prominent. 5.5-7.7 mm .... *nebulosa*

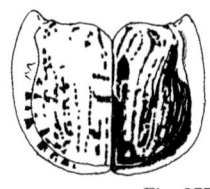

Fig. 357

Distribution: Scattered in southern and eastern England and considered Indeterminate (RDBI). On Chenopodiaceae, also knotgrasses (*Polygonum*), in various habitats.

- Elytral markings not as above. 4.3-8.0 mm 6

6 Convex. Parallel-sided (for tortoise beetles) (Fig. 358). Striae very regular; spaces between striae all at the same height, space between striae 2 and 3 usually wider. 4.3-6.5 mm 7

Confirmatory characters: Underside black, abdomen usually paler at the edges.

- Less convex, more rounded. Spaces between striae 2 and 3 and 4 and 5 raised to form at least a weak ridge towards the front. 5.1-8.0 mm 8

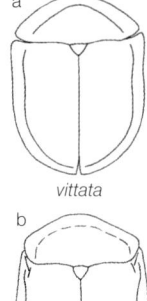

vittata

nobilis

Fig. 358

7   Yellow or pale green (in life with a golden silvery elytral stripe between striae 2 and 6). Elongate-oval. Rear pronotal angles obtuse (Fig. 359). Antennae yellow. Femora entirely yellow or sometimes narrowly darkened at bases. Overall, slightly longer, lighter and smoother-looking. In lateral view, the almost vertical sides of the elytra (below humeral striae) are finely wrinkled with punctures much smaller and shallower than those of the striae above. 5.0-6.5 mm .... *vittata* (bordered tortoise beetle)

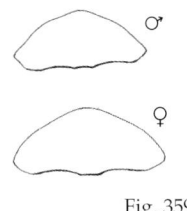

Fig. 359

Distribution: Widespread but patchily distributed on various plants, especially Chenopodiaceae, in a range of habitats, particularly saltmarshes and other coastal locations.

-   Yellow or pale green, sometimes yellow-brownish (in life sometimes has a longitudinal rose-red or metallic gold stripe covering top of elytra), or with blackish suture and some darkened spots; elytra sometimes marked with beautiful crimson horseshoe. Rear pronotal angles broadly rounded (Fig. 360). Front of head, tips of antennae, and basal half of femora black. Overall slightly shorter, darker and rougher-looking. In lateral view, the almost vertical sides of the elytra (below humeral striae) have little or no wrinkling and have punctures only a little smaller and shallower than those of the striae above (except for the margins where punctures are much finer). 4.3-6.0 mm .... *nobilis*

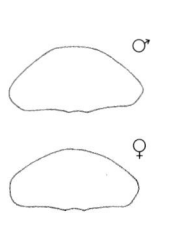

Fig. 360

Distribution: Scarce (Nb) but widely scattered, usually on fat-hen (*Chenopodium album*), glassworts (*Salicornia*), oraches (*Atriplex*) and corn spurrey (*Spergula arvensis*) in various habitats, especially those inland with sandy or chalky soils.

   See Allen (1989) for his description of the differences in elytral sides, general aspect and habitat between *C. vittata* and *C. nobilis*.

8   Legs yellow except for basal half (sometimes more) of femora black. 5.5-8.0 mm 9

-   Legs yellow, sometimes with base of femora slightly darkened, or with some 'smokiness' on parts of tibiae and femora. 5.1-8.0 mm 10

9   Highly rounded. Green or yellowish-green, elytra sometimes with a small dark triangular spot around the scutellum, also usually a small dark spot near the suture (Fig. 361). Rear pronotal angles relatively more acute. 6.0-8.0 mm .... *rubiginosa* (thistle tortoise beetle)
Distribution: Widespread and common on Asteraceae in a wide range of habitats.

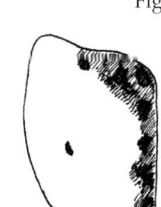

Fig. 361

-   Short-oval. Green or yellowish-green (in life with a variable metallic reflection). Rear pronotal angles relatively more obtuse. Pronotum sometimes with two small dark spots near the rear edge (these may be more extensive). Elytra with a triangular scutellar spot and dark spots on the suture; may form a broad dark sutural band which may merge with the scutellar spot; usually also a small black spot near the middle or side (Fig. 362). 5.5-7.5 mm .... *vibex*
Distribution: Widespread, mainly east of a line from the Severn to the Humber, on Asteraceae in various habitats.

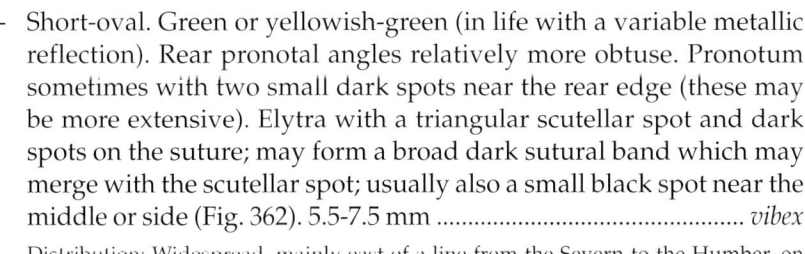

Fig. 362

10 Green or greenish-yellow. One or two reddish spots (may be faint) at the front of elytra. Central epimere yellow, or black with an oblique yellow spot. 5.2-6.5 mm .... *prasina*

Distribution: Scarce (Nb) on yarrow (*Achillea millefolium*) and sneezewort (*A. ptarmica*), possibly also sea campion (*Silene uniflora*), in various habitats.

Central epimere black or green. 5.1-8.0 mm.. 11

11 Green; brownish-red around the scutellum. Central epimere black. Narrow, deep dent at the front of the labrum (Fig. 363). Near each hind angle, rear edge of the pronotum with a distinct tooth (Fig. 364) , the edge between these two teeth being distinctly black. Front edges of elytra between the scutellum and the shoulders also distinctly black, with a series of small, strong, blunt teeth (Fig. 364). May be faint to medium brown darkening along front edge of elytra and around scutellum, sometimes extending along suture (Fig. 365). 5.1-7.0 mm .... *denticollis*

Distribution: Endangered (RDB1); also listed as rare (RDB3). Very sparsely scattered on yarrow (*Achillea millefolium*) on roadside verges, in water meadows and by rivers.

-    Green; pale blood-red around the scutellum (rarely this reddening is absent). Central epimere black or green. Broad, shallow dent at front of the labrum (Fig. 366). Pronotal tooth of *denticollis* may be present, but not with teeth on the front edges of elytra. 5.9-8.0 mm .... *sanguinosa*

Distribution: Very sparsely scattered and apparently rare, but not listed as such. On Asteraceae near water, sometimes on farmland.

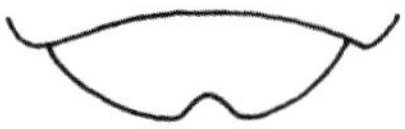

pronotal tooth

small elytral teeth

Fig. 363

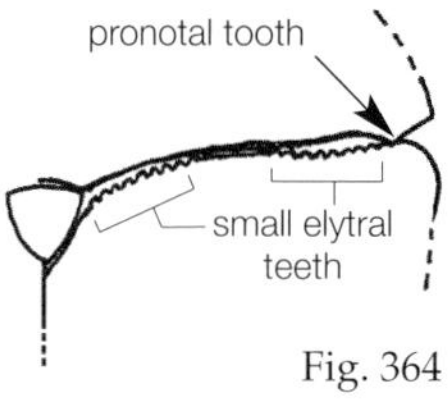

Fig. 364

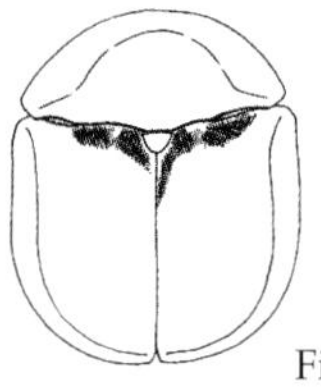

Fig. 365

Fig. 366

References and further reading

Aldridge, R.J.W. & Pope, R.D. (1986). The British species of *Bruchidius* Schilsky (Coleoptera: Bruchidae). *Entomologist's Gazette* **37**: 181-193.

Alexander, K.N.A. (2006). *Ochrosis ventralis* (Illiger) (Chrysomelidae): new Cornish records and a review of its ecology in Britain. *The Coleopterist* **15(3)**: 127-129.

Alexander, K.N.A. (2011). The distribution and status of *Pyrrhalta viburni* (Paykull) (Chrysomelidae) in Scotland. *The Coleopterist* **20(2)**: 96.

Allen, A.A. (1976). Notes on some British Chrysomelidae (Col.) including amendments and additions to the list. *Entomologist's Record and Journal of Variation* **88**: 220-225 and 294-299.

Allen, A.A. (1989). A diagnostic note on two species of *Cassida* L. (Col.: Chrysomelidae). *Entomologist's Record and Journal of Variation* **101**: 205.

Anderson, R., Nash, R. and O'Connor, J.P. (2005). *Checklist of Irish Coleoptera.* InvertebrateIreland Online. Ulster Museum, Belfast and National Museum of Ireland, Dublin.

Bienkowski, A.O. (1997). New distributional records for several Palearctic Chrysomelidae species with some systematic remarks (Insecta: Coleoptera). *Faunitische Abhandlungen (Dresden)* **21**: 91-104.

Bienkowski, A.O. (2004). *Leaf-beetles (Coleoptera: Chrysomelidae) of the Eastern Europe. New Key to Subfamilies, Genera, and Species.* Mikron-print, Moscow.

Biondi, M. (1983). Contributo alla conoscenza delle Alticinae della fauna Italiana (Coleoptera, Chrysomelidae). *Fragmenta Entomologica* **17(1)**: 151-158.

Booth, R.G. and Owen, J.A. (1997). *Chaetocnema picipes* Stephens (Chrysomelidae: Alticinae) in Britain. *The Coleopterist* **6(3)**: 85-89.

Bordy, B. (2000). Coléoptères Chrysomelidae, Volume 3. Hispinae et Cassidinae. *Faune de France* **85**: 250 pp.

Bordy, B. and Doguet, S. (1987). Contribution à la connaissance des Cassidinae de France. Étude de leur spermathèque (Coleoptera, Chrysomelidae). *Nouvelle Revue d'Entomologie* **4(2)**: 161-176.

Buckland, P.C. and Skidmore, P. (1999). *Xanthogaleruca luteola* (Müller) (Chrysomelidae) in Britain. *The Coleopterist* **8(3)**: 97-99.

Bukejs, A. (2010). Leaf-beetles *Oulema septentrionis* (Weise, 1880) and *O. erichsonii* (Suffrian, 1841) (Coleoptera: Chrysomelidae) in Latvian fauna. *Baltic Journal of Coleopterology* **10(1)**: 65-69.

Burakowski, B. (1993). Laboratory methods for rearing soil beetles (Coleoptera). *Memorabilia Zoologica* **46**: 1-66.

du Chatenet, G. (2002). *Coléoptères Phytophages d'Europe 2: Chrysomelidae.* NAP-Editions, Verrières-le-Buisson.

Cizek, P. (2006). *Drepcici (Coleoptera: Chrysomelidae: Alticinae) Ceska a Slovenska.* Kabourek, Zlín.

Cooter, J. and Barclay, M.V.L. (eds.) (2006). *A Coleopterist's Handbook* (4th ed.). Amateur Entomologists' Society, Orpington.

Costesseque, R. (2003). *Les Cryptocephalus de France: Clé de détermination et iconographie* (2nd ed.). Rutilans, Villelongue-dels-Monts.

Cox, M.L. (1981). Notes on the biology of *Orsodacne* with a subfamily key to the larvae of the British Chrysomelidae. *Entomologist's Gazette* **32**:123-135.

Cox, M.L. (1995). Identification of the *Oulema 'melanopus'* species group (Chrysomelidae). *The Coleopterist* **4(2)**: 33-36.

Cox, M.L. (1998). The genus *Psylliodes* Latreille (Chrysomelidae: Alticinae) in the UK. *The Coleopterist* **7(2)**: 33-65.

Cox, M.L. (2000a). The current status of *Psylliodes luteola* (Müller, O.F., 1776) (Chrysomelidae) in the UK. *The Coleopterist* **9(2)**: 55-63.

Cox, M.L. (2000b). Progress report on the Bruchidae/Chrysomelidae recording scheme. *The Coleopterist* **9(2)**: 65-74.

Cox, M.L. (2001). Notes on the natural history, distribution and identification of seed beetles (Bruchidae) of Britain and Ireland. *The Coleopterist* **9(3)**: 113-147.

Cox, M.L. (2007). *Atlas of the Seed and Leaf Beetles of Britain and Ireland*. Pisces, Newbury.

Denton, J. (2009). Beetles of Surrey: First checklist update. *The Coleopterist* **18(1)**: 55-58.

Doguet, S. (1984). Contribution à l'étude des espèces d'Afrique du Nord du genre *Phyllotreta* (Coleoptera, Chrysomelidae). *Nouvelle Revue d'Entomologie* **1(3)**: 243-265.

Doguet, S. (1994). Coléoptères Chrysomelidae, Volume 2. Alticinae. *Faune de France* **80**: 694 pp.

Duff, A.G. (ed.) (2008). *Checklist of Beetles of the British Isles: 2008 edition*. A.G.Duff, Wells.

Foster, G.N., Bratton, J.H., Ewing, A.W., Hodge, P.J. and Nobes, G. (2007). Current status of *Donacia aquatic* Linnaeus (Chrysomelidae) in Britain and Ireland. *The Coleopterist* **16(1)**: 25-34.

Foster, G. and Nelson, B. (2010). Some recent records of Donaciinae in Britain and Ireland. *The Coleopterist* **19(1)**: 15-19.

Foster, G. N., Nelson, B. H. and O Connor, Á. (2009) *Ireland Red List No. 1 – Water beetles*. National Parks and Wildlife Service, Department of Environment, Heritage and Local Government, Dublin.

Fowler, W.W. (1890). *The Coleoptera of the British Islands. Vol 4. Lamellicornia-Serricornia-Longicornis-Phytophaga*. Reeve and Co., London.

Gruev, B. and M. Döberl. (1997). General distribution of the flea beetles in the Palaearctic Subregion (Coleoptera: Chrysomelidae: Alticinae). *Scopolia* **37**: 1-496.

Gruev, B. and Döberl, M. (2005). *General Distribution of the Flea Beetles in the Palaearctic Subregion (Coleoptera, Chrysomelidae: Alticinae). Supplement*. Pensoft, Sofia.

Gruev, B. and Tomov, V. (1998) *Catalogus Faunae Bulgaricae. 3. Coleoptera, Chrysomelidae.* Pensoft, Sofia.

Hammond, P. and Harvey, P. (2011). The exotic seed beetle *Bruchus brachialis* Fahraeus (Coleoptera: Chrysomelidae: Bruchinae) established in South Essex. *Essex Naturalist* **28**: 29-33.

Harrison, T. (2010). *Longitarsus symphyti* Heikertinger, 1912 (Chrysomelidae) new to Britain. *The Coleopterist* **18(2)**: 41-43.

Hincks, W.D. (1950). The British species of the genera *Pyrrhalta* Joannis and *Galerucella* Crotch (Col., Chrysomelidae). *Journal of the Society for British Entomology* **3**: 150-156.

Hodge, P.J. (1997). *Bruchidius varius* (Olivier) (Chrysomelidae) new to the British Isles. *The Coleopterist* **5(3)**: 65-68.

Hoffmann, A. (1945). *Faune de France 44. Coléoptères Bruchides et Anthribides.* Paul Lechevalier, Paris.

Hubble, D. and Murray, D. (2011). First British record of *Smaragdina salicina* (Scopoli, 1763) (Chrysomelidae). *The Coleopterist* **20(1)**: 1-3.

Hůrka, K. (2005). *Beetles of the Czech and Slovak Republics.* Kabourek, Zlín.

Hyman, P.S. & Parsons, M.S. (1992). *A Review of the Scarce and Threatened Coleoptera of Great Britain (Part 1).* JNCC, Peterborough.

IUCN (2010). *2001 IUCN Red List Categories and Criteria version 3.1.* Available from http://www.iucnredlist.org/technical-documents/categories-and-criteria/2001-categories-criteria [update 2010.4, accessed 18/01/2011].

JCCBI (2002). A Code of Conduct for Collecting Insects and Other Invertebrates. *British Journal of Entomology and Natural History* **15(1)**: 1-6.

JCCBI (2008). Statement on the appropriate role of legislation in controlling activities likely to harm specified taxa of terrestrial and freshwater invertebrates, with particular reference to taking and killing. *British Journal of Entomology and Natural History* **21(3)**: 202-204.

Jobe, J.B. and Marsh, R.J. (2012). The status of *Aphthona pallida* (Bach) (Chrysomelidae) in Yorkshire. *The Coleopterist* **21(1)**: 19-20.

Kevan, D.K. (1962). The British species of the genus *Haltica* Geoffroy (Col., Chrysomelidae). *Entomologist's Monthly Magazine* **98**: 189-196.

Kevan, D.K. (1967). The British species of the genus *Longitarsus* Latreille (Col., Chrysomelidae). *Entomologist's Monthly Magazine* **103**: 83-110.

Kingsolver, J.M. (2004). Handbook of the Bruchidae of the United States and Canada (Insecta, Coleoptera). *US Department of Agriculture Technical Bulletin* **1912**, 2 vols.

Kippenberg, H. (1994). Familie Chrysomelidae. In: Lohse, G.A. and Lucht, W.H. (eds.) *Die Kafer Mitteleuropas* Band 14. Goecke and Evers, Krefeld.

Konstantinov, A. (1996). Review of Palearctic Species of *Crepidodera* Chevrolat (Coleoptera, Chrysomelidae, Alticinae). *Spixiana* **19**: 21-37.

Konstantinov, A. (1998). *Revision of the Palearctic Species of* Aphthona *Chevrolat and Cladistic Classification of the Aphthonini (Coleoptera: Chrysomelidae: Alticinae).* Associated Publishers, Gainesville.

Lopatin, I.K. (1984). *Leaf Beetles (Chrysomelidae) of Central Asia and Kazakhstan*. Amerind, New Delhi.

Malumphy, C., Anderson, H. and Eyre, D. (2011). *Rapid assessment of the need for a detailed Pest Risk Analysis for* Chrysolina coerulans *(Scriba)*. Available from http://www.fera.defra.gov.uk/plants/plantHealth/pestsDiseases/documents/chrysolinaCoerulans.pdf [accessed 09/05/12]

Manguin, S., White, R., Blossey, B. and Hight, S.D. (1993). Genetics, taxonomy, and ecology of certain species of *Galerucella* (Coleoptera: Chrysomelidae). *Annals of the Entomological Society of America* **86(4)**: 397-410.

Mann, D.J. and Barclay, M.V.L. (2009). The identification and distribution of *Cryptocephalus biguttatus* (Scopoli) and *C. bipunctatus* (Linnaeus) var. *thomsoni* Weise (Chrysomelidae) in Britain. *The Coleopterist* **18(3)**: 166-181.

Medvedev, L. and Samaderzhenkov, E. (1989). A study of Weise's types of Chrysomelidae (Coleoptera). *Entomologica Basiliensis* **13**: 403-409.

Mendel, H. (1994). *Apteropeda splendida* Allard (Chrysomelidae) new to Ireland. *The Coleopterist* **2(3)**: 70.

Mendel, H. (1998). History of *Cryptocephalus exiguus* Schneider (Chrysomelidae) in Britain. *The Coleopterist* **7(1)**: 7-10.

Menzies, I.S. and Cox, M.L. (1996). Notes on the natural history, distribution and identification of British reed beetles. *British Journal of Entomology and Natural History* **9**: 137-162.

Mohr, K.H. (1966). *Chrysomelidae*. In: Freude, H., Harde, K.W. and Lohse, G.A. (eds.). *Die Käfer Mitteleuropas*. Goecke and Evers, Krefeld.

Morris, M.G. (1970). *Phyllodecta polaris* Schneider (Col., Chrysomelidae) new to the British Isles from Wester Ross and Inverness-shire, Scotland. *Entomologist's Monthly Magazine* **106**: 49-53.

Mutambuki, K. and Harberd, A.J. (2004). *Reference Manual on the Major Insect Pests of Stored Cereal and Pulse Grains in Somalia and their Control*. KARI, Nairobi.

Nadein, K.S. (2007). A Review of the Leaf-Beetle Genus *Psylliodes* Latreille (Coleoptera, Chrysomelidae) from Russia and Neighboring Countries: I. A Key to Subgenera, Species-Groups, and Species. *Entomological Review* **87(3)**: 330-360.

Nelson, B., Walsh, J. and Foster, G.N. (2007). Finding jewels amongst the reeds: a review of the Irish Donaciine beetles (Coleoptera: Chrysomelidae). *Bulletin of the Irish Biogeographical Society* **31**: 117-193.

Oldroyd, H. (1970). *Collecting, Preserving and Studying Insects* (2nd ed.). Hutchinson, London.

Ramos, R.Y. (1976). Las especies de Brúquidos (gorgojos de las leguminosas) de interés agrícola y fitosanitario (Col. Bruchidae) II: Sistemática y biología. *Boletín del Servicio de Defensa contra Plagas e Inspección Fitopatológica* **2**: 161-203.

Ramsay, A.J. (2009). A new hostplant for *Agelastica alni* (Linnaeus) (Chrysomelidae) in Britain and observations of the species in Cheshire. *The Coleopterist* **18(2)**: 149-151.

Reynolds, J.D. and Foster, G.N. (2009). Rediscovery of the chrysomelid beetle *Plateumaris bracata* [sic] (Scopoli) (Coleoptera: Chrysomelidae) in Ireland. *Irish Naturalists' Journal* **30**: 67.

Sage, B. (2009a). *Chrysolina coerulans* (Scriba) (Chrysomelidae) in Norfolk: the second British record. *The Coleopterist* **18(1)**: 6.

Sage, B. (2009b). The second occurrence of *Chrysolina coerulans* (Scriba) (Chrysomelidae) in Norfolk. *The Coleopterist* **18(2)**: 138.

Salisbury, A., Malumphy, C. and Halstead, A.J. (2012). First record of blue mint beetle *Chrysolina coerulans* (Scriba, 1791) (Chrysomelidae) breeding in Britain. *The Coleopterist* 21(1): 35-37.

Sekerka, L. (2008). Revision of the genus *Pilemostoma* Desbroches, 1891 (Coleoptera: Chrysomelidae: Cassidinae: Cassidini). *Zootaxa* **1859**: 40-48.

Shute, S.L. (1975). *Longitarsus jacobeae* Waterhouse (Col., Chrysomelidae) identity and distribution. *Entomologist's Monthly Magazine* **111**: 33-39.

Sinclair, M. and Hutchins, D. (2009). *Aphthona pallida* (Bach, 1856) (Chrysomelidae) is a British species. *The Coleopterist* **18(3)**: 155-157.

Southgate, B.J. (1958). Systematic notes on species of *Callosobruchus* of economic importance. *Bulletin of Entomological Research* **49(3)**: 591-599 + 2 BandW plates.

Stainforth, T. (1944). Reed-beetles of the genus *Donacia* and its allies in Yorkshire (Col. Chrysomelidae). *The Naturalist* **810**: 81-91; **811**: 127-139.

Steinhausen, W.R. (1996). Biological remarks on rearing and and collecting of middle European leaf beetle larvae. In: Jolivet, P.H.A. and Cox, M.L. (eds.). *Chrysomelidae Biology Vol. 3: General Studies*. Academic Publishing, Amsterdam.

Stenhouse, D. (2006). Records of *Agelastica alni* (L.) (Chrysomelidae) in South Lancashire and Cheshire in two successive years. *The Coleopterist*. **15(1)**: 21-24.

Unwin, D.M. (1988). *A Key to the Families of British Beetles*. Field Studies Council, Shrewsbury.

Vig, K. and Markó, V. (2006). Species composition of leaf beetle assemblages in deciduous tree canopies in Hungary (Coleoptera: Chrysomelidae). *Bonner Zoologische Beiträge* **54(4)**: 305-312.

Wanntorp, H.-E. (2009). Svenska bladbaggar: *Oulema septentrionis* (Weise, 1880) och *Cryptocephalus bameuli* Duhaldeborde, 1999, två nygamla arter i den nordiska faunan (Coleoptera, Chrysomelidae). *Entomologisk Tidskrift* **130(1)**: 37-42.

Warchałowski, Λ. (1996). *Übersicht der Westpaläarktischen Arten der Gattung* Longitarsus *Berthold, 1827 (Coleoptera: Chrysomelidae: Halticinae)*. Polish Taxonomical Society, Wrocław.

Warchałowski, A. (2003). *The Leaf-beetles (Chrysomelidae) of Europe and the Mediterranean Area*. Natura Optima Dux Foundation, Warsaw.

Winkelman, J. and Debreuil, M. (2008). *Les Chrysomelinae de France (Coleoptera: Chrysomelidae)*. Rutilans, Villelongue-dels-Monts.

Zaytsev, Y.M. and Medvedev, L.N. (2009). *Lichinki zhukov-listoedov Rossii*. KMK Scientific Press, Moscow.

Online resources

This list presents some general references that may be of use to those wishing to study the chrysomelids of Britain and Ireland. Some cover a wider geographical area and taxonomic range, but include many British and Irish species. This list is not exhaustive; new online projects may appear, while details of those below may change. However, they are correct as of February 2012.

European Chrysomelidae (by Dr Lech Borowiec)
http://www.biol.uni.wroc.pl/cassidae/European Chrysomelidae/list of genera.htm
Wrocław University, Department of Biodiversity and Evolutionary Taxonomy. List of European genera with links to more information, including subfamilies, species and photos, many of which include genitalia.

Watford Coleoptera Group. Chrysomeloidea Gallery
http://www.thewcg.org.uk/thumbnails/Curculionoidea.htm
Images of Orsodacnidae and Chrysomelidae with links to selected species.

Koleopterologie Gallery (by Frank Köhler)
http://www.koleopterologie.de/gallery/index.html
A gallery of beetle photographs from Germany including coverage of the Chrysomelidae.

The Beetle Fauna of Germany (by Christoph Benisch)
http://www.kerbtier.de/cgi-bin/enFOverview.cgi?UFam=Chrysomeloidea
Galleries of beetle photographs from Germany covering the Chrysomelidae and Bruchidae.

The Coleopterist Journal
http://www.coleopterist.org.uk/
A must for serious students of British beetles. Includes the current checklist of species and photo gallery.

Guide to Palearctic Flea Beetle Genera
http://www.sel.barc.usda.gov/Coleoptera/fleabeetles/genera.htm
USDA Systematic Entomology Laboratory's page on Alticinae. Descriptions of 58 genera with a typical example image of each. Includes a link to an online dichotomous key to Palaearctic genera.

Atlas of the Beetles of Russia
http://www.zin.ru/ANIMALIA/COLEOPTERA/eng/atl_chr.htm
Ongoing project by Russian coleopterists at the Zoological Institute of the Russian Academy of Sciences. This link is to the index page of the superfamily Chrysomeloidea.

APPENDIX A. PLANT FAMILIES MENTIONED IN THE TEXT

Asteraceae. Daisy or 'composite' family (also known as the Compositae).

Boraginaceae. Borage or forget-me-not family.

Brassicaceae. Cabbage family; includes various crops.

Cannabaceae. Hop family; includes hemp.

Caryophyllaceae. Pink family.

Chenopodiaceae. Goosefoot family.

Cistaceae. Rock-rose family.

Convolvulaceae. Bindweed family.

Cyperaceae. Sedge family.

Fabaceae. Pea family (also known as the Leguminosae); includes gorse and relatives.

Lamiaceae. Mint family (also known as Labiatae)

Liliaceae. Lily family.

Malvaceae. Mallow family.

Onagraceae. Willowherb family.

Poaceae. Grass family.

Polygonaceae. Dock or knotweed family.

Ranunculaceae. Buttercup or crowfoot family.

Resedaceae. Mignonette family.

Rosaceae. Rose family; includes a wide range of herbs, shrubs and trees.

Scrophulariaceae. Figwort family.

Solanaceae. Nightshade family; includes Potato (*Solanum tuberosum*), tobaccos (*Nicotiana*) and various medicinal plants.

IMAGE CREDITS

A number of line figures have been drawn or redrawn, wholly or in part, from the following sources:

Aldridge & Pope (1986): 57

Bienkowski (2004): 2, 7, 8, 17, 20, 23, 130, 142, 185-187, 192, 193

Cox (1995): 93-96

Cox (1998): 204-209, 214

Cox (2001): 10, 33, 36-39, 41-56

European Chrysomelidae website: 25, 26, 74, 85, 90, 91, 99, 100, 102-110, 113, 115, 116, 118, 119, 121-127, 131, 143-147, 152-161, 163, 164, 175-177, 180-184, 202, 210, 211, 213, 218-220, 226, 227, 231-240, 242-245, 247-255, 257, 260-263, 265, 267, 270-273, 275-284, 286, 288-295, 300-307, 309-312, 314-334, 337, 338, 341, 342, 344, 350-362, 365

Hůrka (2005): 12

Lopatin (1984): 200, 212

Manguin *et al.* (1993): 178, 179

Mann & Barclay (2009): 117, 120

Menzies & Cox (1996): 58, 60-73, 75, 76, 80-84, 86-89

Nadein (2007): 203

Shute (1975): 287

Sinclair & Hutchins (2009): 339, 340

Warchałowski (2003): 148, 149, 221, 224, 228, 241, 274, 296, 298, 308, 313, 347-349

INDEX

Main entries and start of main sections are shown in **bold**. Synonyms are given in *italics*.

abdominalis, Longitarsus 17, 18

absinthii, Longitarsus 17

absynthii, Longitarsus 17, 88, **89**

Acanthoscelides 10

Acanthoscelides obsoletus 10

Acanthoscelides obtectus 10, **28**

Adimonia 15

Adoxus 13

aenea, Chrysomela 14, 52, **60**

aeneicollis, Longitarsus 17, **95**

aeneomicans, Aphthona 17

aerata, Batophila 19, **86**

aerea, Phyllotreta 16

aerosa, Chaetocnema 20, **79**

aeruginosus, Longitarsus 17, **96**

affinis, Bruchus 9

affinis, Plateumaris 8, 11, **37**

affinis, Psylliodes 21, **75**

affinis, Smaragdina 12, **44**

Agelastica 16

Agelastica alni 16, **64**

agilis, Longitarsus 17, **92,** 95, 101

alni, Agelastica 16, **64**

Altica 19, 72, **80**

Altica ampelophaga 19

Altica brevicollis 19, **81**

Altica britteni 19

Altica carinthiaca 19, **82**

Altica coryli 19

Altica ericeti 19, **80**

Altica helianthemi 19, **81**

Altica longicollis 19, 80

Altica lythri 19, **81**

Altica oleracea 19, **81**

Altica palustris 19, **82**

Altica pusilla 19

Altica sandini 19

Altica tamaricis 19

Altica ytenensis 19

Alticini 1, 16, 63, **69**

Amblycerinae 23, **27**

americana, Chrysolina 13, **55**

ampelophaga, Altica 19

analis, Callosobruchus **31**, 32

anchusae, Longitarsus 17, **87**

anglica, Psylliodes 21

Aphthona 17, 71, **106**

Aphthona aeneomicans 17

Aphthona atratula 17, 106, 108, **109**

Aphthona atrocaerulea 17, 106, **108**

Aphthona atrovirens 17

Aphthona coerulea 17

Aphthona cyanella 17

Aphthona euphorbiae 17, 106, 108, **109**

Aphthona herbigrada 17, **107**

Aphthona lutescens 17, **107**

Aphthona melancholica 17, 106, **108**

Aphthona nigriceps 17, **107**

Aphthona nonstriata 17, **107**

Aphthona pallida 17, **107**

Aphthona puncticollis 17

Aphthona venustula 17

Aphthona virescens 17

appendiculata, Macroplea 10, **36**

Apteropeda 21, 71, **109**

Apteropeda globosa 21, **109**

Apteropeda orbiculata 21, **109**

Apteropeda splendida 21, **109**

aquatica, Donacia 8, 10, **38**

arida, Chaetocnema 20, **79**

aridula, Chaetocnema 20

armoraciae, Phaedon 14, **58**

armoraciae, Plagiodera 14

Asiorestia 19

asparagi, Crioceris 11, **41**

ater, Bruchidius 10

ater, Longitarsus 18

atomarius, Bruchus 9, **31**

atra, Phyllotreta 16, 104, **106**

atratula, Aphthona 17, 106, 108, **109**

atriceps, Longitarsus 18

atricillus, Longitarsus 17, **95**

atrocaerulea, Aphthona 17, 106, **108**

atropae, Epitrix 20, 82

atrovirens, Aphthona 17

attenuata, Psylliodes 21, **75**

aucta, Hydrothassa 14

aurata, Crepidodera 20, **83**

aurea, Crepidodera 20, **83**

aureolus, Cryptocephalus 12, **48**

ballotae, Longitarsus 17, **87**

banksi, Chrysolina 13, **57**

Batophila 19, 71, **86**

Batophila aerata 19, **86**

Batophila rubi 19, **86**

bearei, Longitarsus 18

bicolor, Donacia 10

bicolora, Donacia 10, **39**

biguttatus, Cryptocephalus 12, **49**

bilineatus, Cryptocephalus 12, **46**

bipunctatus, Cryptocephalus 12, **49**

braccata, Plateumaris 8, 11, **37**

brachialis, Bruchus 9, **30**

brevicollis, Altica 19, **81**

britteni, Altica 19

Bromius 13, 24

Bromius obscurus 13, **26**

Bruchidius 4, 10, 28, **33**

Bruchidius ater 10

Bruchidius canus 10

Bruchidius cisti 10, **34**

Bruchidius debilis 10

Bruchidius fasciatus 10

Bruchidius incarnatus 10, **33**

Bruchidius olivaceus 10, **34**

Bruchidius unicolor 10

Bruchidius varius 10, **33**

Bruchidius villosus 10, 28, **33**

Bruchinae 1, 9, 23, **27**

Bruchus 9, 10, 28, **29**

Bruchus affinis 9

Bruchus atomarius 9, **31**

Bruchus brachialis 9, **30**

Bruchus ervi 9, **30**

Bruchus fahraei 9

Bruchus loti 9, **29**

Bruchus luteicornis 9

Bruchus pisi 9

Bruchus pisorum 9, **29**

Bruchus rufimanus 9, **31**

Bruchus rufipes 9, **30**

Bruchus velutinus 9

Bruchus viciae 9

brunneus, Longitarsus 17, 18, 98, **99**

brunsvicensis, Chrysolina 13, 56, **57**

caerulans, Chrysolina 13

Callobruchus rhodesianus 32

Callosobruchus 10, 28, **31**

Callosobruchus analis **31**, 32

Callosobruchus chinensis 10, **32**

Callosobruchus maculatus 10, **32**

Callosobruchus pectinicornis 10

Callosobruchus quadrimaculatus 10

calmariensis, Galerucella 15, **68**

Calomicrus 16, **65**

Calomicrus *circumfuscus* 16

Calomicrus circumfusus 16, **65**

Calomicrus *nigrofasciatus* 16

canus, Bruchidius 10

caprea, Lochmaea 15, **67**

capreae, Lochmaea 15

cardui, Sphaeroderma 21

carinthiaca, Altica 19, **82**

Cassida 21, 22, 110, **111**

Cassida chloris 22

Cassida denticollis 22, **114**

Cassida equestris 22

Cassida flaveola 22, **111**

Cassida hemisphaerica 22, **111**

Cassida maculata 22

Cassida murraea 22, **111**

Cassida nebulosa 22, 111, **112**

Cassida nobilis 22, 112, **113**

Cassida prasina 22, **114**

Cassida rubiginosa 22, **113**

Cassida sanguinolenta 22

Cassida sanguinosa 22, **114**

Cassida vibex 22, **113**

Cassida viridis 22, **111**

Cassida vittata 22, 112, **113**

Cassidinae 21, 23, **110**

castaneus, Longitarsus 17, 18

cavifrons, Phratora 15

cerasi, Orsodacne 9, **51**

cerealis, Chrysolina 13, **55**

cerinus, Longitarsus 17, 18

Chaetocnema 1, 20, 70, **78**

Chaetocnema aerosa 20, **79**

Chaetocnema arida 20, **79**

Chaetocnema aridula 20

Chaetocnema concinna 20, **78**

Chaetocnema confusa 20, **78**

Chaetocnema heikertingeri 20

Chaetocnema hortensis 20, **80**

Chaetocnema laevicollis 20

Chaetocnema picipes 20, **78**

Chaetocnema sahlbergii 20, **80**

Chaetocnema subcoerulea 20, **79**

Chalcoides 20

chalcomera, Psylliodes 21, **74**

chinensis, Callosobruchus 10, **32**

chloris, Cassida 22

chloris, Crepidodera 20

chrysanthemi, Mantura 20, **85**

chrysocephala, Psylliodes 21, 76, **77**

Chrysolina 13, 51, **54**

Chrysolina americana 13, **55**

Chrysolina banksi 13, **57**

Chrysolina brunsvicensis 13, 56, **57**

Chrysolina caerulans 13

Chrysolina cerealis 13, **55**

Chrysolina coerulans **54**

Chrysolina crassicornis 13

Chrysolina didymata 13

Chrysolina fastuosa 13, **55**

Chrysolina goettingensis 14

Chrysolina graminis 13, 54, **55**

Chrysolina haemoptera 13, **56**

Chrysolina hellieseni 13

Chrysolina herbacea 13, 54, **55**

Chrysolina hobsoni 13

Chrysolina hyperici 13, **56**, 57

Chrysolina intermedia 13, **54**, 59

Chrysolina latecincta 13

Chrysolina marginalis 13

Chrysolina marginata 13, **57**

Chrysolina menthastri 13

Chrysolina menthrasti 13

Chrysolina oricalcia 13, **56**

Chrysolina orichalcia 13

Chrysolina polita 13, **54**

Chrysolina sanguinolenta 13, **54**, 59

Chrysolina staphylaea 13, **57**

Chrysolina staphylea 13

Chrysolina varians 14, **56**

Chrysolina violacea 14, 52, **55**

Chrysomela 13, 14, 51, 52, **60**

Chrysomela aenea 14, 52, **60**

Chrysomela longicollis 14

Chrysomela populi 14, **60**

Chrysomela tremula 14, **60**

Chrysomela tremulae 14

Chrysomelidae 1, 9

Chrysomelinae 13, 26, **51**

cinerea, Donacia 8, 10, **37**

circumfuscus, Calomicrus 16

circumfusus, Calomicrus 16, **65**

cisti, Bruchidius 10, **34**

clarus, Longitarsus 18

clavipes, Donacia 10, **38**

Clythra 12

Clytra 12, 25

Clytra laeviuscula 12, **45**

Clytra quadripunctata 12, **45**

Clytrini 12, 25, 44

cochleariae, Phaedon 14, **58**

coerulans, Chrysolina **54**

coerulea, Aphthona 17

collaris, Longitarsus 18

concinna, Chaetocnema 20, **78**

concinnus, Phaedon 14, **58**

concolor, Oomorphus 13, **26**

confusa, Chaetocnema 20, **78**

consobrina, Phyllotreta 16, 101, **105**

coriaria, Timarcha 13

coryli, Altica 19

coryli, Cryptocephalus 12, 45, **47**

crassicornis, Chrysolina 13

crassipes, Donacia 10, **40**

crataegi Lochmaea 15, **67**

Crepidodera 19, 20, 73, **82**

Crepidodera aurata 20, **83**

Crepidodera aurea 20, **83**

Crepidodera chloris 20

Crepidodera fulvicornis 20, **83**

Crepidodera helxines 20

Crepidodera nitidula 20, **82**

Crepidodera plutus 20, **83**

Crepidodera smaragdina 20

Criocerinae 11, 24, **41**

Crioceris 11, 24

Crioceris asparagi 11, **41**

cristula, Cryptocephalus 12

cruciferae, Phyllotreta 16, 101, 104, **105**

Cryptocephalinae 12, 25, **44**

Cryptocephalini 12

Cryptocephalus 1, 12, 24, 25, 44, **45**

Cryptocephalus aureolus 12, **48**

Cryptocephalus biguttatus 12, **49**

Cryptocephalus bilineatus 12, **46**

Cryptocephalus bipunctatus 12, **49**

Cryptocephalus coryli 12, 45, **47**

Cryptocephalus cristula 12

Cryptocephalus decemmaculatus 12, **50**

Cryptocephalus duodecimpunctata 41

Cryptocephalus exiguus 12, **46**

Cryptocephalus frontalis 12, **47**

Cryptocephalus fulvus 12, **46**

Cryptocephalus hypochaeridis 12, **48**

Cryptocephalus labiatus 12, **47**

Cryptocephalus moraei 12, **50**

Cryptocephalus nigrocoeruleus 12

Cryptocephalus nitidulus 12, **48**

Cryptocephalus ochrostoma 12

Cryptocephalus parvulus 12, **48**

Cryptocephalus primarius 12, **49**

Cryptocephalus punctiger 12, **45**

Cryptocephalus pusillus 12, 45, **46**

Cryptocephalus querceti 12, **47**

Cryptocephalus sexpunctatus 12, **50**

Cryptocephalus violaceus 12, **48**

cucullata, Psylliodes 21, **74**

cuprea, Psylliodes 21, **77**

curtisi, Macroplea 10

curtus, Longitarsus 17, **100**

cyanella, Aphthona 17

cyanella, Lema 11, **42**

Cyaniris 12

cyanoptera, Psylliodes 21

cynoglossi, Dibolia 21, **70**

debilis, Bruchidius 10

decemlineata, Leptinotarsa 27

decemmaculatus, Cryptocephalus 12, **50**

decemnotata, Gonioctena 14, **61**

dentata, Donacia 10, **41**

denticollis, Cassida 22, **114**

dentipes, Donacia 10

Derocrepis 19

Derocrepis rufipes 19, **73**

Diabrotica 15

Diabrotica virgifera 15, **65**

diademata, Phyllotreta 16, **105**

Dibolia 21

Dibolia cynoglossi 21, **70**

didymata, Chrysolina 13

discolor, Plateumaris 11, **36**, 37

distinguendus, Longitarsus 18

Donacia 10, 11, 24, 35, **37**

Donacia aquatica 8, 10, **38**

Donacia bicolor 10

Donacia bicolora 10, **39**

Donacia cinerea 8, 10, **37**

Donacia clavipes 10, **38**

Donacia crassipes 10, **40**

Donacia dentata 10, **41**

Donacia dentipes 10

Donacia impressa 11, **39**

Donacia lemnae 11

Donacia limbata 11

Donacia linearis 11

Donacia marginata 11, **38**

Donacia menyanthidis 10

Donacia menyanthis 10

Donacia obscura 11, **39**

Donacia sagittariae 10

Donacia semicuprea 8, 11, **40**

Donacia simplex 11, **40**

Donacia sparganii 11, **38**

Donacia thalassina 11, **39**

Donacia typhae 11

Donacia versicolorea 11, **41**

Donacia vulgaris 11, **40**

Donaciinae 8, 10, 24, **35**

dorsalis, Longitarsus 17, **87**

duftschmidi, Oulema 11

dulcamarae, Psylliodes 21, **74**

duodecimpunctata, Cryptocephalus 41

Epithrix 20

Epitrix 20, 72, **82**

Epitrix atropae 20, **82**

Epitrix pubescens 20, **82**

equestris, Cassida 22

equiseta, Macroplea 10

ericeti, Altica 19, **80**

erichsoni, Oulema 11, **43**

ervi, Bruchus 9, **30**

Eumolpinae 13, 26

euphorbiae, Aphthona 17, 106, 108, **109**

exclamationis, Phyllotreta 16, 101, **102**

exiguus, Cryptocephalus 12, **46**

exoletus, Longitarsus 17, **100**

fahraei, Bruchus 9

fasciatus, Bruchidius 10

fastuosa, Chrysolina 13, **55**

fastuosa, Pilemostoma 21, **110**

femoralis, Longitarsus 17

fergussoni, Galerucella 15

ferruginea, Neocrepidodera 19, **84**

ferrugineus, Longitarsus 17, 100, **101**

flaveola, Cassida 22, **111**

flavicollis, Zeugophora 9, 24, **34**

flavicornis, Longitarsus 17, 18, **96**

flavipes, Luperus 16, **67**

flexuosa, Phyllotreta 16, **102**

fowleri, Longitarsus 17, 98, **100**

frontalis, Cryptocephalus 12, **47**

fulvicornis, Crepidodera 20, **83**

fulvus, Cryptocephalus 12, **46**

fuscicornis, Podagrica 20, **84**

fuscipes, Podagrica 20, **84**

fusculus, Longitarsus 18

Galeruca 15, 64, **66**

Galeruca interrupta 15

Galeruca laticollis 15, **66**

Galeruca tanaceti 15, **66**

Galerucella 15, 66, **68**, 69

Galerucella calmariensis 15, **68**

Galerucella fergussoni 15

Galerucella grisescens 15

Galerucella lineola 15, **68**

Galerucella nymphaeae 15, **68**

Galerucella pusilla 15, 68, 69

Galerucella sagittariae 15, **68**

Galerucella tenella 15, 68, **69**

Galerucinae 1, 3, 15, 25, **63**

Galerucini 15, 63, **64**

gallaeciana, Oulema 11

Galleruca 15

ganglbaueri, Longitarsus 17, **93**

Gastroidea 14

Gastrophysa 14, 51, 52, **57**

Gastrophysa polygoni 14, **57**

Gastrophysa viridula 14, **57**

glabra, Hydrothassa 14, **59**

globosa, Apteropeda 21, **109**

goettingensis, Chrysolina 14

goettingensis, Timarcha 13, 52, **53**, 55

Gonioctena 14, 53, **60**

Gonioctena decemnotata 14, **61**

Gonioctena olivacea 14, **60**

Gonioctena pallida 14, **61**

Gonioctena rufipes 14

Gonioctena viminalis 14, **61**

gracilis, Longitarsus 18, 91, **93**, **97**

graminis, Chrysolina 13, 54, **55**

grisescens, Galerucella 15

Gynandrophtalma 12

Gynandrophthalma 12

Haemonia 10

haemoptera, Chrysolina 13, **56**

halensis, Sermylassa 16, **64**

Haltica 19

hannoverana, Hydrothassa 14

hannoveriana, Hydrothassa 14, **59**

heikertingeri, Chaetocnema 20

helianthemi, Altica 19, **81**

hellieseni, Chrysolina 13

Helodes 14

helxines, Crepidodera 20

hemisphaerica, Cassida 22, **111**

herbacea, Chrysolina 13, 54, **55**

herbigrada, Aphthona 17, **107**

Hermaeophaga 19

Hermaeophaga mercurialis 19, **72**

hintoni, Phyllotreta 16

Hippuriphila 20

Hippuriphila modeeri 20, 70, **73**

hobsoni, Chrysolina 13

holsaticus, Longitarsus 18, **88**

hortensis, Chaetocnema 20, **80**

hospes, Psylliodes 21

humeralis, Orsodacne 9, **51**

Hydrothassa 14, 53, 54, **59**

Hydrothassa aucta 14

Hydrothassa glabra 14, **59**

Hydrothassa hannoverana 14

Hydrothassa hannoveriana 14, **59**

Hydrothassa marginella 14, **59**

hyoscyami, Psylliodes 21, **74**

hyperici, Chrysolina 13, **56**, 57

Hypocassida 21

Hypocassida subferruginea 21, 110

hypochaeridis, Cryptocephalus 12, **48**

impressa, Donacia 11, **39**

impressa, Neocrepidodera 19, **84**

incarnatus, Bruchidius 10, **33**

instabilis, Psylliodes 21

intermedia, Chrysolina 13, **54**, 59

interrupta, Galeruca 15

jacobaeae, Longitarsus 17, 18, **96**

junci, Prasocuris 14, **59**

kutscherae, Longitarsus 18, **94**

labiatus, Cryptocephalus 12, **47**

Labidostomis 12, 25

Labidostomis tridentata 12, **44**

laevicollis, Chaetocnema 20

laevis, Longitarsus 18

laeviuscula, Clytra 12, **45**

Lamprosoma 13

Lamprosomatinae 13, **26**

Laria 9

latecincta, Chrysolina 13

laticollis, Galeruca 15, **66**

laticollis, Phratora 15, **62**

laticollis, Psylliodes 21, **76**

Lema 11

Lema cyanella 11, **42**

Lema puncticollis 11

lemnae, Donacia 11

Leptinotarsa decemlineata 27

lichenis, Oulema 11

lilii, Lilioceris 11, **41**

Lilioceris 11

Lilioceris lilii 11, **41**

limbata, Donacia 11

linearis, Donacia 11

lineola, Galerucella 15, **68**

lineola, Orsodacne 9

Lochmaea 15, 65, **67**

Lochmaea caprea 15, **67**

Lochmaea capreae 15

Lochmaea crataegi 15, **67**

Lochmaea suturalis 15, **67**

Lochmaeata 15

longicollis, Altica 19, 80

longicollis, Chrysomela 14

longicornis, Luperus 16, **67**

longiseta, Longitarsus 18, **92**

Longitarsus 17, 70, **86**, 91

Longitarsus abdominalis 17, 18

Longitarsus absinthii 17

Longitarsus absynthii 17, 88, **89**

Longitarsus aeneicollis 17, **95**

Longitarsus aeruginosus 17, **96**

Longitarsus agilis 17, **92**, 95, 101

Longitarsus anchusae 17, **87**

Longitarsus ater 18

Longitarsus atriceps 18

Longitarsus atricillus 17, **95**

Longitarsus ballotae 17, **87**

Longitarsus bearei 18

Longitarsus brunneus 17, 18, 98, **99**

Longitarsus castaneus 17, 18

Longitarsus cerinus 17, 18

Longitarsus clarus 18

Longitarsus collaris 18

Longitarsus curtus 17, **100**

Longitarsus distinguendus 18

Longitarsus dorsalis 17, **87**

Longitarsus exoletus 17, **100**

Longitarsus femoralis 17

Longitarsus ferrugineus 17, 100, **101**

Longitarsus flavicornis 17, 18, **96**

Longitarsus fowleri 17, 98, **100**

Longitarsus fusculus 18

Longitarsus ganglbaueri 17, **93**

Longitarsus gracilis 18, 91, **93**, 97

Longitarsus holsaticus 18, **88**

Longitarsus jacobaeae 17, 18, **96**

Longitarsus kutscherae 18, **94**

Longitarsus laevis 18

Longitarsus longiseta 18, **92**

Longitarsus luridus 18, 88, 89, **90**, 98

Longitarsus lycopi 18, **94**, 99

Longitarsus medicaginis 18

Longitarsus melanocephalus 18, **94**

Longitarsus membranaceus 18, 86, 98, **100**, 101

Longitarsus nasturtii 18, **95**

Longitarsus nigerrimus 18, **88**

Longitarsus nigricollis 17

Longitarsus nigrofasciatus 18, **91**

Longitarsus obliteratoides 18, 88, **90**

Longitarsus obliteratus 18, 88, **90**

Longitarsus ochroleucus 18, 86, **97**

Longitarsus parvulus 18, 86, **89**

Longitarsus patruelis 18

Longitarsus pellucidus 18, **98**

Longitarsus piciceps 17, 18

Longitarsus plantagomaritimus 18, 88, **89**, 94

Longitarsus poweri 18

Longitarsus pratensis 18, **97**

Longitarsus pulex 18

Longitarsus pumilus 18

Longitarsus pusillus 18

Longitarsus quadriguttatus 18, **88**, **89**

Longitarsus reichei 18, **92**, **97**

Longitarsus rubiginosus 18, **101**

Longitarsus rufescens 17

Longitarsus rutilus 18, **101**

Longitarsus senecionis 17

Longitarsus strigicollis 100

Longitarsus succineus 18, 86, **98**

Longitarsus suturalis 17

Longitarsus suturellus 19, **93**

Longitarsus symphyti 1, 19, 95, **98**

Longitarsus tabidus 17, 18, 19, **91**

Longitarsus teucrii 18

Longitarsus thoracicus 19

Longitarsus waterhousei 17

loti, Bruchus 9, **29**

Luperomorpha 16

Luperomorpha xanthodera 16, **71**

Luperus 1, 16, 65, **67**

Luperus flavipes 16, **67**

Luperus longicornis 16, **67**

Luperus rufipes 16

luridipennis, Psylliodes 21, **77**

luridus, Longitarsus 18, 88, 89, **90**, **98**

luteicornis, Bruchus 9

luteola, Psylliodes 21, **75**, 77

luteola, Xanthogaleruca 15, **66**

lutescens, Aphthona 17, **107**

lycopi, Longitarsus 18, **94**, **99**

Lythraria 19

Lythraria salicariae 19, **71**

lythri, Altica 19, **81**

Macroplea 10, 35, **36**

Macroplea appendiculata 10, **36**

Macroplea curtisi 10

Macroplea equiseta 10

Macroplea mutica 10, **36**

maculata, Cassida 22

maculatus, Callosobruchus 10, **32**

Mantura 20, 72, **85**

Mantura chrysanthemi 20, **85**

Mantura matthewsii 20, **85**

Mantura obtusata 20, **85**

Mantura rustica 20, **85**

marcida, Psylliodes 21, **77**

marginalis, Chrysolina 13

marginata, Chrysolina 13, **57**

marginata, Donacia 11, **38**

marginella, Hydrothassa 14, **59**

matthewsii, Mantura 20, **85**

medicaginis, Longitarsus 18

Megalopodidae 1, 9, 24, **34**

melancholica, Aphthona 17, 106, **108**

melanocephalus, Longitarsus 18, **94**

melanopa, Oulema 11

melanopus, Oulema 11, **42**, 43

Melasoma 14

membranaceus, Longitarsus 18, 86, 98, **100**, 101

menthastri, Chrysolina 13

menthrasti, Chrysolina 13

menyanthidis, Donacia 10

menyanthis, Donacia 10

mercurialis, Hermaeophaga 19, **72**

Mniophila 21

Mniophila muscorum 21, **69**

modeeri, Hippuriphila 20, 70, **73**

moraei, Cryptocephalus 12, **50**

murraea, Cassida 22, **111**

muscorum, Mniophila 21, **69**

mutica, Macroplea 10, **36**

Mylabris 9

napi, Psylliodes 21, **76**, 77

nasturtii, Longitarsus 18, **95**

nebulosa, Cassida 22, 111, **112**

nemorum, Phyllotreta 16, 101, **104**

Neocrepidodera 19, 73, **84**

Neocrepidodera ferruginea 19, **84**

Neocrepidodera impressa 19, **84**

Neocrepidodera transversa 19, **84**

nigerrimus, Longitarsus 18, **88**

nigriceps, Aphthona 17, **107**

nigricollis, Longitarsus 17

nigripes, Phyllotreta 16, **105**

nigrocoeruleus, Cryptocephalus 12

nigrofasciatus, Calomicrus 16

nigrofasciatus, Longitarsus 18, **91**

nitidula, Crepidodera 20, **82**

nitidulus, Cryptocephalus 12, **48**

nobilis, Cassida 22, 112, **113**

nodicornis, Phyllotreta 16, 101, **106**

nonstriata, Aphthona 17, **107**

nymphaeae, Galerucella 15, **68**

obliteratoides, Longitarsus 18, 88, **90**

obliteratus, Longitarsus 18, 88, **90**

obscura, Donacia 11, **39**

obscura, Oulema 11, **43**

obscurus, Bromius 13, **26**

obsoletus, Acanthoscelides 10

obtectus, Acanthoscelides 10, **28**

obtusata, Mantura 20, **85**

ochripes, Phyllotreta 16, 101, **102**

ochroleucus, Longitarsus 18, 86, **97**

Ochrosis 19

Ochrosis ventralis 19, **73**

ochrostoma, Cryptocephalus 12

oleracea, Altica 19, **81**

olivacea, Gonioctena 14, **60**

olivaceus, Bruchidius 10, **34**

Oomorphus 13

Oomorphus concolor 13, **26**

orbiculata, Apteropeda 21, **109**

oricalcia, Chrysolina 13, **56**

orichalcia, Chrysolina 13

Orsodacna 9

Orsodacne 9, 24, **51**

Orsodacne cerasi 9, **51**

Orsodacne humeralis 9, **51**

Orsodacne lineola 9

Orsodacnidae 1, 9, 26, **51**

Orsodacninae 26, **51**

Oulema 11, 24, **42**

Oulema duftschmidi 11

Oulema erichsoni 11, **43**

Oulema gallaeciana 11

Oulema lichenis 11

Oulema melanopa 11

Oulema melanopus 11, **42**, 43

Oulema obscura 11, **43**

Oulema rufocyanea 11, **42**

Oulema septentrionis 11, **43**

pallida, Aphthona 17, **107**

pallida, Gonioctena 14, **61**

palustris, Altica 19, **82**

parvulus, Cryptocephalus 12, **48**

parvulus, Longitarsus 18, 86, **89**

patruelis, Longitarsus 18

pectinicornis, Callosobruchus 10

pellucidus, Longitarsus 18, **98**

Phaedon 14, 53, **58**

Phaedon armoraciae 14, **58**

Phaedon cochleariae 14, **58**

Phaedon concinnus 14, **58**

Phaedon regnianum 14

Phaedon tumidulus 14, **58**

phellandrii, Prasocuris 14, **59**

Phratora 15, 53, **62**

Phratora cavifrons 15

Phratora laticollis 15, **62**

Phratora polaris 15, **62**

Phratora vitellinae 15, **62**

Phratora vulgatissima 15, **62**

Phyllobrotica 15

Phyllobrotica quadrimaculata 15, 24, **65**

Phyllodecta 15

Phyllotreta 4, 16, 71, **101**

Phyllotreta aerea 16

Phyllotreta atra 16, 104, **106**

Phyllotreta consobrina 16, 101, **105**

Phyllotreta cruciferae 16, 101, 104, **105**

Phyllotreta diademata 16, **105**

Phyllotreta exclamationis 16, 101, **102**

Phyllotreta flexuosa 16, **102**

Phyllotreta hintoni 16

Phyllotreta nemorum 16, 101, **104**

Phyllotreta nigripes 16, **105**

Phyllotreta nodicornis 16, 101, **106**

Phyllotreta ochripes 16, 101, **102**

Phyllotreta punctulata 16, **106**

Phyllotreta sinuata 16

Phyllotreta striolata 16, **103**

Phyllotreta tetrastigma 16, **102**, **103**

Phyllotreta undulata 16, **104**

Phyllotreta vittata 16

Phyllotreta vittula 16, **104**

Phytodecta 14

piciceps, Longitarsus 17, 18

picina, Psylliodes 21, **75**, 77

picipes, Chaetocnema 20, **78**

Pilemostoma 21, 110

Pilemostoma fastuosa 21, **110**

pisi, Bruchus 9

pisorum, Bruchus 9, **29**

Plagiodera 14, 51

Plagiodera armoraciae 14

Plagiodera versicolora 14, **52**

plantagomaritimus, Longitarsus 18, 88, **89**, 94

Plateumaris 11, 35, **36**

Plateumaris affinis 8, 11, **37**

Plateumaris braccata 8, 11, **37**

Plateumaris discolor 11, **36**, 37

Plateumaris sericea 11, **37**

Plectroscelis 20

plutus, Crepidodera 20, **83**

Podagrica 20, 72, **84**

Podagrica fuscicornis 20, **84**

Podagrica fuscipes 20, **84**

polaris, Phratora 15, **62**

polita, Chrysolina 13, **54**

polygoni, Gastrophysa 14, **57**

populi, Chrysomela 14, **60**

poweri, Longitarsus 18

prasina, Cassida 22, **114**

Prasocuris 14, 53, **59**

Prasocuris junci 14, **59**

Prasocuris phellandrii 14, **59**

pratensis, Longitarsus 18, **97**

primarius, Cryptocephalus 12, **49**

Psylliodes 4, 21, 69, **74**, 77

Psylliodes affinis 21, **75**

Psylliodes anglica 21

Psylliodes attenuata 21, **75**

Psylliodes chalcomera 21, **74**

Psylliodes chrysocephala 21, 76, **77**

Psylliodes cucullata 21, **74**

Psylliodes cuprea 21, **77**

Psylliodes cyanoptera 21

Psylliodes dulcamarae 21, **74**

Psylliodes hospes 21

Psylliodes hyoscyami 21, **74**

Psylliodes instabilis 21

Psylliodes laticollis 21, **76**

Psylliodes luridipennis 21, **77**

Psylliodes luteola 21, **75**, 77

Psylliodes marcida 21, **77**

Psylliodes napi 21, **76**, 77

Psylliodes picina 21, **75**, 77

Psylliodes sophiae 21, **76**

Psylliodes weberi 21

pubescens, Epitrix 20, **82**

pulex, Longitarsus 18

pumilus, Longitarsus 18

puncticollis, Aphthona 17

puncticollis, Lema 11

punctiger, Cryptocephalus 12, **45**

punctulata, Phyllotreta 16, **106**

pusilla, Altica 19

pusilla, Galerucella 15, 68, **69**

pusillus, Cryptocephalus 12, 45, **46**

pusillus, Longitarsus 18

Pyrrhalta 15

Pyrrhalta viburni 15, **66**

quadriguttatus, Longitarsus 18, **88**, 89

quadrimaculata, Phyllobrotica 15, 24, **65**

quadrimaculatus, Callosobruchus 10

quadripunctata, Clytra 12, **45**

querceti, Cryptocephalus 12, **47**

regnianum, Phaedon 14

reichei, Longitarsus 18, **92**, 97

rhodesianus, Callobruchus 32

rubi, Batophila 19, **86**

rubidum, Sphaeroderma 21, **110**

rubiginosa, Cassida 22, **113**

rubiginosus, Longitarsus 18, **101**

rufescens, Longitarsus 17

rufimanus, Bruchus 9, **31**

rufipes, Bruchus 9, **30**

rufipes, Derocrepis 19, **73**

rufipes, Gonioctena 14

rufipes, Luperus 16

rufocyanea, Oulema 11, **42**

rustica, Mantura 20, **85**

rutilus, Longitarsus 18, **101**

sagittariae, Donacia 10

sagittariae, Galerucella 15, **68**

sahlbergii, Chaetocnema 20, **80**

salicariae, Lythraria 19, **71**

salicina, Smaragdina **44**

sandini, Altica 19

sanguinolenta, Cassida 22

sanguinolenta, Chrysolina 13, **54**, 59

sanguinosa, Cassida 22, **114**

semicuprea, Donacia 8, 11, **40**

senecionis, Longitarsus 17

septentrionis, Oulema 11, **43**

sericea, Plateumaris 11, **37**

Sermyla 16

Sermylassa 16

Sermylassa halensis 16, **64**

sexpunctatus, Cryptocephalus 12, **50**

simplex, Donacia 11, **40**

sinuata, Phyllotreta 16

Smaragdina 12, 25

Smaragdina affinis 12, **44**

Smaragdina salicina **44**

smaragdina, Crepidodera 20

sophiae, Psylliodes 21, **76**

sparganii, Donacia 11, **38**

Sphaeroderma 21, 71, **110**

Sphaeroderma cardui 21

Sphaeroderma rubidum 21, **110**

Sphaeroderma testaceum 21

Sphaeroderma testaceum 21, **110**

splendida, Apteropeda 21, **109**

staphylaea, Chrysolina 13, **57**

staphylea, Chrysolina 13

strigicollis, Longitarsus 100

striolata, Phyllotreta 16, **103**

subcoerulea, Chaetocnema 20, **79**

subfasciatus, Zabrotes **27**

subferruginea, Hypocassida 21, 110

subspinosa, Zeugophora 9, **34**

succineus, Longitarsus 18, 86, **98**

suturalis, Lochmaea 15, **67**

suturalis, Longitarsus 17

suturellus, Longitarsus 19, **93**

symphyti, Longitarsus 1, 19, 95, **98**

tabidus, Longitarsus 17, 18, 19, **91**

tamaricis, Altica 19

tanaceti, Galeruca 15, **66**

tenebricosa, Timarcha 13, **53**

tenella, Galerucella 15, 68, **69**

testaceum, Sphaeroderma 21

testaceum, Sphaeroderma 21, **110**

tetrastigma, Phyllotreta 16, **102**, **103**

teucrii, Longitarsus 18

thalassina, Donacia 11, **39**

thoracicus, Longitarsus 19

Timarcha 13, 51, 52, **53**

Timarcha coriaria 13

Timarcha goettingensis 13, 52, **53**, 55

Timarcha tenebricosa 13, **53**

transversa, Neocrepidodera 19, **84**

tremula, Chrysomela 14, **60**

tremulae, Chrysomela 14

tridentata, Labidostomis 12, **44**

tumidulus, Phaedon 14, **58**

turneri, Zeugophora 9, **34**

typhae, Donacia 11

undulata, Phyllotreta 16, **104**

unicolor, Bruchidius 10

varians, Chrysolina 14, **56**

varius, Bruchidius 10, **33**

velutinus, Bruchus 9

ventralis, Ochrosis 19, **73**

venustula, Aphthona 17

versicolora, Plagiodera 14, **52**

versicolorea, Donacia 11, **41**

vibex, Cassida 22, **113**

viburni, Pyrrhalta 15, **66**

viciae, Bruchus 9

villosus, Bruchidius 10, 28, **33**

viminalis, Gonioctena 14, **61**

violacea, Chrysolina 14, 52, **55**

violaceus, Cryptocephalus 12, **48**

virescens, Aphthona 17

virgifera, Diabrotica 15, **65**

viridis, Cassida 22, **111**

viridula, Gastrophysa 14, **57**

vitellinae, Phratora 15, **62**

vittata, Cassida 22, 112, **113**

vittata, Phyllotreta 16

vittula, Phyllotreta 16, **104**

vulgaris, Donacia 11, **40**

vulgatissima, Phratora 15, **62**

waterhousei, Longitarsus 17

weberi, Psylliodes 21

xanthodera, Luperomorpha 16, **71**

Xanthogaleruca 15

Xanthogaleruca luteola 15, **66**

ytenensis, Altica 19

Zabrotes subfasciatus **27**

Zeugophora 9, 24, **34**

Zeugophora flavicollis 9, 24, **34**

Zeugophora subspinosa 9, **34**

Zeugophora turneri 9, **34**

Zeugophorinae 9, 24, **34**